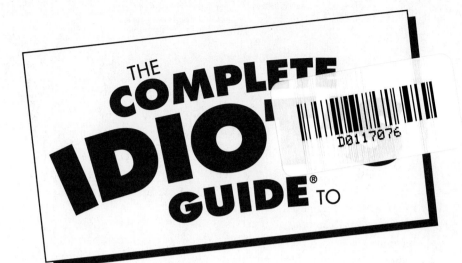

THE
COMPLETE
IDIOT'S
GUIDE® TO

D0117076

Playing the Harmonica

Second Edition

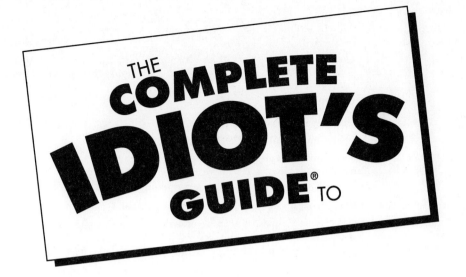

THE COMPLETE IDIOT'S GUIDE® TO

Playing the Harmonica

Second Edition

by William Melton and Randy Weinstein

ALPHA

A member of Penguin Group (USA) Inc.

Dedicated to the memory of DeFord Bailey (1899–1982), whose genius on the harp was exceeded only by the courage, grace, and dignity he brought to every day of his life.

ALPHA BOOKS

Published by the Penguin Group

Penguin Group (USA) Inc., 375 Hudson Street, New York, New York 10014, U.S.A.

Penguin Group (Canada), 10 Alcorn Avenue, Toronto, Ontario, Canada M4V 3B2 (a division of Pearson Penguin Canada Inc.)

Penguin Books Ltd, 80 Strand, London WC2R 0RL, England

Penguin Ireland, 25 St Stephen's Green, Dublin 2, Ireland (a division of Penguin Books Ltd)

Penguin Group (Australia), 250 Camberwell Road, Camberwell, Victoria 3124, Australia (a division of Pearson Australia Group Pty Ltd)

Penguin Books India Pvt Ltd, 11 Community Centre, Panchsheel Park, New Delhi—110 017, India

Penguin Group (NZ), cnr Airborne and Rosedale Roads, Albany, Auckland 1310, New Zealand (a division of Pearson New Zealand Ltd)

Penguin Books (South Africa) (Pty) Ltd, 24 Sturdee Avenue, Rosebank, Johannesburg 2196, South Africa

Penguin Books Ltd, Registered Offices: 80 Strand, London WC2R 0RL, England

Copyright © 2006 by William Melton and Randy Weinstein

International Standard Book Number: 1-59257-465-3
Library of Congress Catalog Card Number: 2006925727

08   8   7   6   5

Interpretation of the printing code: The rightmost number of the first series of numbers is the year of the book's printing; the rightmost number of the second series of numbers is the number of the book's printing. For example, a printing code of 06-1 shows that the first printing occurred in 2006.

Printed in the United States of America

Most Alpha books are available at special quantity discounts for bulk purchases for sales promotions, premiums, fund-raising, or educational use. Special books, or book excerpts, can also be created to fit specific needs.

For details, write: Special Markets, Alpha Books, 375 Hudson Street, New York, NY 10014.

Publisher: *Marie Butler-Knight*
Editorial Director: *Mike Sanders*
Managing Editor: *Billy Fields*
Acquisitions Editor: *Paul Dinas*
Development Editor: *Ginny Bess Munroe*
Production Editor: *Megan Douglass*
Copy Editor: *Jan Zoya*

Cartoonist: *Chris Eliopoulos*
Book Designers: *Trina Wurst/Kurt Owens*
Cover Designer: *Bill Thomas*
Indexer: *Brad Herriman*
Layout: *Brian Massey*
Proofreader: *Aaron Black*

Contents at a Glance

Appendixes

Contents

Foreword

When I first started playing blues harmonica in the 1960s, it was like stepping into the unknown. Not only were there no serious books available on the subject, even if I had been able to afford them, but the whole business was literally shrouded in mystery and there was nobody around who was either willing or able to shed any light on it. Blues-harp players were like a kind of secret society, and they didn't initiate novices particularly readily. When I finally managed to locate a fellow player who was prepared to share a few of his "secrets" with me, I was so delighted at simply encountering another harp enthusiast that I never did get around to picking his brain. I ended up figuring everything out for myself, and later (this is the hard part) I had to unlearn many counterproductive habits I had acquired through ignorance and the lack of suitable teachers. That was what initially prompted me to write *The Harp Handbook* in the late 1980s; I hoped to spare others some of the frustration and time-wasting I'd gone through myself. Things have come a long way since then, and there has never been a better time to take up the harmonica than right now.

For one thing, the harmonica community itself has opened up and developed in ways that would have been unimaginable 20 years ago. Blues, country, folk, jazz, and classical players now coexist in an atmosphere of mutual respect and admiration. The emergence of new playing techniques and styles has truly expanded the musical scope of the instrument. Finally, high-quality learning material and competent teachers have changed the way the harmonica is taught.

This brings us to the work you hold in your hands. *The Complete Idiot's Guide to Playing the Harmonica, Second Edition*, manages to combine all the necessary "how to's" with a wealth of detailed background information that should satisfy the curiosity of any but the most obsessed of aspiring harmonicists. It wisely doesn't promise you instant virtuosity or a career in show business. However, I assure you that if you take the time to work systematically through the techniques and exercises contained in these pages, you will not only end up knowing an awful lot more about the harp than you ever imagined you might want to, but you'll certainly also be able to play it well enough to impress your friends, family, and neighbors. You should have a lot of fun in the process, too!

William Melton and Randy Weinstein have succeeded in compiling an informative and well-thought-out guide to this frequently underestimated instrument, covering a vast range of topics and relating them to popular musical styles such as folk, blues, rock, country, and Celtic. Whether discussing basic playing techniques, or offering advanced tips on how to strut your stuff to your best advantage at a jam session or in a band context, this book is a down-to-earth, easy-to-understand, practical, and comprehensive teaching aid for anyone thinking of exploring the weird and wonderful world of the harmonica. The rest is up to you, so grab your harp and blow the back off it!

—Steve Baker, Wintermoor, Germany, August 2001

Steve Baker is one of the leading blues harmonica players on the European scene, and one of the finest exponents of the instrument in the world. Born and raised in London, he now lives near Hamburg, Germany, and has been a full-time professional harmonicist since 1975. Over the years, he has also become a kind of harmonica guru for numerous up-and-coming young players. In addition to the thousands of gigs and studio recordings Steve has played, he is Hohner's international consultant for diatonic harmonicas and the author of *The Harp Handbook* (distributed worldwide by Music Sales Corporation), acclaimed as the most comprehensive work on the diatonic harp to date. He regularly writes for *Easyreeding*, *American Harmonica Newsmagazine*, and *Harmonica Player* magazine. Steve recently published the first harmonica tutorial CD-ROM, "Interactive Blues Harp Workshop," and a new book-and-CD package, *Blues Harmonica Playalongs* (both available from Mel Bay Publications). His website is www.stevebaker.de.

Introduction

Let's start with two important things that we want you to remember as you go through this book and learn to play the harmonica.

First, music is supposed to be fun. In this regard, playing the harmonica is no different from playing any other musical instrument. It's safe to assume that you didn't decide to play the harmonica to add to your stress levels, so although we've approached the harmonica as a serious instrument requiring practice and commitment, we've also tried to *not* take our instrument or ourselves *too* seriously. We encourage you to do likewise.

Please feel free to go through this book as quickly or slowly as you choose, and practice as much or as little as suits you. No one is going to chastise you for not practicing every day. There are no tests to be passed or failed. If you don't let this new hobby become another job, you just might stick with it long enough to get pretty good.

Second, playing the harmonica is all about emotion and spontaneity springing from the depths of your heart and soul. Technique, while critically important to getting that righteous sound, has always been secondary. We *will* teach you the technique you need to play the harmonica very well. We will *try* to take you beyond merely reading or playing the music—all the way to *feeling* the music. However, when all is said and done and you've dutifully practiced your way through all the chapters, the music you make will come just as much from what's inside of you as from the pages of this book. So, by all means, let your inside out.

How to Use This Book

In this book, you learn how to play the *diatonic* harmonica, which is by far the most commonly played harmonica in blues, rock, country, folk, and other popular styles of music. The book is put together pretty simply: we cover all the important topics, and we start with easy things and then move on to more difficult ones. It's divided into four parts.

Part 1, "The Harmonica: It's No Toy," gives you a strategy for becoming a harmonicist. We tell you how to get the most out of your harp and yourself by practicing smart. You'll also learn all about how the instrument works, the types of harmonicas there are, and how to choose the right one for you and keep it playing the way you want it to for a long time.

Part 2, "Let's Get Blowin'," introduces you to the tablature system so that you can play the harp even if you don't read music. You can learn how to use your lips, head, hands, and other parts of your body to get the right sounds from your harmonica. And, oh yes, you get to play notes and chords and practice making music with some familiar tunes.

Part 3, "Steppin' Up," is where you can learn to read music if you want to and get into the techniques that will give you the sounds that drew you to the harmonica in the first place: tongue-blocking and note-bending, in particular. We then give you the basics on chord progressions and how to use them, show you how you can play in different keys on the same instrument, and explain the different diatonic harmonica tunings.

Part 4, "It's Showtime!" introduces you to blues and improvisation techniques: call-and-response, riffs, and licks. You'll also learn how to play country, rock, Celtic, and Appalachian fiddle tunes on your harp. There's a whole chapter on getting a band together (and keeping it together) and what you need to know about amplifiers and how to use them to your best advantage. In the Showtime! Finale chapter you get to play a variety of songs in different styles that will employ everything you've learned and all the technique you've developed. You'll be amazed at how far you've come!

There are also two appendixes at the back of the book (where else would they be?) that provide lots of good information on the harmonica world; Appendix A, "Complete Glossary of Harp Terms," and Appendix B, "Resources," which includes harmonica websites, catalogues, and online stores specializing in harmonicas and related supplies, other harmonica books and instruction guides, harmonica organizations and events, harmonica publications, custom harmonica and repair specialists, and CDs we recommend. You definitely should use these resources and take advantage of some of the websites, organizations, and harmonica publications that are readily available to you.

And last, but by no means least, this second edition of *The Complete Idiot's Guide to Playing the Harmonica* includes a CD for you to play along with. This is a fantastic learning tool that enables you to hear all of the most important exercises and songs included in this book. You can start by playing the songs along *with* the harmonica, then (when you're ready) cut out the harmonica and play along on your own with the instrumental backup.

Extras

In our never-ending quest to be both informative and amusing, we've included four types of margin notes that give you additional bits of information along your way through the book:

def•i•ni•tion

Definitions of terms that are used in the nearby text.

Blues Clues

Important tips, tricks, and words of wisdom that will enhance your learning experience.

Don't Harp On It

Warnings about potential problems or things you should avoid doing.

Straight from the Harp

Little tidbits of harmonica trivia that you probably haven't heard before.

We also include numerous practice exercises throughout the book in special exercise boxes so that you can easily find them when you want to return to a chapter for more practice on a particular technique.

Acknowledgments

A special thank you to Paul Dinas and Ginny Munroe, acquisitions editor and development editor respectively, for this book, who both have contributed as much or more to completing it as have the authors.

Trademarks

All terms mentioned in this book that are known to be or are suspected of being trademarks or service marks have been appropriately capitalized. Alpha Books and Penguin Group (USA) Inc. cannot attest to the accuracy of this information. Use of a term in this book should not be regarded as affecting the validity of any trademark or service mark.

Part 1

The Harmonica: It's No Toy

The harmonica has not always enjoyed a stellar reputation in the music world. It still doesn't among many so-called serious musicians, who tend to dismiss an instrument that costs less than $25 as a toy. Yet the harmonica's roots make it one of the oldest musical instruments in the world, and today it's probably the most popular instrument in the world in terms of the quantity sold and the number of musicians who actively play it.

Unlike many "more respectable" instruments, the harmonica is successfully used to play a wide range of different music styles. Although it can be learned at a beginning to intermediate level surprisingly quickly, the nuances and techniques required to play at the virtuoso level make it one of the most difficult instruments in the world to master.

In these chapters, we give you tips on how to practice and become a good player. We also explore the harmonica's rich history, particularly on the American music scene, and its current place in today's world of music. You can learn about the numerous types and styles of harmonicas, and how to maintain, tune, and repair the ones you buy.

Chapter 1

Versatile, User Friendly, and Fun

In This Chapter

- A dozen good reasons to play the harmonica
- What you'll need to get started
- Ten tips on how to get the most out of practicing

Let's start by asking this: what are we going to call this little instrument? Its most common, and perhaps official, name is the harmonica. It's also called a lot of other things: harp, mouth organ, French harp, tin sandwich, Louisiana or Mississippi sax, and of course there are numerous other names for it in other countries. After "harmonica," *harp* probably is the most commonly used term in the United States, particularly favored by blues, rock, and country musicians. In this book, we use the terms harmonica and harp interchangeably. You may feel a bit silly at first referring to your new purchase as a harp, which most people associate with angels (and not too many angels are known to have played the harmonica). But as your interest progresses from a hobby to a passion, you'll start feeling the music that made the harmonica the quintessential all-American instrument. The term harp will start to feel right, and it'll roll right off your tongue, along with the riffs, licks, and calls and responses you can learn in this book.

Whatever you want to call it, the harmonica is part of the American music scene in a big way. And now *you* are going to be part of that scene. This chapter gives you some good reasons to play the harp and some practice tips that'll help you get as good as you want to get, as fast as you want to get there.

Why Play the Harp?

So you want to learn to play the harmonica. Do you know why? Think about it for a moment. Why not the piano? Or the guitar? Or … tennis? If you ponder this for a few minutes, you'll probably find some hidden little memory that's surfaced and prompted you to decide to learn the harp and explore your musical side. The harmonica is part of all our memories.

Think about the movies or television programs you've seen that have a harmonica played by a character or as background music in an important scene. Think about the music you've heard on the radio or on CDs that had a harmonica providing a key element of the melody, harmony, or rhythm. Think back to your childhood and remember visits to your grandparents' farm or camping with your friends. Did someone pull out a harmonica and play some good music to sing along with? Fast forward to your favorite musical artists, whether rock, blues, country, Celtic, or whatever. Didn't they, or one of their band members, play the harmonica in some of your favorite songs?

You might not understand why you want to learn to play the harmonica until you dig deep into your memory. One thing is certain: from this point on, you'll hear and notice the harmonica being played everywhere, even in movies and songs that you may have seen or heard many times without having noticed it before. Now it can be part of your own personal musical experience.

The authors were introduced to the harmonica by different paths. Randy's passion was ignited by his early exposure to the harp masters of the postwar Chicago blues style. William started his musical life as a classical musician, playing the clarinet, French horn, and classical accordion (yes, classical accordion, not polkas).

You'll find that as you learn more about playing your harmonica and you're able to play some good music, it will give you hours of pleasure and fun times with your friends.

If you have doubts about whether you can, and should, learn to play the harp, here's our list of a dozen good reasons to embark on this adventure:

1. The harmonica is incredibly inexpensive. You can buy a pretty good diatonic harmonica for under $25 (and a really good one for around $100), and after you start playing with other musicians, you'll need only four or five harps in different music keys to play just about any song that comes up.

2. The harmonica is supremely portable. Front pocket, back pocket, shirt pocket, coat pocket, briefcase, purse: there is never any excuse for being caught without your harp. You naturists can even get harmonica cases with neck loops for those naked *jam* sessions in the woods. Because of its portability, the harmonica can be played in more circumstances than any other instrument. Only singing and whistling give you more choices of venue.

3. The harmonica is amazingly versatile. You can play blues, bluegrass, folk, country, jazz, classical, Celtic, Cajun, European, ethnic, Oriental, and any other kind of music that comes to mind. Name one other musical instrument that is so versatile. Some of these styles require a specially tuned harmonica to hit the right notes for that style, but you can be certain that whatever you need isn't going to break the bank.

---

def•i•ni•tion

"**Harp** 1. A plucked string instrument consisting of a resonator, and arched neck and strings of graded length 2. A harmonica."
—*Merriam Webster's Collegiate Dictionary*

---

def•i•ni•tion

A **jam** is a gathering of musicians and vocalists who play many different songs spontaneously. Usually, the participants take turns selecting the songs and rotate playing the lead melodies. Some jam sessions encourage improvisations over songs or even freeform improvisation.

Your harmonica should look something like this. If it doesn't, then you need to get a new one. Read Chapter 3 before you go shopping.

4. The harmonica is an emotional instrument. (We don't mean that it's prone to unexpected breakdowns or blow-ups.) It is an extremely expressive instrument when mastered even at an intermediate level. You can express your full range of emotions through your harp, and you can bring those emotions to your audience. You can make them feel what you want them to feel.

5. The harmonica is an ancient instrument. Its earliest versions were invented by the Chinese thousands of years ago. These are the same people who brought us fireworks, the printing press, and a bunch of other good things while the rest of the world was wandering around lost in the Dark Ages. They simply wouldn't have invented it if it hadn't been such a good idea.

6. You can get pretty good on the harp with little or no formal training. You could even become one of the world's great harp masters. It's been done several times. A few lessons might be a good idea, but they're not essential if you make good use of this book.

7. Harpists are colorful and eccentric people. Some of the master harpists have led lives and lifestyles that go way beyond the typical American's experience. As you learn to play your harp, you'll notice some changes coming over you. At first it may be something small, like neglecting to shave some mornings or wearing the same underwear two days in row. But gradually, you'll notice that you, too, are becoming colorful and eccentric, at least relatively speaking: the harmonica can't make a silk purse out of a sow's ear or an immensely colorful person out of a drone.

8. It doesn't take a village. You don't need an orchestra, band, group, accompanist, or anyone else to create some good music, enjoy yourself, and entertain others. As you'll discover, it's a great rhythm instrument as well as a great melodic instrument and is thus ideal for solo performance.

Straight from the Harp

The harmonica is the instrument of choice for U.S. presidents. Woodrow Wilson and Calvin Coolidge were avid harmonicists who were known to play regularly in the White House. Ronald Reagan practiced his harmonica while recovering from his gunshot wounds suffered during an assassination attempt.

9. The harmonica is everywhere. It is the world's most popular musical instrument. Practically everyone owns one. If you don't believe this, try something the next time you are at a movie or the symphony or having dinner in a restaurant. Just stand up, pull out your harp, hold it up proudly, and ask people to show you theirs. Be ready to write down names and telephone numbers because these are people you can jam with.

10. The harmonica is a mysterious instrument, so harmonica players are mysterious people. The harmonica's history is a little murky, with considerable disagreement as to what happened when and who did it. When you see someone playing the harmonica in a park or on the street, you automatically wonder whether he or she is a famous musician—or spent 20 years in a state penitentiary. If you want to add just a hint of mystery to your aura, play the harmonica.

11. If you play the harp, you get to have a cool nickname. People named Gregory, Arnold, Mike, Bill, and Tom don't play the harp, at least not for long. People named Sonny Boy, Wild Child, Toots, Bullet, Jelly Roll, Sugar Blue, and Howling Wolf play the harp. Start thinking about this right now. By the time you've finished this book, you're going to need a nickname.

12. Playing the harmonica is a great aerobic exercise. It's one of the better and certainly most pleasurable forms of aerobic exercise imaginable. With a bit of practice, you'll be the envy of every yogi in town.

Straight from the Harp

The harp is so all-American it is even part of baseball lore. "The Great Harmonica Incident" in 1965 was precipitated by Yogi Berra's decision to fine infielder Phil Linz $200 for disturbing the other Yankee players on the team bus with his harmonica playing. There was such an outcry from fans that the Yankees ended up rescinding the fine and giving Linz money for harmonica lessons to try to improve his playing.

Becoming a Player

Okay, you selected this book over all the other harmonica instruction guides in the store and invested a few dollars to purchase our combined wit, wisdom, and advice. We don't want you to end up thinking you wasted your money, so here's some advice on how to get the most from this book.

Probably the most important thing we can say is that we hope you don't have unrealistic expectations. Purchasing this book in and of itself doesn't really get you anything. You won't make any progress in playing the harp by merely reading your *Complete Idiot's Guide* before you go to bed. Learning a musical instrument just doesn't work that way. This book provides you with knowledge based on our experience, but the only way you can get good is to practice hard. The critical word is *practice*.

This book is heavily oriented toward practice and playing. All the chapters include healthy doses of practice exercises and songs. There are also two special "Music Break" chapters designed to give you an opportunity to consolidate your technique and skills.

In compiling the music, we've used songs we hope you'll recognize and enjoy playing. This always makes learning music easier and more enjoyable, and you'll get a charge out of it when your family hears you practicing and recognizes the tune. We also include some great songs that you might not know but sound great on the harp.

Don't Harp On It _____

Please don't let this new activity in your life get too serious or technical. You're doing it most likely because your day job is driving you crazy or otherwise filling your life with tension. Sure, you have to practice hard, but remember that you're supposed to be having fun. Don't get frustrated or discouraged if you don't progress as quickly as you would like to. One of the things we show you is how much fun you can have while you refine your skills.

Some of the songs you learn in the early chapters appear again later in the book, incorporating the new techniques and skills you've acquired along the way. That's when you'll clearly see (and hear) how your practice is paying off.

Getting Geared Up

To get started, you won't need to spend much money beyond what you pay for this book and a harmonica if you don't already have one. If you don't, your first harmonica will cost you less than $25. It should be a diatonic major harp in the key of C. Most of the book's exercises for diatonic harmonica are written in C, but if you already have a harmonica and it's in a different key, that's okay. Chapter 3 explains why and tells you what you need to know about choosing harmonicas. You may decide to add three or four more diatonic harmonicas in different music keys as you progress through the book, but it's not a requirement.

If you decide to learn the chromatic harmonica, it will require a serious upgrade in your inventory of harmonicas. But even that will cost you less than $150. You'll also want to buy some good harp CDs to listen to and play along with. If you reach the point where you want to play out in the world, you'll want a harp mike and some relatively inexpensive maintenance and repair items described in Chapter 4. As we've said, the harp is an incredibly inexpensive instrument to get started on. And it won't cost a whole lot more as you increase your skills and expand your repertoire and playing opportunities.

Straight from the Harp

Although *your* first harmonica will be inexpensive, this hasn't been true for every beginner. In the 1930s, the Hohner Company presented a harmonica to Pope Pius XI that had solid-gold faceplates and was encrusted with ivory and jewels. It certainly cost more than $25.

Practice Smart to Get Good Fast

Listen, and then practice. Practice, and then listen. Learning to play the harmonica revolves around these two key words. This is true for all musical instruments, but the listening aspect is particularly important for the harp. The harp can produce an extremely broad range of sounds, and different artists have developed styles and sounds that are unique to them. Listening closely is the key to emulating these styles and sounds and then moving on to develop your own.

Learning to play a harmonica or other musical instrument is not rocket science. We don't want to make it seem too complicated or intellectual. No matter how little musical talent you may think you possess, your persistence and commitment will pay off. You *will* learn to play the harmonica very well.

Basically, practicing smart to get good fast can be boiled down to the following 10 simple practice tips:

Don't Harp On It

Although there's an unlimited number of opportunities to practice your harp, don't make "while driving your car" one of them. You'll get a lot of strange looks, and it is dangerous. Trust us on this. We've tried it.

- ◆ **Develop a routine and consistency.** Set aside certain times during the week when you know you'll be practicing. This is like exercising or anything else. It helps to have a schedule that provides consistency in your practice routine. However, unlike exercising, practicing your harmonica is something you'll look forward to doing.

- ◆ **How much should you practice?** As much as you enjoy it. Remember, this isn't your day job. You should practice as long and as often as you want to and continue to enjoy it. If, however, you don't enjoy practicing at least 45 to 60 minutes a day, you probably aren't going to make much progress. (You don't always need to squeeze your entire daily practice into one session; you can accomplish a lot in a series of short, focused sessions scattered throughout your daily activities.) You should start somewhat slowly and build up to a regular practice schedule. You might be surprised at how much of a workout playing the harmonica is for your lips, tongue, and mouth muscles, not to mention your lungs and diaphragm. Also, it's a good idea to take off one day a week to give your mouth, lips, and lungs a rest.

Blues Clues

Try to practice at the same time every day and on the same days every week. For example, establish a routine in which practicing is the first thing you do when you get home every day, or something you do for an hour right before you go to bed. Getting into a routine helps develop steady progress and prevents you from going backward. You should practice at least 45 to 60 minutes per day if you want to make any serious progress. This can be done in one long practice session, a series of focused 10- to 15-minute sessions, or a combination of both.

def•i•ni•tion

A **gig** is a booking or paid engagement for a musician, usually for a single performance.

- ◆ **At what pace should you go through this book?** The pace you are comfortable with. Unless you have an imminent *gig* or recording session, there is no reason you need to practice at any pace other than your own. Obviously, you should go through the exercises and songs in the order they are presented. New techniques and skills are introduced along the way, and you need to become proficient at each of them before you move on to the next. When you get to a "Music Break" chapter, spend enough time on the exercises and songs to feel comfortable playing them before moving on. Then come back to them a little later after you've learned something new. You'll discover that you can play them much better than before.

- ◆ **Maintain a little variety in your routine.** Don't spend your entire practice session working on just one technique, exercise, or song. You'll get bored and you may get discouraged if you're not getting it right. Spend 10 minutes or so on one thing, then 10 minutes or so on something else, and then go back to the first thing. You should always work on three or four different areas simultaneously, and perhaps break them out into different practice sessions so that you can focus exclusively on the area at hand.

◆ **Where should you practice?** This is one of the great things about the harmonica. It can always be within your reach. You don't have to go home to practice. Although it's a good idea to conduct your regular practice sessions at home so that you can develop the correct posture and breathing techniques, you can hold a spontaneous practice session just about anytime and anywhere: sitting in your car, lunchtime in the park, or airport departure lounges. Even a spare 10 minutes can be usefully and enjoyably utilized blowing on your harp.

◆ **Listen to and play along with CDs.** This is a great way to perfect your technique and style and to learn the styles and techniques of the masters. Appendix B lists some good harp CDs you can play along with and provides the music key for each of the songs. And of course this book has its own CD, described in Appendix C, which includes many of the songs found in this book. You'll also find some digital audio products listed that enable you to loop sections of a song and to slow down its speed. These tools are ideal for accurate transcription of the songs you're listening to. Don't limit yourself to one style; try a little blues, a little country, a little bluegrass. The harp is a versatile instrument, and you should embrace that versatility in your playing. And remember what we said at the beginning of this section: don't forget to listen. You won't learn as much as you can unless you put your harp down and listen.

◆ **Record yourself.** This is one of the most important practice tips we can give you. You'll be amazed at how different you sound when you hear yourself on tape. It will give you the opportunity to evaluate your playing critically, which will greatly accelerate your progress. Oh, and by the way, don't forget to listen to the tapes. Replay them again and again, listening closely to your technique, playing style, and sound. Retape the same thing, listen again, and you'll hear the improvement.

◆ **Start playing with others as soon as possible.** There is no substitute for playing live with other musicians. It doesn't have to be anything too grand. If you check at work, you might be surprised at how many of your colleagues have musical backgrounds and would enjoy the opportunity to play. You can put an ad in the music section of your local newspaper and check the postings at local music stores. Many neighborhoods have local "porch jams," where musicians of different experience levels get together and play for the pure enjoyment of making music. You'll be welcome in these jams regardless of your skill level. If your neighborhood doesn't have one, why don't you be the one to start it?

◆ **Take some lessons.** This certainly isn't required. Many great harpists have never had a lesson in their life. But it can't hurt, and chances are you'll learn something new. This is particularly true if you've achieved an intermediate skill level and want to go on to a higher level. If nothing else, a skilled instructor can introduce you to some fresh ideas that will add diversity to your playing style. Also, don't necessarily limit yourself to harp players; there's a lot to learn in terms of style and musical interpretation from other instrumentalists and vocalists.

Straight from the Harp

Just Me and My Harp

*Just me and my harp
She's all that I need
Keep her close to my heart
'Cause she sets me free
When I'm feelin' low
Or my day's gone all
    wrong
Pull her out for a blow
Let her play a sweet song
She don't let me down
She don't tell me no
Don't give me no frown
Always up for the show
She's all that I got
But she's there every time
Wish they all was as hot
As this old harp of mine
Just give me my harp
She's all that I need
Keep her close to my heart
'Cause she sets me free*

—Old blues poem about a man and his harp. Author unknown.

◆ **Be spontaneous.** Remember: the harp is the ultimate unstructured, free-style music instrument. You don't have to be restrained by anyone else's ideas of what music should be. What you play on the harp, more than on any other instrument, should be a pure reflection of your soul. Your goal is *not* to merely play the music. Your goal is to *feel* the music. Music should be an extension of your mood at the moment, and you should let your emotion flow freely through your harp. As you're practicing your songs or playing with CDs or other musicians, don't hesitate to let your emotion lead your music where it wants to go. You'll find that you play the same song differently each time, depending on how you're feeling at that particular moment. That's what the harmonica is all about.

> **Blues Clues**
>
> **Practice being spontaneous.** Although this is something of an oxymoron, it's a great way to develop a free-flowing, spontaneous style of play. Set your CD changer to random selection, load it up with CDs of different styles of music, and let it rip. You won't know which song is coming next, so you'll have to adjust your style and technique quickly and often. This is great preparation for professional jam sessions, which can get pretty hot and fast paced. You want to be able to keep up.

The more you practice, the better you're going to get. If you stick with it and practice long and hard enough, you'll become a very good harp player. It could even happen in as little as six months from when you get started. It will take much longer to get even close to a master level, but you don't have to ever reach that level. The harmonica world needs only so many masters. Within six months from the date you purchased this book, you could find yourself entertaining others with good quality music, playing professionally in a band if you want to, and generally having a good time with your music.

The Least You Need to Know

◆ The harmonica is incredibly versatile, portable, and inexpensive.

◆ Listen and practice; practice and listen.

◆ Develop a practice routine and go at your own pace.

◆ Don't merely play the music—*feel* the music.

◆ Be spontaneous and have fun.

In This Chapter

- ◆ A little history about a little instrument
- ◆ The role of the harmonica in early American music
- ◆ The harmonica today: the world's most popular instrument

Throughout history, musical instruments have come and gone as various civilizations reached their zenith only to fade in favor of a conqueror or other successor with its own distinct culture and music. The musical instruments of ancient civilizations look and sound strange by today's standards, but they were an important part of the social life of some earlier society. Why these instruments die, only to be replaced in subsequent societies with completely different instruments, is an interesting historical question that, you'll be glad to know, we have no intention of exploring in this book. We just want you to note that the harmonica not only has survived several thousand years of human progression and occasional regression, but has also migrated across different civilizations while constantly adapting itself to reflect prevailing musical tastes. Its roots can be traced from America back through nineteenth-century Europe to ancient China, making it perhaps the oldest instrument played in today's music world (and its free-reed ancestors, in much the same form as their earliest versions, are still played today throughout Asia).

In this chapter, we sketch the history of the harmonica from its oriental origins to its place in the modern world of music. Then we explore its role in the development of early American music styles and examine why it was and still is the perfect instrument for the sounds and rhythms that exemplify the American music experience.

In the Beginning: Oriental Blues

Historians generally agree that the harmonica's earliest ancestor was invented in China, but they disagree as to who invented it and when. Some maintain that Emperor Huang Tri came up with the concept for the first instrument, the *sheng*, as early as 4500 B.C.E. Others contend that it was in fact Empress Nyu-kwa who deserves credit for inventing this instrument around 3000 B.C.E. We strongly suspect that the *sheng* actually was invented for either of these royal personages by one of the Royal Eunuchs. Why? Partly because we just can't visualize a Chinese emperor or empress toiling away over the Royal Workbench. But mostly because eunuchs never got credit for anything and, well, they didn't have much else to do with their time, did they?

Whoever came up with the idea, the *sheng* was an immediate hit in the royal household and quickly spread throughout China and more distant areas of Asia. It then began to spread westward with the opening of trade routes and was being played by Turks and Persians by the sixth century.

The *sheng* was one of the first *free-reed* instruments. Its reeds were fixed at one end and free to vibrate at the other. The length of the reed determined the pitch of the tone. Modern-day free-reed instruments include the harmonica, accordion, and concertina. Each of them has many different freestanding reeds of various lengths to create different pitches. Compare them with a typical fixed-reed instrument, such as a clarinet or saxophone. With these instruments, the reed is fixed within, and vibrates against, a mouthpiece. There is only one reed in the instrument. The pitch of a note is determined by the length of the tube attached to the mouthpiece. Different pitches are created by opening and closing holes in the tube.

Much like its descendant the harmonica, the *sheng* was a highly expressive instrument that could be played with great versatility. It could be mellow or shrill, and *sheng* players used many of the same techniques you will learn in this book: vibratos, bending, and trilling. (Unlike the modern harmonica, however, the *sheng* plays the same notes on both inhale and exhale.)

def•i•ni•tion

A **free-reed** instrument uses freestanding reeds to create different tones. The reed is a strip of leather or metal that is attached at one end and free to vibrate at the other. The flow of air makes the free end vibrate. The length of the strip determines the tone: a longer reed produces a lower tone and, conversely, a shorter reed produces a higher tone.

Europe Adopts (and Adapts) the Free Reed

Traders reputedly brought *shengs* back to Europe as early as the seventeenth and eighteenth centuries, but a French missionary, Pere Amiot, is generally credited with getting the free-reed ball rolling in Europe in the late 1770s. Numerous experiments were undertaken to create free-reed variants of the original *sheng*. The most notable of these was 16-year-old Christian Buschman's invention of a musical box consisting of 15 "blow-only" pipes with freestanding reeds. Called an *aura*, it's considered the first modern-day harmonica. Buschman secured a patent on this device in 1822, thus earning himself the title "inventor of the harmonica."

A few years later, a mysterious fellow named Josef Richter invented the *vamper*. If the truth be told, this instrument was much closer to the modern-day harmonica than any of the others: the player could both blow and draw (i.e., breathe in) to play different notes, *and* chords could be played due to the unique ordering of notes (using the same concept still found on diatonic harmonicas today). Richter is still the namesake for the most common tuning for diatonic harmonicas today.

By the 1830s, these free-reed instruments had become popular enough to be commercially produced in Germany, Austria, and Switzerland. A young clock-maker named Matthias Hohner began manufacturing harmonicas in 1857, and he and his family built 650 harmonicas in that first year of production. Hohner was much more than an artisan; he was a very good businessman who soon controlled the harmonica trade in Europe. Yet the greatest contributing factor to his success was nothing so grand. It was the simple act of corresponding with relatives who had emigrated to America. They convinced him to ship a box of harmonicas to them in the early 1860s, and a harmonica empire was born.

Hohner: Harmonicas for the Huddled Masses

Hohner's relatives got that first box of harmonicas, sold them quickly for 10¢ apiece, and ordered more—many more. The harmonica quickly found a market in America and spread both west and south, where it found its true roots.

The harmonica actually followed two divergent paths to popularity in American music, two paths that initially were defined by racial lines. However, despite their divergence, musicians from each genre soon began to borrow from the other's styles. Eventually, any racial distinctions disappeared and the two paths, to a large extent, merged.

Among the European immigrants and their descendants, the harmonica was adopted for new American folk music that was a combination of Old- and New-World sounds and rhythms. Much of the early American folk music was rooted in the popular music and dance tunes brought to America by European immigrants. Here, it was all mixed together into a melting pot of music, with a touch of American independence, freedom, and attitude added for flavor. The style of play was primarily what we now call *straight harp*, and the little harmonica became the instrument of choice for cowboys, homesteaders, soldiers, travelers, and everyone else who wanted to carry their music with them but couldn't sing. It was incorporated into American folk bands and, together with the fiddle and banjo, became a driving force at barn dances, saloons, weddings, festivals, and campfire sing-alongs.

def•i•ni•tion

The **straight harp** is a style of playing the harmonica, also called the first position, in which the harmonica is played in the same music key as it is tuned to. This style of playing consists primarily of blowing notes, as opposed to drawing, and is the dominant style of play for folk, bluegrass, and Celtic music. A more modern-day musician who exemplifies the straight harp style of play is Bob Dylan.

Many notable characters from American folklore took up the harmonica to pass the time between gunfights and poker games or while lingering in jail cells. Wyatt Earp and Billy the Kid supposedly both played the harmonica, and Jesse James's life reputedly was saved once by a harmonica in his shirt pocket that deflected a bullet. Davey Crockett was said to have played the harmonica for the Alamo defenders (it is unclear who survived to report this).

At about this same time, African slaves in the South were given their freedom. They had brought from Africa many diverse styles of music characterized by intricate rhythms and notes not found in European music. Africans introduced notes commonly referred to today as "blue notes" and also "falling tones" (a slurring style of singing in which the pitch of notes would drop), which today give blues, gospel, and jazz much of their distinctive flavor. African rhythms became combined with the "work songs" and hymns Africans learned in America. Add their tradition of musical storytelling passed from generation to generation, and you have the birth of the blues.

The slaves also brought from Africa a hand-held mouth instrument called a *quill* that was able to produce the same style of falling tones as the human voice. As the harmonica spread to the South, they soon learned that similar falling tones could be produced on this new instrument. This was one of the first steps in the development of the style of playing known as *cross harp*, which is the dominant style of play for modern blues and is also widely used in rock and country music.

def•i•ni•tion

> The **cross harp,** or second position, is a style of playing the harmonica in which it is played in a key five notes higher than the key it is tuned to. For example, a song in the key of G would be played on a C-tuned harmonica. This style of playing consists primarily of drawing notes, as opposed to blowing, and is characterized by pulling the tone of the notes downward to create a "bending" effect. This position is also known as the blues-harp position. The key concept of playing the harp in different positions and its relationship to the "circle of fifths" is discussed in Chapter 13.

In the 1890s, Hohner began to aggressively market the harmonica in other parts of the world, and by World War I, the British Musicians' Association was distributing harmonicas to every British soldier on the front. At the same time, every German soldier was being provided with a Kaiser Wilhelm model for Christmas.

Harmonicas from Sea to Shining Sea

Meanwhile, back in America, the popularity of the harmonica continued to grow and branch out into different areas of music. The harmonica's story in twentieth-century America can be divided into several stages, during which particular styles of music utilizing the harmonica became popular.

The Pre–World War II Era

The period from 1910 to 1940 is sometimes referred to as the harmonica's golden age. This period was characterized not only by the continued growth in the harp's popularity in blues and folk music, but also by the emergence of numerous harmonica bands. They started to spring up around the country in the early 1920s, mostly as harmonica youth bands complete with uniforms in the style of marching bands. As these young musicians matured, so did their venues. Harmonica bands became a staple of vaudeville and concert halls in the 1930s, and their repertoires were incredibly diverse, spanning ethnic songs, pop tunes, jazz standards, and light classical pieces. The best known of these bands probably was Borrah Minevitch and the Harmonica Rascals, which was a popular fixture on stages around the country for 25 years.

At the same time, radio and movies were competing for the attention and dollars of audiences, and the harmonica quickly moved into these media. One of the most popular early radio stars was DeFord Bailey, who played folk and blues (as well as train and animal imitations) for the *Grand Ol' Opry* show out of Nashville. In the 1940s, Sonny Boy Williamson II also gained great popularity with his *King Biscuit Flour Hour* in which he played the harmonica in between plugging sacks of flour.

The other significant pre-war harmonica development was the emergence of the first harmonica soloists focusing on classical music. This was made possible by the invention in 1924 (by Hohner, of course) of the chromatic harmonica. Unlike other harmonicas, which could play all 12 notes in the scale only by using techniques such as bending and overblowing, the chromatic harmonica could play all 12 notes through simply blowing and drawing and pushing a button on the side of the instrument to sharpen or flatten the notes. This development opened up an entirely new world of music to harmonica players. The first to gain notoriety playing this new harmonica was Larry Adler, who performed classical music in concert halls as the featured soloist with some of America's greatest orchestras.

The harmonica world was on a roll.

World War II

In the last half of the 1930s, more than 30 million harmonicas had been sold in the United States, but almost all of them had come from the small village of Trossingen in Germany, site of Hohner's production facilities. America's entrance into World War II brought the import of these harmonicas, and the harmonica craze, to a screeching halt. With an embargo in effect, harpists now turned their attention to figuring out how to repair what had previously been considered throwaway instruments. In the process of learning how to fix their busted harmonicas, players began to learn how to improve and customize them.

The '40s and '50s

The end of World War II was good for at least one German company, Hohner, as its huge American market reembraced the little instrument. New styles of music appeared on the scene, and the harmonica again proved its versatility in becoming an important element of these styles.

It was at this time that the harmonica had its first major hit on a national scale. The Harmonicats' recording of "Peg O' My Heart" was the number-one best-selling record of 1947 and went on to sell over 25 million copies. This success (plus the prospect of adding thousands of new dues-paying members) led the American Federation of Musicians to "declare" the harmonica a legitimate instrument and invite harp players to join.

Straight from the Harp

Larry Adler, one of the all-time great classical and pop music harmonicists, was rejected at the age of 10 by Baltimore's Peabody Conservatory of Music on the grounds of "lack of talent." He went on to perform the harmonica as the featured soloist with some the world's greatest orchestras, including the New York Philharmonic.

Straight from the Harp

"If I don't blow my harp, I hurt. God put that on me to make me play."
—DeFord Bailey, harp master, 1899–1982, in *Harmonicas, Harps and Heavy Breathers* by Kim Field (Cooper Square Press, 2000), a superb history of the harmonica and American music.

Perhaps the best-known harmonica performance of the 1960s was by a decidedly amateur musician named Wally Schirra, who smuggled a Hohner Little Lady harmonica onto *Gemini IV* and played "Jingle Bells" for the world on December 16, 1965. The harmonica thus became the first musical instrument played in outer space, and Schirra's harmonica is enshrined at the National Air and Space Museum in Washington, D.C.

But the most important post-war event, as far as the harmonica was concerned, was conducted with much less fanfare. During a 1951 recording session, Marion "Little Walter" Jacobs amplified his harp by cupping it together with a radio microphone and playing through a guitar amplifier. This produced a dynamic, deep-throated sound that alternated between a gritty rawness and a fluid, swooping quality reminiscent of the saxophone as played in jazz and R&B. Suddenly, the harmonica took center stage on the Chicago blues scene. This sound became the standard for blues harp playing and was a major contributing factor in catapulting blues music and blues harpists, such as James Cotton and Junior Wells, onto the national scene.

During this same period, the chromatic harmonica players continued to carve out a niche in the jazz and, to a lesser extent, classical arenas. Larry Adler was still the master of this scene in America right up until he was branded a communist and blacklisted during the dark period of the McCarthy hearings. He left his native country and emigrated to the United Kingdom. At the same time that America was exiling Adler to Europe, a Belgian named Jean "Toots" Thielemans arrived in New York City, and he went on to become one of the greatest jazz harmonicists of all time. Also in the early 1950s, John Sebastion became the first harmonicist to focus exclusively on classical music.

The '60s

The 1960s was a decade of revolution in American society and music. It was during this era that the harmonica once again captured the imagination of the American public, and sales soared. It seemed that, regardless of the style of music, the harp was a featured instrument. The Beatles might have been responsible for instigating this new craze with their 1963 release of "Love Me Do," featuring John Lennon playing the harmonica (who was tutored by the great Delbert McLinton prior to recording). The "British invasion" was on, and much of it was harmonica-centric. Ironically, many of the British rockers of the 1960s drew their inspiration from the rhythms and sounds of the American blues masters, and to a large extent these invaders can be credited with the "discovery" of American blues music by mainstream America.

The harmonica's resurgence, fueled by the marriage of rock and blues music, continued throughout the decade of the '60s. Almost every British band featured a harp player, and American bands, such as Creedence Clearwater Revival, took up the instrument as well. Harmonica virtuoso Paul Butterfield became the main progenitor of a style known as "blues-rock," and his signature harmonica style became a prevalent influence on many later players. Bob Dylan also introduced a new music sound and a new style of harmonica playing. His music was a poetic combination of rock and folk themes, and while he certainly wasn't the first musician to emphasize straight (blowing) harp, his style of play nevertheless was totally unique and Dylanesque. Charlie McCoy brought his own style of harp playing to the country music world, and he went on to become the first nonguitar instrumentalist to win the Country Music Association's Instrumentalist of the Year award.

The Harmonica in Today's Music World

Although the harmonica's influence has ebbed and flowed, it's continued to be an important part of the American and world music scene. Today, approximately 2 million harmonicas are sold each year in the United States alone, with annual worldwide sales exceeding 10 million. There are estimated to be over 40 million people in the United States who have played the harmonica. Hohner itself has produced well over 1 billion harmonicas since its first year when its founder painstakingly built the first 650. No matter how you slice it, the harmonica is the most popular instrument in the world.

Classic Harmonicas

The latest burst in popularity and sales probably was fueled by the John Belushi/ Dan Ackroyd movie, *The Blues Brothers*, and blues music continues to be the most visible driving force for the harmonica. However, it also has an extremely strong presence in rock, country, bluegrass, and folk music, and a growing popularity in the world of jazz.

Although the harmonica bands have largely faded from the scene, there are plenty of old and new legends still blowing their harps. Kim Wilson (The Fabulous Thunderbirds), Lee Oskar, Howard Levy, Rick Estrin (Little Charlie and the Nightcats), Charlie Musslewhite, Charlie McCoy, Norton Buffalo, John Popper (Blues Traveler), Magic Dick, Rod Piazza, Terry McMillan, Toots Thielemans, Billy Branch, William Galison, Jason Ricci, Charlie Leighton, Carey Bell, Paul DeLay, and Peter "Madcat" Ruth are just a few of the masters who have become household names within and beyond the harmonica community.

Harmonica players not only have been blowing their harps—they've also been getting seriously organized. The Society for the Preservation and Advancement of the Harmonica (SPAH) was founded in Detroit in 1962. It has become the preeminent international organization promoting and supporting the harmonica, complete with quarterly newsletters and an annual convention.

Straight from the Harp

The Hohner company has produced over 1,500 different models of harmonicas, including its 48-chord rhythm model, which is listed in the *Guinness Book of World Records* as the world's largest harmonica. It has established a museum in Trossingen, Germany, that displays over 25,000 harmonicas.

On a final note, harpists finally seem to be making inroads into the world of formal music education. City University of New York has become the first university to qualify the harmonica for credit toward a degree program. This university is a short subway ride from The Juilliard School of Music, so who knows where this will lead.

The Least You Need to Know

◆ You don't *need* to know any of the facts in this chapter, but it will give you a good feel for the history of your instrument.

Chapter 3

The First Step: Spend a Little Money

In This Chapter

- Important criteria for selecting your harmonica
- A look at the different styles and tunings that are available
- Comparing major brands and models
- Additional harp stuff to spend your money on

The first step in learning how to play the harmonica is to spend a little money, and we do mean a little. You can get started playing the harp with a $25 investment in equipment, and continue playing the harp for a lifetime without ever having to break the bank.

Up till now, all harmonicas probably looked pretty much the same to you. In this chapter, you'll learn that …

- There are various styles of harmonicas used to play different styles of music.
- For each style, there are numerous versions with different features and tunings.
- Within each version, there are significant differences among the available models in terms of quality, sound, and price.

We help you choose your first harmonica and provide some useful information to guide you in future purchases. Most of your choices, however, will be based on personal preference. There's a wide range of harmonicas available out there, all with different sounds and characteristics. No one style or model is ideal for every person or every situation. As you progress, you should experiment with different types of harmonicas from different manufacturers and build your harp inventory based on your own playing style and preferences.

Decisions: Getting the Best Buy

Purchasing a harmonica should involve much more than walking into a music store and selecting the one with the best-sounding name or best-looking case. Just because a harmonica is inexpensive doesn't mean you can buy one without understanding what you're getting. There are many important criteria to be taken into account to ensure that you get the right harp *for you*. Most of the following points refer to the diatonic harmonica, the first type to learn.

Keys and Tunings

Harmonicas are tuned to play different notes. The collection of notes available on a harmonica is usually identified as a *key*, such as the key of C-major. Basically, that means on a C-major harmonica, you can play all the notes for the major scale that starts with the note C. (We discuss the music theory underlying the concept of keys in Chapter 10.) So one of the first things to do is determine the key of the harmonica you want to purchase. Unfortunately, it gets much more complex than this.

There are harmonicas tuned to both diatonic and chromatic scales, and within the diatonic category you'll find harmonicas tuned to major scales, harmonic minor scales, and natural minor scales (as well as specialized tunings that aren't 100 percent compatible with any scale). We thoroughly explain what set of notes each scale type refers to in Chapter 10. These tunings come in a variety of "hole lengths," ranging from harmonicas with 4 holes to 16 holes. Then there are the specialized tunings of tremolo, octave, chord, and bass harmonicas. Within these categories of tunings, you'll find that different manufacturers often tune specific notes differently to achieve a desired sound (such as flattening or sharpening certain notes slightly to get a more "bluesy" or a brighter sound, respectively) or to produce a smoother-sounding chord. The point is this: you need to know exactly what style of harmonica and tuning you want before you buy.

Blues Clues

Although all diatonic harps are designed similarly, subtle differences affect their sound: materials used for the reed and reed plate, comb material and size, hole and chamber size, and reed size and thickness. For example, harps with wooden combs are considered to have a "warmer" tone. Metal combs tend to produce a bright tone. Harps with large holes and chambers play louder. The larger the reed surface area, the louder and more responsively the harp plays. The thinner the reed plate, the easier it is to bend notes. Usually it's easier to just buy one and play it for a while than to try to figure out what it's going to sound like before you buy it.

Musical Style

Do you want to play blues, rock, country, bluegrass, folk, Celtic, or something else? For the first three, you tend to play in cross harp, so you would purchase a harp that produces a full (fat) tone and is built for strong bends and overblowing.

For the latter three, you would likely play in straight harp, so you might prefer a brighter, cleaner sound. If you want to play jazz and/or classical, you probably will want a chromatic harmonica.

Sound Quality

The sound quality of a harmonica is affected by the materials it's constructed from, its workmanship, its tunings, the size of its holes and chambers, and other factors relating to its physical attributes. However, the most important factor affecting sound quality is what's going on with your own lips, tongue, mouth, throat, and diaphragm. In other words, you can achieve a good tone on any harmonica (excluding the really cheap models) if you use good technique and you work at it. Remember, though, that various models of the same style of harmonica usually sound quite different if they have different manufacturers, so the issue usually isn't whether a harmonica has good sound quality, but whether it produces a sound you like when *you* play it. The best way to discover which harmonicas produce the right sound for you is to experiment with different models instead of always buying the same one. You probably will end up with "different horses for different courses," meaning you'll prefer certain harmonicas for heavy blues and other harmonicas for bluegrass, country, and so on, depending on the type of sound you want to produce.

Durability

Durability is largely determined by the quality of the materials and workmanship that go into the manufacture of a harmonica. You can pretty much count on harmonicas manufactured by any of the companies discussed later in this chapter (see the table in the section "The Choice Is Yours" later in this chapter) to be of good quality and therefore to be suitably durable. Probably the biggest factor affecting a harmonica's durability is how you play and care for it. Heavy bends and overblowing cause your reeds to wear out faster, and failure to take care of your harp (as discussed in Chapter 4) definitely shortens its life expectancy.

Comb

You now can purchase harmonicas with combs (the center portion with the holes) made from wood, plastic, or metal. This choice truly is a matter of preference. All three produce slightly different tones. Many harpists still prefer the classic tone produced by a wooden comb, but plastic combs have become very popular in recent years. Harmonicas with wooden combs have a reputation for swelling and shrinking, and thus are prone to leaking air and are not as durable as plastic or metal combs. Both plastic and metal combs definitely are easier on the lips than wooden ones. The metal combs tend to produce the brightest tones but are the most expensive.

Maintainability

Hohner, Lee Oskar, Suzuki, and Hering all manufacture reed-plate replacement kits for at least some of their harmonicas. (In the case of Hohner, reed-plate replacement kits are available for its new Modular System models.) This gives you the ability to easily replace a reed plate when one or more reeds wear out for about half the price of purchasing a new harmonica. You also can use replacement reed plates to customize your harmonica with a special tuning by combining top and bottom reed plates that aren't available together from the manufacturer. Lee Oskar also offers replacement combs, cover plates, and a harmonica repair toolkit in addition to reed plates. These replacement reed plates and parts greatly enhance your ability to repair your harmonicas and extend their playing life.

Availability

You can't purchase what you can't find. Hohner and Lee Oskar seem to dominate the harmonica distribution market as far as music stores are concerned, although most of the brands mentioned in this chapter can be found fairly easily. All of them are also available at the online stores and catalogues listed in Appendix B (often at a superior price even after shipping charges).

Don't Harp On It

Don't become wedded to a particular brand or model of harmonica. Try different ones and become familiar with their playing characteristics. No single brand or model gives you the best sound for every style and occasion (although we hasten to add that many very skilled harpists find a harp with that certain sound they really like, and they continue to refurbish and play it for decades).

Price

The price of a harmonica usually, but not always, tells you something about the quality of its materials and workmanship. As with everything else in this world, you get what you pay for. We suggest you skip the cheaply made diatonic models priced under $10 and begin your harp career with something in the $20 to $30 range. Cheap harmonicas leak air and are difficult to play, and they won't last.

More Decisions: Tunings for Every Occasion

We've discussed diatonic and chromatic harmonicas several times, so you've probably figured out the difference between them. In case you haven't, here's a summary:

♦ A diatonic harmonica is tuned to a seven-note scale selected from the 12 tones available in standard Western tuning. It typically repeats this scale three times at successively higher pitch ranges. Each of these repetitions is commonly known as an octave. Thus the most common diatonic harps have three octaves of seven-note scales. Other notes can be played only by bending or overblowing these available notes. Diatonic harmonicas come in major and minor tunings as well as special tunings that are slight variations of the traditional major tuning. Diatonic harmonicas commonly are used for blues, rock, country, bluegrass, and folk music.

♦ A chromatic harmonica contains all 12 notes of the chromatic scale, including all sharps and flats (the black keys on a piano). It does this by including two sets of reed plates tuned a half step apart. The player switches from one set to the other by pushing a spring-action button, which raises the tone a half step. Chromatic harmonicas tend to be used mostly for classical and jazz music, but as chromatic harmonicas can play every note of any scale, they're suitable for practically any style of music and have even become a popular choice for blues.

♦ In addition to diatonic and chromatic harmonicas, several other styles of harmonica are available: tremolo, octave, bass, and chord. The tremolo and octave harmonicas are the more popular of these specialized styles.

Blues Clues _____

After you've learned a song on a diatonic harmonica, you would use exactly the same positions to play that song on any other key of any identically tuned harmonica. The notes would be different, but the positions would be exactly the same. For example, if you can play "Silent Night" on a C-major diatonic harp, you would play it exactly the same on a G-major, or on any other major diatonic harp.

This chapter (and most of the instructions, exercises, and songs in this book) focuses primarily on diatonic harmonicas.

The principal diatonic tunings you need to be familiar with are as follows:

♦ **Major diatonic.** This is the traditional tuning for a diatonic harmonic, based on Richter's original tuning from the 1820s. It is clearly the most commonly played harmonica and is used for blues, rock, country, bluegrass, folk, and just about every other style of music. It often is played in the second or cross-harp position, meaning it is played in a different key than the key the harmonica is tuned to. For example, if you play cross harp on a C-major diatonic harmonica, you'll be playing in the key of G and primarily emphasizing the draw notes. Following is the note layout for a C-major diatonic harmonica:

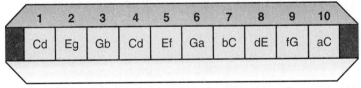

The capital letters are blow notes and the small letters are draw notes.

♦ **Melody Maker.** The Melody Maker (by Lee Oskar) is a variation of the traditional major diatonic tuning, specifically designed for playing single-note melodies. It's for playing in the cross-harp position, so it's labeled with its cross-harp key rather than the straight-harp key.

♦ **Country Tuned diatonic.** This Hohner harp is tuned the same as the traditional major diatonic, except that the fifth-hole draw note is raised a half step. As the name implies, it's a good harp for playing country music.

◆ **Natural minor diatonic.** Five notes are flattened from the traditional major diatonic tuning for this harp, with the result that both blow and draw chords are minor. This harmonica is used for minor blues, rock, and reggae music. The natural minor diatonic is designed for playing in cross harp and thus is labeled in its cross-harp key.

◆ **Harmonic minor diatonic.** This is a great harp for playing Eastern European, "gypsy," Greek, and other ethnic music that requires the classic minor tuning. This harp is designed for playing in the straight-harp position and is labeled in its straight-harp key.

◆ **Steve Baker Special.** This version of the Hohner Marine Band model is an extension of the standard major diatonic tuning. Three holes added at the low end provide an additional octave for playing low bend notes.

◆ **Valved diatonic.** On a traditional diatonic harmonica, it's possible to produce draw bends on holes 1 through 6 and blow bends on holes 7 through 10 to play notes that are not available with the harmonica's standard tuning. With a valved diatonic, it's possible to produce *blow bends* on holes 1 through 6 and *draw bends* on holes 7 through 10 to achieve a chromatic capability through bending. Suzuki manufactures a valved diatonic called the ProMaster.

We discuss advantages of alternate tunings and provide demonstrations of Melody Maker, natural minor, and harmonic minor tunings in Chapter 14.

The Choice Is Yours

You have an almost unlimited array of good-quality harmonicas made by numerous manufacturers to choose from. Prices for diatonic harmonicas generally range from $5 up to around $75, while some chromatics cost over $750. We've suggested that you plan to spend $20 to $30 for your first harmonica. Actually, you can play for years and become a very good, professional harpist without *ever* having to spend more than this amount on your harps.

The following table describes some of the more popular diatonic models in the recommended price range, give or take a few dollars. Information and pricing on more (and less) expensive diatonic harmonicas are readily available through the online stores and catalogues listed in Appendix B. Other good brands and models are available in the recommended price range, but the goal is *not* to present an entire harmonica catalogue in this chapter, merely to provide some basic information about some of the popular models we're familiar with.

Under the Keys column, the designation *All* indicates that the harp is available in all 12 keys: C, C sharp, D, E flat, E, F, F sharp, G, A flat, A, B flat, and B. All the harps listed in this table are the standard 10-hole model.

All these harmonicas are manufactured of high-quality materials and with workmanship by vendors who stand behind their products.

Survey of Diatonic Harmonicas

Hohner

Model	Tuning	Comb	Keys	Comments
Marine Band	major	wooden	All + high G and low D, E, E flat, F	✓ the original harp and still ticking ✓ covered slots help bluesy sound
Golden Melody	major	plastic	All	✓ good for single notes
Special 20	major	plastic	All + high G and low D, E, E flat, F, F sharp	✓ airtight ✓ one of the most popular models
Special 20	country	plastic	All	✓ same as above, but Country Tuned fifth-hole draw note gives country flavor
Pro Harp	major	plastic	All	✓ part of Hohner's new Modular System ✓ very airtight ✓ replacement reed plates
Blues Harp	major	wooden	All	✓ also Modular System model ✓ wood resists swelling ✓ replacement reed plates

Lee Oskar

Model	Tuning	Comb	Keys	Comments
Major	major	plastic	All + high G and low F	✓ airtight ✓ large chambers ✓ tuned slightly sharp for bright single-note sound ✓ replacement reed plates
Melody Maker	melody	plastic	A, C, D, E, G: labeled in cross harp key	✓ same comments as for major ✓ good for playing single-note melodies ✓ tuning sharp key on cross harp
Natural Minor	natural minor	plastic	All-minor: labeled in cross-harp key	✓ same comments as for major ✓ ideal for playing minor blues, rock, and reggae
Harmonic Minor	harmonic minor	plastic	All-minor	✓ same comments as for major ✓ good tuning for East European and other ethnic music

Survey of Diatonic Harmonicas (continued)

Suzuki

Model	Tuning	Comb	Keys	Comments
ProMaster	major	metal	All high G and low F	✓ a little more expensive but a quality harp and also comes in valved version ✓ replacement reed plates
Blues Master	major	plastic	G, A, C, and D	✓ high-quality construction
Folkmaster	major	plastic	All	✓ good value

Hering

Model	Tuning	Comb	Keys	Comments
Golden Blues, Hering Blues, and Black Blues	major	plastic	All	✓ same harmonica with different cover plates ✓ replacement reed plates ✓ longstanding international reputation ✓ only recently available in United States and Canada

Huang

Model	Tuning	Comb	Keys	Comments
Star Performer	major	plastic	All	✓ surprisingly good in view of low price ✓ somewhat inconsistent ✓ tone considered too thin and trebly by some
Silvertone Deluxe	major	plastic	All	✓ even less expensive than Star Performer ✓ good value even though very inexpensive compared to other listed harps ✓ same tone issue as Star Performer

What to Buy Now and What to Buy Later

Let's make this easy. For now, to get the most out of this book, you should purchase any of the following harmonicas in the key of C-major:

Lee Oskar

Hohner Special 20

Hohner Pro Harp

Hohner Blues Harp

Hohner Marine Band

Hohner Big River

All of them are well constructed and airtight. They have plastic combs, with the exception of the Blues Harp and Marine Band, which have wooden combs. They're in the right price range. They're readily found in music and online stores and in catalogues. The Lee Oskar and Hohner Pro Harp and Blues Harp models have replacement reed plates available. The C-major tuning is a good starting point because it falls in the middle of the range between the highest and lowest keys and you don't have to mess with sharps and flats right away.

In the future, the first thing you'll probably do is to buy additional keys of major diatonic harmonicas, possibly G, A, D, and F to start with. (Together with your original C-major harp, you'll then have cross-harp keys of G, D, E, A, and C, which are popular blues keys.) When you add to your instrument collection, don't always stick with the same brand and model of harp. Experiment and plot your own course based on where your music takes you. It'll be fun!

> **Blues Clues**
>
> You might just not be able to find the right harp for you through normal channels. Have no fear; you can commission a harp artisan to custom-build a harp to your specific wants and needs. They aren't cheap, but you'll get exactly what you want. Several custom harp artisans are listed in Appendix B.

Harmonica Stuff

While you don't *have* to spend a lot of money to become a good harp player, unlimited shopping opportunities are available for those desiring to do so. Harp players are like all other musicians. They are constantly buying new toys and upgrading or replacing perfectly good equipment. It's a universal truth that musicians always spend all their music earnings on some new piece of equipment or other music paraphernalia, whether they need it or not.

A few ideas for purchases down the road are …

- More harmonicas.
- Lots of harp CDs.
- Harmonica repair toolkits.
- Harmonica neck holders.
- More harmonicas.
- Carrying cases and stage stands for all those harmonicas.
- Microphones and amplifiers (discussed in Chapter 16).
- Harmonica belt (for holding all those harmonicas).
- Timing device (such as a metronome).
- Practice machine (for recording and slow playback).
- Play-along CDs (fun and extremely educational).
- Key chains, T-shirts, caps, and so on.
- Still *more* harmonicas.

If you feel something burning a hole in your pocket, you can visit any of the online stores and catalogues listed in Appendix B to put the fire out.

The Least You Need to Know

◆ Start out with a C-major diatonic harp.

◆ Don't buy cheap.

◆ Try different tunings, brands, and models as you progress.

◆ Understand the harp's tuning *before* you buy (you can't return it).

◆ The most important criterion for a harp is that *you* like the sound when *you* play it

Chapter 4

My Harp Will Go On

In This Chapter

- How the little thing works
- Breaking it *in* without breaking it
- Basic, everyday care
- Self-repairing and tuning for a longer lifespan
- Solving common problems

Yes, your harp will go on and on, but only if you take care of it. The harmonica is not an expensive instrument. You can buy very good diatonic harmonicas for less than $25 in most music stores. This is both good and bad. It's good because you can replace a harmonica without a huge hit to your wallet. It's bad because you can replace a harmonica without a huge hit to your wallet. Hey, $25 is $25, and if you really get into your harp playing, you might end up with 10 or more harmonicas in various keys and styles. Why not make them last as long as possible? If you just use some of the common-sense tips set out in this chapter, you can double or triple the life of your harmonica. And by the way, when your harp really is on its last blows, *don't throw it away*. We mean it, and you'll understand why by the end of this chapter.

Harmonica Physics: Good Vibrations

In one sense, the harmonica is just like every other musical instrument: it creates sound when one or more of its parts vibrate. In a harp (and all other free-reed instruments), the vibration is caused by air flowing across a reed that is connected at one end and free to vibrate at the other. In the final analysis, music is nothing more than a bunch of vibrations—some of them good and some of them not so good.

Working Parts

Now is a good time to get that harmonica you purchased back in Chapter 3 out of its box. Take a look at it and you'll immediately see that it has two metal faceplates on the top and bottom, a set of 10 small holes on one side of a plastic, wooden, or metal "comb," and a large opening on the other side. You are going to blow into the harmonica on the side with the 10 small holes, but you probably had already figured this out.

Okay, let's take a look inside. You're probably not quite ready to be taking your harmonica apart and putting it back together, so you can just look at the following harmonica diagram:

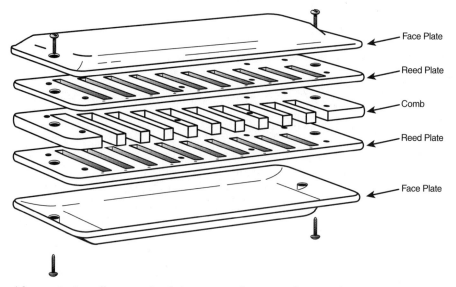

A harmonica is really a very simple instrument. It consists of (1) two faceplates, (2) two reed plates, and (3) a plastic, wooden, or metal comb.

You'll see three major parts inside the harmonica: two metal plates with reeds, and a plastic, wooden, or metal comb. Each of the metal plates has 10 slots, and thin strips of metal called reeds are attached at one end of each slot. You'll notice that on the upper plate, the reeds are attached under the plate (inside the comb) and at the end toward the mouthpiece. On the lower plate, the reeds are attached on top of the plate (outside the comb) and at the end away from the mouthpiece.

This configuration is what gives you the ability to play 20 different notes on the 10-hole diatonic harmonica. (Actually, in later chapters, you can learn how to play many more than 20 notes through bending techniques.) When you blow into one of the 10 holes, air enters the chamber in the comb and escapes through the slot in the top reed plate, causing the attached reed to vibrate. When you draw air into the same chamber, it enters through the bottom slot and the attached reed on the bottom plate vibrates. Each of the reeds is cut to a different length, meaning it's tuned to a different note. The longer the reed, the lower the pitch, and conversely, the shorter the reed, the higher the pitch.

Notes and Keys

If you followed our instructions and purchased a C-major diatonic harmonica, the frontal view will look like this:

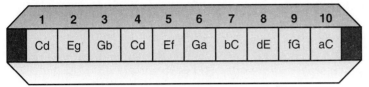

1	2	3	4	5	6	7	8	9	10
Cd	Eg	Gb	Cd	Ef	Ga	bC	dE	fG	aC

You can play the designated notes on your C-major diatonic harp. Blow notes are in capital letters; draw notes are in small letters.

Don't get hung up on the letters. They're just the most common way to identify different notes. The C on your harmonica produces a note that is equivalent to a note called C on a piano, saxophone, or xylophone, for that matter. All harmonicas have the first position (straight harp) key printed on the front. Some, such as Lee Oscar harmonicas, have the second position (cross-harp) key printed on the side. The 10 holes on your harmonica are usually numbered for you, too, with "1" being the lowest note and "10" the highest. This numbering is supplied only so you don't embarrass yourself and launch into a great *riff* while holding your harp upside down.

One last point before we move on to care and maintenance tips. Why are the harmonica notes set out in the order shown in the diagram? Why aren't they simply set out in a scale, like a piano keyboard? This goes back to our old friend Richter and the vamper he invented in the 1820s. One of Richter's objectives was to create a wind instrument that could play harmonious groups of notes (called chords) that could provide chordal accompaniment as well as melodies for songs with simple harmonic structures. Notice on the diagram the repetition of the pattern C-E-G in the blow position. Go ahead and blow on your harp now. Hear that sweet harmonious sound? Congratulations! You're playing a chord known as the C-major triad, one of the most prevalent chords in European and American folk music.

Now let's take a look at the draw notes. Even though their order does not repeat the way the blow notes' order does, blowing on any group of them produces a great-sounding chord different from the one produced when you blow. Give it a try. The notes on a diatonic major harmonica are set out in such an order that you can play more than one note at a time and produce chords in keys that are complementary to the harmonica's key (in our case, C).

In general, the ordering of notes on diatonic major harmonicas produces chords that complement the tonal patterns of blues, folk, bluegrass, and country music.

def•i•ni•tion

A **riff** is a short solo or interlude in which an instrumentalist plays the melody line or other improvised lead. Riffs often are played between, and complementary to, vocal lines or as a transition between verses. Riffs also are sometimes called *licks* (or *motifs* by classical musicians). Techniques for playing riffs are covered in Chapter 14.

Be Gentle at First

It probably is a good idea to blow on your harp a little gently at first, but the need to "break in" a harp is somewhat exaggerated. Start out in the middle, playing long blow and draw notes. The higher and lower notes are more difficult to play on a new harmonica, so ease your way up and down the harmonica until you can feel the reeds loosening up. This is about it as far as breaking in the harmonica is concerned. As you get better, you'll discover that the harmonicas you play become "broken in" to your particular style.

One more thing about breaking in your harmonica: in case you've heard that harmonicas are supposed to be soaked in whiskey, and you're looking forward to blowing all night on a Jack Daniels–flavored harp—forget it. Whiskey (or water or beer for harpists on tight budgets) often was used "in the old days" to soak new harps with wooden combs. The liquid swells the wood, making the harp more airtight and increasing its volume. Soaking, however, also ultimately ruins the reeds and the wood, thus significantly shortening the harp's useful life. Some harpists still soak their wooden harps in whiskey (it doesn't do a thing for a harp with a plastic or metal comb except ruin it), but unless you need to pull a new wooden harp right out of its box to play a gig (not a good idea for a lot of reasons), you probably should just break your harp in the gentle and slow way we outlined.

Don't Harp On It

Don't overblow your new harmonicas at first. Break them in slow and easy. Start in the middle and avoid playing loud or hard until you can feel the reeds loosening up. This extends their longevity.

Preventing Harp Disease

It's somewhat amazing how much longer your harmonica will last if you just use a little common sense in caring for it. It's even more amazing how many harpists do so little to take care of their harmonicas. If you just follow the tips in the next sections, you'll significantly reduce the number of problems you encounter with your harps.

Care and Not Feeding

The following are some basic ways to extend the life of your harps by taking care of them and avoiding harp abuse:

- **Keep your harmonicas away from extreme temperatures.** That includes automobiles sitting out in direct sunlight with the windows closed. This advice is true for all instruments and musical equipment.

- **Don't eat or drink while you're playing.** The food and drink particles will be blown directly into your harp. This is the quickest way to get a reed clogged.

- **Don't play with your head pointed down all the time.** It causes saliva to run from your mouth into the harmonica. This is the second quickest way to get a reed clogged.

- **Never let anyone else blow on your harp.** Unless it's someone you'd feel comfortable doing some pretty serious kissing with, keep your harp to yourself. That probably rules out most harp players you know.

- **Always keep your harmonicas in their cases when they're not being played.** It protects them from moisture and dust.

- **Before you put your harp back in its case, dry off the surface and slap it around a little.** Hit it against your leg or the palm of your hand with the hole-side down. That loosens any particles and helps dry it out.

Keeping It Clean

You should periodically clean your harps. This is particularly true for the ones you play the most. Every month or so (again, for each harp, it depends on how much you play it), take your harmonica apart and give it a good cleaning, using hydrogen peroxide solution or isopropyl alcohol. You'll notice the areas that need cleaning the most—usually a build-up of gunk in the openings of the holes and around the reeds. Be very careful while cleaning around the reeds. Use a Q-Tip and don't bend the reeds or increase or decrease their gapping (the space between the reed and reed plate). A soft toothbrush can be used to clean larger parts, such as the faceplates and comb. Soap and warm water can be substituted for hydrogen peroxide solution or isopropyl alcohol, but you'll have to be particularly careful about rinsing and drying the parts.

If a hole stops working properly, one of the following cleaning techniques will probably do the trick:

1. Try slapping it hard against your leg or hand. This usually shakes out any particles that are obstructing airflow or blocking a reed.

2. If it still isn't working, try removing the faceplates and inspecting the offending reed. You might see whatever is blocking the reed and be able to carefully remove it with a toothpick or a Q-Tip soaked in isopropyl alcohol.

3. If the hole *still* is not working, it's okay *as a last resort* to hold your diatonic harp under running water for a few seconds. That helps free up any gunk or saliva that could be blocking a reed. Be sure to shake the harp completely dry and wipe off all moisture after doing this.

If you follow the advice in this section, you'll have fewer problems and your harmonicas will last significantly longer. By the way, just how long *will* your harps last? That depends. If you're a casual player, your harps could last several years. If you're a professional who's blowing your harps every day, some might last only two to four weeks before some major repair work or a replacement is required.

Blues Clues

Don't forget that your harmonica comes with a warranty. If it doesn't work, you can send it back to the manufacturer for repair or replacement. Don't delay, because any continued usage will void the warranty, and don't try to take it back to the store where you purchased it. Health laws prohibit the exchange of mouth-blown instruments at retail stores. Avoid all this by testing the harmonica before you buy it. Most retail music stores have a harmonica tester that can be used to make sure all the reeds are working correctly.

Four Repair Techniques You Can Learn

A lot of harpists figure that, having tried everything mentioned above without success, it's simply time to purchase a new harmonica. For diatonic harmonicas, this isn't necessarily wrong thinking. There does come a point when you have to question how much effort you're willing to invest to avoid spending $25 on a new harmonica. But it means giving up on a harmonica that might have been playing just right for you, and breaking in a new one all over again. Also, $25 multiplied by the number of harmonicas you own can quickly become a fairly large cash outlay. Why not learn a few easy repair techniques that won't take a lot of time but might save you a lot of money?

There are four types of repairs you can undertake with minimal cost and effort: gapping, tuning, replacing individual reeds, and replacing reed plates. You can piece together all the tools and materials you need at home or a hardware store, or you can purchase very effective jeweler's tools (like small hammers, files, pliers, screwdrivers, and tweezers) from websites such as www.jewelertools.com.

Minding the Gap

Occasionally the gap between a reed and the reed plate becomes too large or small, or the reed might become slightly misaligned in relation to its slot. This likely will be evidenced by a buzzing sound (misaligned reed), an unresponsive or sticking reed (gap too small), or a "windy" sounding reed (gap too large).

This gap is too large.

This gap is too small.

This gap is just right.

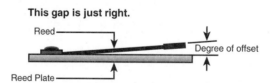

The gap should be about the same thickness as the reed itself.

Remove the faceplates and inspect the reeds on each reed plate. If the broken reed is on the bottom reed plate, you need to unscrew the comb-reed plate assembly to inspect the bottom reeds. The reeds should all be aligned straight in relation to the slots. Identify the reed that is not working correctly. If it's too weak or breathy, then the gap needs to be decreased. If it chokes up too easily, then the gap needs to be increased. If you don't have the special pick that comes in a harmonica toolkit, you can use a toothpick or pin to *very carefully* pry, nudge, or press the reed into the proper position. If the reed is misaligned vis-à-vis the slot, you should use the toolkit's alignment tool to align the reed correctly on top of the slot. You also can use needle-nosed pliers or a jeweler's pliers or wrench to carefully rotate the attached end of the reed (where the metal plug holds it in place) until it is correctly aligned.

Tuning

Harmonica reeds go out of tune with extended use, particularly if you're a hard blower, but it isn't all that difficult to tune an out-of-tune reed. Harmonica toolkits include a scraping tool for this task, or you can use a very fine file. If the pitch of the reed is flat, you can *lightly* file or scrape the unattached end of the reed to raise the pitch. If the pitch is sharp, you can file or scrape the attached end of the reed to lower the pitch. Don't get carried away. It takes only a little filing or scraping to alter the reed's pitch. You should be filing or scraping metal away from the flat surface of the reed, not from the edge (you are *not* trying to shorten the reed). You should support the reed with something like a razor blade so that you don't accidentally push it down through the slot. If you don't have perfect pitch (and most of us don't), you can match the pitch to the corresponding note on a pitch pipe or electronic tuner.

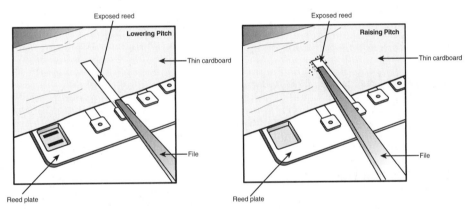

a) To lower the pitch, scrape the attached end of the reed. b) To raise it, scrape the unattached end. Scrape metal from the flat surface of the reed. Do not shorten the reed by scraping the edges.

Replacing Individual Reeds

This isn't all that easy to do, but if you're handy with tools, have good eyes, and saved all those old harmonicas like we told you to, you can replace a blown or cracked reed with a reed from another harmonica.

1. Find a reed from an old harmonica, preferably the same pitch so you don't have to try to tune it.

2. Push it out of the reed plate from the bottom using an awl or other sharp tool, like a pin punch. You also might be able to get it out of the reed plate using needle-nosed pliers from the top, or a combination of both. The reed and the metal plug should come out together.

3. Then use the same technique to remove the bad reed from the reed plate you're repairing. Align the replacement reed so that it's properly

Blues Clues

Replacement reed plate kits cost about one half the price of a new harmonica and can be purchased at music stores or online at manufacturers' and other harmonica vendors' websites. Many of them are listed in Appendix B.

positioned over the slot on this reed plate and push the plug into the hole. Make sure the replacement reed is properly aligned and that it's flush with the reed plate, and then lightly hammer the plug from both sides with a jeweler's hammer or squeeze the plug lightly with needle-nose pliers until it's firmly secured.

4. Finally, gap the reed as described in the preceding "Minding the Gap" section.

Replacing reeds is a lot of work, and it's a little tricky to get right. If you're going to attempt it, make sure you purchase the proper tools described in this chapter.

Replacing the Entire Reed Plate

The easiest way to deal with an out-of-tune or blown reed is to simply replace the entire reed plate. This can easily be done with most modern harmonicas by removing a reed plate from a discarded harmonica and using it to replace a bad one in the same key (assuming the reed plate you need wasn't the one that went bad on the discarded harmonica). Alternatively, some harmonicas, including Lee Oskar, Hohner, Suzuki, and Bushman models, are designed so that the reed plates can be replaced with new ones available from the manufacturer.

Quandaries and Queries

Before you run to a repair shop with your harp, check out the following chart to see if the problem is something you can solve yourself.

Quandaries and Queries

Quandary/Query	Possible Cause	Solution/Answer
Unresponsive/slow reed	1. Particle, gunk, or saliva is blocking reed vibration.	1. Slap harmonica against leg or hand.
		Or take harmonica apart and use toothpick/pin to clear reed or clean blocked reeds with Q-Tip and isopropyl alcohol.
	2. Or reed gap is too small.	2. Increase gap of reed using gapping tool or toothpick/pin.
Windy sound when playing	1. Reed gap is too large.	1. Decrease gap of reed using gapping tool or toothpick/pin.
	2. Your lips are leaking.	2. Close your mouth tighter.
Buzzing or vibrating sound when playing	1. Reed is not aligned correctly over the slot.	1. Correct reed alignment using alignment tool or small jeweler's needle-nosed pliers or wrench.
	2. You have a screw loose.	2. Turn head to side and try to shake screw out through ear hole.

Quandary/Query	Possible Cause	Solution/Answer
Should I soak my harmonica in whiskey to break it in?		No. This ultimately will ruin your harp. Just break it in the nice and slow way.
How do I keep saliva out of my harmonica while playing?		1. Periodically slap your harmonica against your leg or hand. 2. Play with your nose pointed at the ceiling.
The pitch of a note is flat.	The reed is out of tune.	Tune the reed sharper by lightly scraping the unattached end with a scraping tool or small file.
The pitch of a note is sharp.	The reed is out of tune.	Tune the reed flatter by lightly scraping the attached end with a scraping tool or small file.
Do I need to clean my harmonicas?		Absolutely. Follow the instructions in this chapter.
My harmonica tastes like chocolate.	Your kid has been playing it while eating a candy bar.	Hide it better while you're at work.
My harmonica tastes like whiskey.	You've been soaking it.	Stop it. We told you not to do that. You'll ruin it.
No matter what I do, there's a note that just won't play right.	The reed is blown or fatigued beyond repair.	Replace individual reed or entire reed plate. Follow the instructions in this chapter.
What should I do with my old harps that don't work right anymore?		Save them. You can use them as a source of replacement parts. They also make interesting Christmas tree ornaments.
The notes I'm trying are coming out all wrong.	You probably are playing the wrong key harmonica or are holding it upside down.	Be cool and get yourself to play straightened out. Hope that no one notices. If they do, mumble something about playing in the fourth position.
Some of the holes on my new harmonica don't seem to play right.	This is common with new harmonicas particularly for high notes and the low draw holes.	Break your harp in gently as described in this chapter.
The audience suddenly gets an uncomfortable, pained look.	You've just played a hideously wrong note.	It's okay. Next time around, play it wrong again but louder. The audience will think you're skillfully innovative instead of merely untalented.
Do "chicks" usually go for harp players?		No, not unless you're also the lead singer.

continues

Quandaries and Queries (continued)

Quandary/Query	Possible Cause	Solution/Answer
Where can I get the tools I need to maintain and repair my harp?		Buy one of the harp toolkits, or you can purchase jeweler's tools.
What can I do to maintain and repair my chromatic harmonicas?		The best source of information on maintaining and repairing chromatic harmonicas is *Make Your Harmonica Work Better* by Douglas Tate (Centerstream, 1999). We've also listed several professional harmonica repair centers in Appendix B.

The harmonica is sometimes referred to as "the people's instrument," and one of the reasons is that almost anyone can afford to own and maintain one. Treat your harps with care, do simple repairs yourself, and hey, if you have to buy a replacement, you can do it for a song.

The Least You Need to Know

◆ Treat your harp like a precision-engineered musical instrument, because it is.

◆ Don't give up on your instrument if it breaks down. You can usually fix it.

◆ Never throw it away. There's always something you can use it for.

◆ When all else fails, just buy a new harp. At least you tried.

Part 2

Let's Get Blowin'

Learn how harmonica players play music without having to know how to read music, using a tablature system, and start learning how to play it correctly, coordinating your tongue, lungs, lips, hands, throat, diaphragm, and feet. Get off to a correct start by practicing the techniques we describe until you feel comfortable with them, and start having some fun playing more notes and playing faster.

Chapter 5

Harp Talk

In This Chapter

- ◆ What the straight arrows mean in the tablature system
- ◆ What the "Bs" mean
- ◆ What the hollow circles mean

There are a lot of good reasons to learn to read traditional music notation. Music is the only true international language. The music notation system that originated in Europe has come to be used throughout most of the world. If you want to learn how to read music, you can, in Chapter 10.

The good news is that you don't *have* to know how to read music to become a very good harp player. Many of the best harpists in the world can't read a note, and they get along just fine with their ears and instincts. The harmonica world has developed a very simple, easy-to-read tablature system for playing music. Actually, it's developed a multitude of tablature systems, so when you play from other harmonica books, you'll need to learn the particular tablature system used in those books.

What's Going On Here?

Playing the harp (or any other instrument for that matter) is not just about playing notes and tunes. You can't make real music until you learn a multitude of musical and physical techniques and practice them, over and over. The three chapters that follow teach you how to do that. In this chapter, we help you become familiar with your instrument and with the *tablature* system.

Before we begin, let's take a closer look at what you're playing. Remember that the blow notes are designated by capital letters and the draw notes by small letters.

def•i•ni•tion

A **tablature** system is any notation system that does not use standard music notation to designate notes and rhythms to be played. Harmonicas, guitars, and drums all have tablature systems that are used as an alternative to standard music notation. There are several different styles of harmonica tablature. You should always check the front of any new harmonica book for an explanation of the tablature system used in that book.

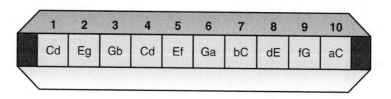

Examine this drawing closely. You'll see that all the blow notes are C, E, and G. This means that no matter where you blow on the harp, you'll get the elements of a C-major chord. The draw notes are even more interesting. Depending on which holes you draw, you'll create a G-major chord, a G-seventh chord, a D-minor chord, a partial F-major chord, or, if you draw any combination including both the 6- and 7-holes, a really ugly chord. All these chords, with the exception of the last ugly one, are used along with the C-major chord in many kinds of folk and popular music.

Go ahead and blow, then draw, on each hole on your harmonica. Note that for all the holes up through the 6-hole, the draw note is higher than the blow note. This pattern reverses with the 7-hole, and all draw notes from the 7-hole up are lower than the blow note. Last, you'll see that the only place on the harmonica where you can play a complete C-major scale is by starting at the 4-blow-hole and going up through the 7-draw-hole. Then you have to reverse the order of your blows and draws at the 7-hole.

Also note that holes 1 to 3, 4 to 7, and 8 to 10 are each separate octaves. Each repeats all or most of the seven notes of the diatonic scale but at successively higher pitch ranges.

All of this might seem meaningless right now, but as you learn the tonal patterns of your harmonica and start to play songs in different styles, you'll understand why your harmonica is designed the way it is.

The Tablature System

Fortunately, all the tablature systems work in the same way. They just use different symbols to represent the various components of harmonica tablature. These components are as follows:

♦ What note to play

♦ How long to play it

- Whether or not you should bend the note
- How much you should bend it
- When to use the slide button on a chromatic harmonica

What Note to Play

In this book, we use numbers to designate the hole you should play on the harp, and up or down arrows to indicate whether you should blow or draw. An up arrow together with the number 4 indicates that you should blow on the 4-hole. A down arrow together with the number 5 indicates that you should draw on the 5-hole. A column of two or three numbers indicates that you should play the designated holes as a chord. Following is a sample of how this tablature system works:

Single notes:

↑	↓	↑	↓	↑	↓	↓	↑
4	4	5	5	6	6	7	7

Chords:

↑	↓	↑	↓	↑	↓	↑	↓	↑
4	4	5	5	6	5	5	4	4
3	3	4	4	5	4	4	3	3
2	2	3	3	4	3	3	2	2

Example of up and down arrows.

How Long to Play It

We're using short stems on the arrows to indicate that a note should be played short, and longer stems to indicate that a note should be held longer. Three different stem lengths are used, as follows:

↑ ↓ = short note (one beat or less)

↕ ↕ = medium note (usually two beats)

↕ ↕ = long note (usually four beats)

For ease of reading, we place a single slash across the stem of the middle-length arrow and a double slash across the stem of the longest arrow.

The shortest stem generally indicates that the note should be held for one beat or less. Notes with the middle-length stem should be held two beats, and notes with the longest stem should be held four beats. We say "generally" because harmonica tablature is not an exact science. True music notation has a multitude of different note lengths, and it is impossible to replicate all of them within the limitations of harmonica tablature. You're going to have to feel your way through this to a certain extent, using the stem lengths only as a general guide.

This kind of tablature really encourages you to listen to versions of the song you want to play. Your ear is capable of perceiving rhythms with much greater precision than your eyes.

We're using vertical lines to separate *measures* so that you can pick up the rhythm of the song you're playing. Measures indicate recurring subgroups of the stream of notes. The first note of each measure usually is accented slightly (that is, played with more force). This is what gives the music its "beat." If you play eight beats and accent the first and fifth beat more than the others, you would say that you had counted out two measures with four beats in each measure.

def•i•ni•tion

In music, a **measure** is a unit used to separate notes into rhythm patterns and a uniform number of beats. There are typically three or four beats per measure, although there can be more or less. The measures establish a rhythm and accent pattern for the music. For example, the first beat in each measure usually is accented, giving the music a rhythm that you can tap your foot or dance to. A measure is also referred to as a *bar*. You'll sometimes hear songs referred to by the number of measures in the song, such as 12-bar blues or a 32-bar ballad.

If you're supposed to *rest* (not play) at any point in a measure, we use an "R" for *rest* to indicate that you do not play.

Should You Bend the Note?

Notes that should be bent are indicated with a B next to the hole number. We do not use these Bs or teach you how to bend notes until Chapter 12.

1B   2B   3B   4B   8B   9B

How Much Should You Bend It?

Later, you will learn to do single bends, double bends, and triple bends of notes. We use a B^2 by the hole number to designate a double bend and B^3 to designate a triple bend. Don't worry about what this means now. We explain it in Chapter 12.

B = single bend

B^2 = double bend

B^3 = triple bend

When to Use the Slide Button on a Chromatic Harmonica

The chromatic harmonica has a slide button that you push to play certain non-diatonic notes. Notes on which you should push the slide button are indicated by placing the hole number inside a hollow circle, as follows:

Blues Clues

As you learn to play songs, start to make them your own. Experiment with your new skills. Add some notes and chords here and there. Slide around a little. Try a little syncopation (i.e., accent the off beat instead of the beat you tap your foot with) and different rhythms. Have some fun and impress your friends.

↑ ↑ ↓ ↓ ↑ ↑ ↓ ↑ ↑ ↓ ↓ ↑
5 ⑤ 5 ⑤ 6 ⑥ ⑥ 7 ⑦ 7 ⑦ 8 8

Example of chromatic tablature with slide-button notes placed in hollow circles.

Some Familiar Tunes

Now, let's play three familiar songs using harmonica tablature. At this point, you have not learned *how* to play the harmonica using correct technique, but we want you to get a preliminary feeling for how the tablature system works. So for now, don't worry about how you sound. Just follow the arrows and make your first harmonica music.

Blues Clues

We have included a CD in this edition of the book. Many of the exercises and songs from the book are played on the CD so that you can hear what they should sound like. They are designated with a CD icon: ●. See Appendix C for a description of the CD and our supplementary website, as well as a listing of all exercises and songs that are included on the CD.

● Mary Had a Little Lamb

↑	↓	↑	↓	↑	↑	↑		↓	↓	↓		↑	↑	↑
5	4	4	4	5	5	5		4	4	4		5	6	6

↑	↓	↑	↓	↑	↑	↑	↑	↓	↓	↑	↓	
5	4	4	4	5	5	5	4	4	4	5	4	4
4	3	3	3	4	4	4	3	3	3	4	3	3
3	2	2	2	3	3	3	2	2	2	3	2	2

● Twinkle Twinkle Little Star

↑	↑	↑	↑	↓	↓	↓		↓	↓	↑	↑	↓	↓	
4	4	6	6	6	6	6		5	5	5	5	4	4	4

↑	↑	↓	↓	↑	↑	↑	↑	↑	↓	↓	↑	↑	
6	6	5	5	5	5	4	6	6	5	5	5	5	4

↑	↑	↑	↑	↓	↓	↓		↓	↓	↑	↑	↓	↓	
4	4	6	6	6	6	6		5	5	5	5	4	4	4
3	3	5	5	5	5	5		4	4	4	4	3	3	3
2	2	4	4	4	4	4		3	3	3	3	2	2	2

● When the Saints Go Marching In

R	↑	↑	↓	↑		R	↑	↑	↓	↑		R	↑	↑	↓	↑	↑	↑	↑	
R	4	5	5	6		R	4	5	5	6		R	4	5	5	6	5	4	5	4
				5						5						5	4	3	4	3
				4						4						4	3	2	3	2

R	↑	↓	↑	↑	↑	↑	↓	↑	↓	↓	↑	↑	↑	↓	↑	
R	5	4	4	4	5	6	6	6	5	5	6	5	4	4	4
											5	4	3	3	3
											4	3	2	2	2

"Mary Had a Little Lamb," "Twinkle Twinkle Little Star," and "When the Saints Go Marching In" (using both single notes and chords), all in harmonica tablature.

We use the preceding harmonica tablature system for all the exercises and songs in the rest of the book. It's somewhat limited and cumbersome, so we try to use songs that are familiar to you. Starting with Chapter 10, we also include the traditional music notation. Its versatility and scope enable us to use a wider variety of songs in the remainder of the book. You choose which system you prefer to follow, but we strongly encourage you to take the time to go through Chapter 10 and learn to read music. We promise it will be time well spent.

The Least You Need to Know

- ◆ The numbers tell you which hole to blow or draw.
- ◆ An up arrow means blow, and a down arrow means draw.
- ◆ The length of the arrow's stem indicates how long the note should be held.
- ◆ Long vertical lines are used to separate measures, so you can establish the beat.
- ◆ An "R" means to give it a rest.

Chapter **6**

Body Language

In This Chapter

◆ The importance of correct posture
◆ Positioning your hands correctly
◆ Focusing your airstream
◆ Breathing exercises that improve your tone
◆ Controlling your mouth and lips

Your body is such an important aspect of playing the diatonic harp because, from a purely mechanical standpoint, the harp is a very limited instrument. It's designed to play only 20 notes, and cannot play the chromatic notes in any key. You use your body to overcome these limitations. In a sense, you're playing your body more than you're playing the harmonica. The result is an extremely versatile instrument unrestrained by its mechanical limitations.

Don't simply skim through this chapter and move on. It's more difficult to unlearn bad habits than it is to learn correct ones. What we tell you about how to stand, breathe, and position your hands, mouth, and lips will give you a solid foundation for learning the increasingly difficult techniques in the chapters that follow.

The harp is not a rigid instrument, and you shouldn't take on the formal demeanor of a symphony orchestra musician. Harp music is best when it flows freely from your heart, and your body needs to be loose and relaxed for that to happen. Relax, enjoy yourself, and move at a comfortable pace. Before you start practicing, clear your mind of any distractions. Free yourself from thinking about your daily issues. Pretend you're entering Disney World, where you can check your everyday problems at the gate. After you're finished playing, you might be surprised to discover a fresh, more positive outlook. That's part of the magic of playing the harp.

Stand Up Straight! Suck in That Gut!

Posture is simple. It's best to play standing up because it ensures that you breathe deeply from your diaphragm. Stand erect with your back straight. If you prefer to play seated, sit up straight and keep your stomach and chest cavities open and relaxed.

You may have seen pictures of harpists in instruction books, overdemonstrating their interpretation of proper posture. If you get carried away with this, you'll look like Barney Fife playing the harmonica. That's not the goal.

Don't Harp On It

Remember, harmonica players are cool. You've got to look cool to feel cool, and you've got to feel cool to play cool. Pay attention to your posture, but don't tense up and don't get too wrapped up in how you're standing or sitting. Your audience will be listening to you more than they'll be watching you. Stand however you need to stand to get the sound you want to get.

Keep Both Hands on the Harp

The reason that the harmonica sometimes is called a "tin sandwich" is that you hold it just like a sandwich, as follows:

1. Fit the harmonica (with the hole numbers on top) into the V of your left hand, supporting it between the thumb and middle finger. Keep your fingers on top pressed together, and leave about one-half inch of open space between the edge of the harmonica and your forefinger (this is so there's enough space to get a good lip grip on the harp).

2. The right hand is used to create effects. Cup it under the harmonica with the heels of both hands together and the fingers of the right hand curled slightly upward. Keep the fingers of your left hand pressed together and positioned so that when you lift them, they close with the back edge of your right hand and envelop the front of the harmonica.

3. Try blowing into the harmonica while simultaneously raising and lowering your right hand. If you're doing it correctly, you'll hear a *tremolo* effect as you close your right hand together with the left. Make sure you're bringing your hands together and completely closing off the front of the harmonica. The goal is to get a good airtight seal. Keep the heels of your two hands together while you're doing this. Try doing this fast and slow, and get comfortable with the hand positioning.

It takes a while before your hand placement feels completely natural. As you become more familiar with it, you might experiment with positioning your right hand until it feels comfortable for you. Some harpists keep the right hand more to the right side of the harp and slide it over in front when they want to

def·i·ni·tion

A **tremolo** effect is a wavering sound produced by playing the same note on the double set of reeds of a tremolo harmonica. Each set of reeds on this diatonic harmonica is tuned to slightly different pitches of the same note, resulting in the tremolo effect.

create an effect. As you try different positions, you'll notice that the tone of the harp is affected by even slight alterations in your hand positioning. You generally should strive for the fullest (sometimes called "fattest") tone possible. Then, as you progress, you'll learn how to use your hand positioning to alter your tone from full to "thin" as desired.

If you're left-handed and feel more comfortable reversing the hand positioning, that's okay, but you won't be able to play a chromatic harmonica from this reversed position, as the slide button is on the right side.

 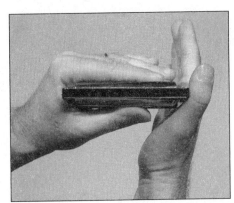

Closed and open hand positions.

Take Some Deep Breaths

Fortunately, breathing is something you've been doing all your life, and you don't have to learn a completely new way of breathing to play the harmonica.

The main thing about breathing and playing the harp is to breathe *from the diaphragm.* All this means is that you need to breathe fully and draw the air into your lungs past your chest. Your stomach, not your chest, should expand as you breathe. When you exhale, you should push from your stomach. This technique gives you a controlled and focused flow of air going both ways.

We don't mean you should breath *hard;* on the contrary, you want to breathe about the same way you do when you talk. Playing the harmonica doesn't take a lot of air; it just takes a controlled and focused stream of air. This is particularly true when you're first learning to play. It's very easy to blow too hard and choke off the reed so that it makes no sound at all.

While playing, you should never completely expel air from your lungs or have your lungs completely full of air. Leaving a bit of room for expansion and contraction makes it easier to smoothly transition between playing draw and blow notes.

Here's how to focus your airflow:

1. Place the harmonica fully into your mouth with your lips firmly over the edges on both the top and bottom. Don't be timid about putting the harmonica all the way in. It's not to be played from the outside of the lips.

> **Blues Clues**
>
> You can create a slightly more difficult hand effect by using your right hand like a mute on a trumpet. This involves trapping air in your tightly closed hand as you blow or draw a note, and then opening the hand quickly at the same time that you stop the flow of air. This creates a *wah-wah* effect like a trumpet's mute.

2. Focus on blowing air *through* the harmonica rather than into it, and, when you're breathing in, drawing air all the way *through* the harmonica into your lungs. This is just another way of training yourself to provide a controlled and focused flow of air without having to think about it.

The quality of your airflow is critical for creating a good sound, particularly for the high notes and low draw notes. You'll practice them when you start playing single notes in Chapter 7

Breathing Exercise

For now, just practice breathing into the harmonica, blowing and drawing.

1. Start by playing long blows followed by long draws. Hold them out as long as you can and then immediately reverse the flow of air and start again.

2. Move up and down the harmonica, playing long blow and draw notes. Concentrate on your stomach and on blowing *through* the harmonica both ways. This technique gives the controlled, focused airflow you need for a good sound.

3. Gradually speed up the changes from blowing to drawing until you're alternating quickly—several times a second. Then gradually slow down again.

4. Repeat this pattern again and again, always concentrating on your stomach and on blowing through the harmonica.

You'll probably feel yourself running out of air, even if you're a swimmer or jogger used to controlled breathing. Playing the harmonica is a different type of breathing from the breathing used in those physical activities. As you practice playing, your breathing will improve and you'll learn to control the airflow as necessary to create a good sound without running out of breath.

So what's your nose contributing to all of this? Not much, actually. You don't want to breathe through your nose, any more than you would breathe through your nose to blow out a candle or blow through a straw. With practice, you'll learn how to use your nose to release air pressure and to draw in extra air when needed for an upcoming lengthy blow phrase. For now, keep your nose out of it.

Blues Clues _____

If you're a spiritually oriented person and are into yoga, harmonica breathing should come pretty easily to you. The basic techniques of harmonica breathing and yoga breathing are the same, except that you can get chords with the harmonica; *pranayama* only enables you to produce single notes.

Blues Clues _____

A controlled, focused stream of air is the starting point for a good harp sound. You should think of the air as starting in your belly and flowing out through your mouth into and *through* the harmonica. On its return route, it passes *through* the harmonica again and all the way down into your belly. Don't let it stop in your mouth or in the harmonica. Keep it moving.

Open Wide and Say "Oooh"

The type of sound you produce with your harp is directly related to how your lip position affects your airflow. You'll get the idea when you do the following:

Place the harmonica fully into your mouth, not quite touching your teeth. The inside of your lips should be resting on the top and bottom of the harmonica, not on the front. You don't play the harmonica from the front or with the outside of your lips. Your lips should be covering the entire half-inch space on top of the harp and touching the edge of your forefinger and thumb.

Note that the harp is fully in the mouth so that the insides of the lips are resting on the top and bottom of the instrument.

Generally speaking, the deeper you can place the harp in your mouth and still play single notes, the better. This lip positioning enables you to produce the airflow required for full-bodied sounds and strong bends. Do not angle the harmonica in your mouth, at least at first. That would obstruct your airflow and make playing the low draw notes and high notes even more difficult.

As you become more comfortable playing the harp, you might experiment with its angle to test the differences in sound.

As you learn to play the more difficult techniques such as playing fast riffs and moving quickly from high to low notes, your harp will be moving sideways in your mouth. Note that we didn't say your *head* would be moving; *your harp will be doing the moving.*

Use your hands to slide your harp against your lips; don't use your head to slide up and down the harp. Watch yourself in a mirror, and you'll quickly understand what we mean. Think of your lips as a stationary point, with you bringing

Don't Harp On It

If you have a mustache or beard, be careful. It's best to keep them trimmed. Your facial hair definitely can get caught in the gaps between the faceplates and the comb, which makes moving on to the next note rather painful.

def•i•ni•tion

A **trill,** also called a *shake* or *warble,* is the alternation of two adjacent notes on the harmonica caused by either moving the harmonica quickly sideways with the hand or shaking the head quickly from side to side, depending on which technique is preferred. The notes will blend together and sound almost like a single note.

the hole you're playing to that point. When you get into your music, obviously your whole body will be moving, but between your harmonica and your head, it's the harmonica that will be moving. (The only possible exception to this is when performing a *trill,* which sometimes is played by shaking or vibrating the head instead of moving the harmonica. The techniques for trilling are discussed in Chapter 8.)

When you first start playing, you might have problems with air leaking between the corners of your lips and the harmonica, and your lips will tire easily. The more you practice, the stronger your lips will become, and the leaking problem will resolve itself. At first, you may need to concentrate on pushing the harp back against the corners of your lips, but eventually they'll form a natural seal with the edge of the harp.

Before we close this chapter and move on to more advanced techniques, try blowing a long note through your harmonica while silently saying *a-e-i-o-u.* As you say each vowel, you'll notice a slight change in your lips and mouth that, in turn, produces a slight variation in the sound you're producing. It's not particularly important right now, but it demonstrates how even slight variations in your technique can alter your sound.

The Least You Need to Know

◆ Play relaxed.

◆ Breathe from your belly and *through* the harp.

◆ Concentrate on producing a controlled, focused airflow.

◆ Don't just nibble at your harp. Put it all the way into your mouth. The insides of your lips should be resting on the top and bottom of the harp.

◆ Again, play relaxed.

Chapter

Playing Your First Notes

In This Chapter

◆ Using your mouth, tongue, and lips to create music

◆ Learning to play chords and single notes

◆ Using tongue twisters to produce different sounds and rhythms

◆ Producing a beautiful tone

In this chapter, you'll discover that playing the harmonica uses and requires more control over your lips, mouth, and tongue than you ever imagined. Many of the techniques we describe will not come naturally or be learned immediately. It'll require practice and patience on your part, but stick with it. We promise that all of the techniques will be second nature to you by the time you finish this book.

Let's Start with Some Chords

It's somewhat ironic that the harmonica is so often used to play chords because, unlike other instruments such as piano or string instruments, the harmonica has a very limited range of available chords. Nevertheless, you often hear the harmonica used primarily to provide backup chords or rhythms, and even harmonica solos usually are a mixture of chords and single notes. This is probably because, even though the selection of chords may be limited, the sounds created by playing chords on a harmonica can be quite unique and agreeable to the ear.

Playing chords is much simpler and more natural than playing single notes. You simply open your mouth wide enough to cover four, three, or two holes, and then blow and draw (remembering to use the breathing technique and lip positioning described in Chapter 6).

Let's look again at the diagram of the C-major diatonic harmonica:

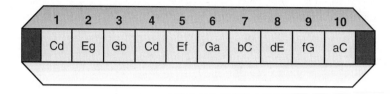

Now, to play chords:

1. Take your harmonica and use the forefinger of your right hand to cover up all the holes except the 1-2-3 holes.

2. Bring the harp to your lips (keeping your finger in place) and blow through the 1-2-3 holes. You just created a C-major chord (C, E, G).

3. Use the forefingers of both hands to cover all the holes except 4-5-6. Blow through these holes. Another C-major chord (C, E, G).

4. Cover different combinations of holes with your fingers and blow through the uncovered holes.

Every chord you blow is some combination of notes creating a C-major chord.

1. Now cover all the holes except 1-2-3 and draw. You've just played a G-major chord (D, G, B).

2. Cover all the holes except 2-3-4-5 and draw. This creates a G-seventh chord (G, B, D, F).

3. Cover all holes except 5 and 6 and draw. This note is a partial F-major chord (F and A, but missing the C).

If you look at the draw notes on the diagram, you'll see that most combinations produce a G-major, G-seventh, or partial F-major chord. That means, when you play a C-major diatonic harmonica, you have at your disposal the notes required to play C-major, G-major, G-seventh, and partial F-major chords. These chords will get you through a lot of songs in your typical jam sessions.

You also have two draw combinations of D, F, and A (4-5-6 holes and 8-9-10 holes), which produce a D-minor chord. Finally, there's the possible draw combination of A and B (6- and 7-holes), which produces an ugly sound that really isn't a chord at all.

Chord Exercise Number 1

1. Try playing various combinations of three-note chords without using your fingers to block the holes. Try both blow and draw chords. Look at the numbers first to determine which holes you want to play. Start by blowing or drawing from the 1-hole and counting up to the first hole of the chord you want to play. As you get more comfortable with the hole positions, you won't need to do this. If you aren't certain you're playing the correct three notes, go back to blocking the holes you don't want with your fingers. That way, you can check your notes.

2. Practice the preceding exercise, moving up and down the harmonica, until you can play three-note chords comfortably without counting holes up from the 1-hole and without using your fingers to block holes. The goals are to be able to (1) simply look at the hole numbers and place the harmonica correctly in your mouth so that you can play the desired chord, and (2) control your lip opening so that you can consistently play a three-note chord.

Chord Exercise Number 2

1. Now do exactly the same thing you did in the previous exercise, but practice playing partial two-note chords. This requires you to slightly decrease the size of your lip opening. Do everything else just as you did to play three-note chords.

2. When you're comfortable playing two-note chords and can control your lip opening to play them consistently, practice alternating between three-note chords and two-note chords. You'll slightly increase or decrease the size of your lip opening to achieve this. First, practice it by stopping the flow of air between each chord, adjusting your lip opening and playing the next chord. Then practice alternating between three- and two-note chords by adjusting your lip opening without stopping the airflow.

Chord Exercise Number 3

1. Try drawing once on the 1-2-3 holes and then blowing twice. Repeat this slowly, and then gradually speed up. As you get faster, accent the draw note. Raise the fingers on your right hand to close off the front of the harp, and open your hand on your accented draw note. Keep closing it on the blow notes and reopening it on the draw note. Go faster and faster. Now go to the 3-4 (or 4-5) holes and draw a long note. Tighten your lips and slightly pinch, or cut off, the airflow on this draw note. Open your hand as you start the draw, close when you pinch the airflow, and open it again as you continue the draw. Do you hear that train a-comin'? Is it comin' round that bend?

2. After you've tried accelerating and decelerating, pick a comfortable tempo and play this exercise. Try to play it at that tempo for as long as you can. It can be a slow tempo. What you want to focus on is keeping a steady beat.

'Tis Nobler to Pucker or Tongue?

One of the great deliberations among harmonica scholars is the impassioned debate over whether single notes should be played by puckering or tongue blocking. There seems to be no consensus among the harmonica intellectuals or the great masters, and many use both techniques in combination.

We come down on this issue firmly in the middle, because you need to know how to do both.

It's best to start with puckering, partly because it's easier. However, it also has some other advantages. You can more easily produce a clean, melodic sound with this technique, particularly on the high notes, and it's easier to bend notes using puckering. But you obviously don't always want a clean, melodic sound on the harp. Tongue blocking allows for a fuller sound and deeper bends. It also opens up a new world of sounds and effects that you can create playing your harp. Particularly when you play heavy blues, you'll want to use tongue-blocking techniques to produce the raw, heavy sounds that often exemplify that style of music. For this, you need to produce special effects such as tongue-block octaves, tongue-block chords, and tongue-block tremolos. We get into these effects in Chapters 11 and 12. For now, we'll focus on how to produce basic single notes using both the puckering and tongue-blocking techniques.

Blues Clues

There's a third method of playing the harp called "U-blocking" or "tube tonguing." It's achieved by curling your tongue like a tube around the hole you want to play, thus blocking the holes on both sides of the one you're playing. If you're one of those people who can curl your tongue into a tube, you might want to try this. It allegedly produces a nice, full tone. However, you can't bend notes very easily or play tongue-blocking special effects using this method.

Puckering

If you can whistle, even badly, then you can pucker. If you can blow through a straw, you can pucker. If you can't do either, then move on down to the paragraph on tongue blocking.

You started out playing three-note chords. You slightly decreased the size of your lip opening and played two-note chords. Now you're merely going to slightly decrease the size of your lip opening again and produce single notes.

Try this on your 5-hole:

1. Blow a long note, and then draw a long note. Move up and down your harp playing single blow and draw notes. Concentrate on getting a clean, clear, rich tone. If your opening is too wide, air will bleed into one of the other holes and your tone will not be clean.

2. Practice playing only long notes, holding them as long as you can. Make sure they're clean, clear, and rich. Remember the breathing techniques and lip positioning discussed in Chapter 6. It doesn't take a lot of air to create the tone you want. Listen for leaking air, particularly on the high notes, and seal your outer lips more tightly around the harmonica if this is a problem (but don't clamp them—stay relaxed).

Straight from the Harp

The pucker method of playing single notes also is referred to as the "whistle" or "lipping" method.

Don't Harp On It

Do *not* puff out your cheeks. That creates a pocket where air can accumulate instead of moving into and through the harmonica, and it messes up your airflow and lip positioning. Besides, it makes you look stupid.

3. As you do this, you'll hit a point when you're consistently playing your single notes with the right kind of tone. Then it's okay to start practicing shorter notes, again concentrating on achieving the same clean, clear, and rich tone.

As you move up to the higher notes, you'll discover that they're more difficult to play, partly because the reeds for high notes are shorter and not as flexible. Your problems with high notes, however, are primarily caused by using too much air when you blow and draw. You must narrow your airflow even more to play the high notes on a harmonica, and blow and draw with less force than on the lower notes.

The low draw notes are often difficult to play with a good tone on a new harmonica, too. They may sound airy at first. You'll need to focus and control your airflow for these two notes more than for your other draw notes. That doesn't mean drawing the air *harder*; on the contrary, you might need to cut back the flow of air on the draw notes to get a good tone. The low draw holes will improve as they get broken in and you start working with them on bends, but they'll always be a little more contentious than your other draw holes. It's just part of harp playing.

Single-Note Exercise Number 1

Start at the 4-hole and play this:

4-blow, 4-draw, 5-blow, 5-draw, 6-blow, 6-draw, 7-draw, 7-blow

Note the reversal of the pattern at the 7-hole. You just played a C-major scale. Now start at the 1-hole and slowly blow/draw your way all the way to the 10-hole so that you understand the pattern of the notes.

Tongue Blocking

Tongue blocking is much more difficult to master than puckering. The basic concept is to use the tip of your tongue to block all holes on the left side of your mouth, while directing a stream of air out the right side of your mouth through one hole. Easier said than done. Take a look at the following diagram to get an understanding of what should be happening inside your mouth:

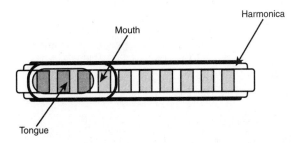

You won't pucker your lips for this technique. Instead, you'll position them much the same way as for a three-note chord. Go ahead and play some chords in this position. Then place your tongue gently against the harmonica and block

> **Blues Clues**
>
> For both puckering and tongue blocking, you want to play smoothly and fluidly. Don't break your airflow between notes; move from one note to the other while keeping it steady.

all the holes except the one to the right. Use only the tip of your tongue. You don't need much tongue to block the airflow to the two holes on the left. Try blowing and drawing through this one open hole. You will probably hear more than one note, or a sputtering sound. That just means you need to practice correctly placing your tongue so that you block all the notes except one, and leave that one hole totally unobstructed. You might notice a note leaking through on the left side. Make sure you're totally blocking the airflow on the left side of your mouth with your tongue. You also may notice that your tone sounds more pinched than when you pucker. That means you're slightly blocking the airflow through the hole you're trying to play. You need to adjust your tongue a little to the left.

Practice playing long notes first, exactly as you did with the puckering technique. Do we need to say it again? Remember your breathing techniques and lip positioning. Remember to focus on producing a controlled, focused airflow. Move up and down the harmonica, playing all the notes with both blow and draw. Then start playing shorter notes. This technique takes longer to master than puckering, but the goal is the same: a clean, clear, rich tone. Also, as difficult as this might be to believe, your tongue and lips have to stay relaxed during this whole process or your tone will not be what you want it to be.

Single-Note Exercise Number 2

1. Practice playing long and short single notes, switching periodically from puckering to tongue blocking. Then play long notes and switch from puckering to tongue blocking and back several times while playing the notes. Do this by slightly increasing the size of your lip opening and gently placing your tongue against the notes that have just been opened up. Try to do it without breaking the airflow or allowing any additional notes to leak through.

2. Now play a series of notes using the puckering technique, and immediately play the same series again using tongue blocking. This is good practice for later when you'll need to switch from puckering to tongue blocking to achieve different sounds and effects.

Single-Note Exercise Number 3

1. Now add chords to the mix. Practice playing combinations of single notes and chords, moving from puckered single notes to two- and three-note chords and back to tongue-blocked single notes. As with the preceding exercise, this is good practice for playing more complex songs later.

2. Don't just randomly jump from one style to another. Move up and down the harmonica in a pattern and play several series of notes in one style, and then play the same series in a different style. For example, play any five- to ten-note pattern of your liking in puckered single notes, then play the same pattern using two-note chords, then three-note chords, and last, tongue-blocked single notes.

More Tonguing Techniques

Tah-tah is more than merely the way some people say good-bye. It's also a very important harmonica tonguing technique. So are *dah-dah*, *ta-ka ta-ka*, *cha-chugga-cha-chugga*, and many other tonguing techniques you may create from time to time to achieve a desired effect.

Some of the more common tonguing techniques are …

♦ **Tah-tah.** The basic tonguing technique used when blowing. The tongue touches the back of the teeth to create this effect.

♦ **Dah-dah.** The basic tonguing technique used when drawing. The tongue touches the top of the mouth slightly above the teeth for this technique.

♦ **Cha-chugga-cha-chugga.** This can be used for blowing or drawing. It's good for creating a trainlike rhythm or very fast notes. You can play faster notes using this tonguing technique than with either *tah-tah* or *dah-dah*.

♦ **Ta-ka ta-ka.** Similar in effect to *chugga-chugga*, *ta-ka ta-ka* tends to be used with single notes whereas *chugga-chugga* is more effective with chords. *The William Tell Overture* (or the *Lone Ranger* theme song, if you prefer) uses a variation of this technique.

♦ **Drdrdrdrd dah dah drdrdrdrd dah dah.** Seriously, this tongue roll is a good, standard drum-roll–style tonguing technique that can be used to create a rhythm effect.

♦ **Create your own.** Experiment with different syllables to create different rhythm patterns. Use the consonant sounds "h," "k," "t," and "d" interspersed with the vowel sounds "a," "oo," and "i." Here's your first one: *doo-dikiti-doo-dikiti-doo-dikiti*. Form the syllables with your mouth—do not vocalize them. Now create your own rhythm patterns.

Tonguing Technique Exercises

Practice all the preceding techniques on your harmonica until you feel comfortable doing them. You can use any combination of notes you like. At first, practice them individually; then try playing different combinations of techniques, moving from one to the other. Start nice and slow and then build up speed. You'll have more difficulty with the draw tonguing techniques at first, but they'll come to you with practice. Try keeping a consistent tempo when doing this to develop a good feel for a steady beat.

Good Vibratos

You can greatly enhance your sound by learning and using several *vibrato* techniques. Your hand, tongue, throat, or diaphragm can all be used to create a vibrato effect that gives your tone a warmer, more expressive quality.

def•i•ni•tion

A **vibrato** is a slight tremulous or oscillating effect characterized by rapid variations in pitch or volume. On a harmonica, you can create it by using your hand, tongue, throat, or diaphragm.

Vibratos have the following characteristics:

- **Hand vibrato.** The most common vibrato technique. A vibrato effect can be achieved using your right hand to create an airtight cup in front of the harmonica. The heel of your right hand should always be flush with the heel of your left hand. Flutter your right hand, slowly at first and then faster, and you'll hear a tremolo sound. The key is to make the "cup" as airtight as possible when the right hand is closed. Watch yourself in the mirror as you practice this technique. There should be no gaps between the fingers of your right hand, and you must completely close the right hand together with the left to achieve the correct effect.

- **Tongue vibrato.** Also a fairly easy vibrato to create. Simply blow or draw any long note and vibrate or wiggle your tongue up and down in your mouth as fast as you can. You'll immediately hear the vibrato effect this produces.

- **Throat vibrato.** A more difficult vibrato technique that will take you some time and practice to master. When describing how to create a throat vibrato, we have variously heard and read that you should try to re-create the "machine gun" sound you used the make when you were a kid, make a "seal sound" in your throat, or imitate an Elmer Fudd style of laughing. Actually, all these seem a bit harsh on the throat. We think it's simpler to merely *ha-ha-ha-ha* while you're playing, like a light cough coming from the back of your throat. The difficulty is in making the sound come from the back of your throat, instead of merely cutting off the air with each vibrato. Your airflow should continue steadily throughout the vibrato. By making the *ha-ha-ha-ha* sound in the back of your throat, you're constricting your throat muscles and thus slightly altering (but not stopping) the airflow. You should be able to feel your throat constricting with your right hand if you're doing this technique correctly. As we said, it won't come to you immediately. It will take practice and patience. Practice it with long notes, both blowing and drawing. It's easier to do blowing than drawing, so your draw vibratos will be slower and more tentative at first. Place the fingers of your right hand on your throat while first practicing this technique so that you can feel your throat constricting when you do it correctly. As you master the technique, you'll begin to hear the notes change pitch slightly with each vibrato.

- **Diaphragm vibrato.** This vibrato technique is the easiest to describe but the most difficult to learn. Relatively few harp players use it. Simply put, all you have to do to achieve a diaphragm vibrato is to alternate between tightening and loosening your lower stomach muscles. If you're in good enough shape to do this, you'll immediately hear the vibrato effect caused by the changes in the airflow. It's fairly easy to do slowly but very difficult to do at a speed that creates a meaningful vibrato effect.

When mastered, a diaphragm vibrato often produces a more open (less pinched) sound than a throat vibrato.

Don't Just Stand There! Stomp Your Foot!

Yes, you should tap your toe or stomp your foot with the music while you're playing. This gets you into it and helps you maintain your rhythm and tempo. If you're playing in a group, it helps keep you all together. Besides, toe tapping and foot stomping get you in the right mood to play and help loosen you up. If we have to explain techniques for moving your foot to the music, you probably are not going to get very far in your music career.

Ten Tips to Top Tone

1. Place the harmonica deep inside your mouth.

2. Keep your lips loose and relaxed.

3. Practice long notes, starting soft, then getting loud and then soft again.

4. Play clean single notes. You have plenty of time to learn how to play "sloppy" notes on purpose later.

5. Use your diaphragm for breathing.

6. Maintain a controlled, focused, even airflow.

7. Keep the air passages open. Don't pinch the airflow.

8. Concentrate on being fluid, not choppy.

9. Use vibratos to enhance your tone.

10. Place the harmonica deep in your mouth and practice saying "Ten tips to top tone" while blowing into the harp and playing long notes. Then practice the same phrase while drawing. Blowing will be easier than drawing at first. Make sure you keep a focused, controlled airflow. Start slow and then build up speed until you can say it five times in a row really fast, both blowing and drawing. This exercise does absolutely nothing for your tone, but if you can perfect it, you'll know the kind of stupid human trick that might get you on the David Letterman show.

The Least You Need to Know

- Whether you're playing chords, puckered single notes, or tongue-blocked single notes, always maintain a controlled, focused flow of air.

- It's important to be able to play both puckered and tongue-blocked single notes if you want to play the cross-harp blues techniques we teach you in later chapters.

- Throat and diaphragm vibratos are very difficult techniques to master, but they'll set you apart from the crowd.

- For good tone, use all the techniques you've been taught—and practice, practice, practice.

Chapter 8

Playing More and Faster Notes

In This Chapter

- ◆ Tips for playing high notes
- ◆ Doing that headshake thing
- ◆ Sliding around and dropping off
- ◆ Playing fast notes—very fast notes
- ◆ Hanon exercises for the harp

In this chapter, we hone your skills at playing notes in the straight harp position on your harmonica. We work on your accuracy and speed and teach you how to play a few "embellishments" that add flavor and style to your technique. Don't try to go too quickly with the exercises and songs in this chapter. Increase your speed *only* when you can play them cleanly and accurately.

Playing High Notes

There's nothing too complicated about playing the higher notes on your harp. You need to remember only three things:

- ◆ The reeds and slots for the high notes are smaller, and it takes less, not more, air to get a good tone out of a high note (particularly on a new harmonica).
- ◆ Similarly, your airflow needs to be even more focused for playing high notes. Consider how you must tighten your pucker and narrow your airflow to whistle high notes. Whether you pucker or tongue block your high notes, the concept is the same. You want a more focused, narrower airstream.

♦ Your blow and draw notes are reversed starting at the 7-hole; that is, the blow note is higher than the draw note starting at the 7-hole. Thus, you need to "reverse" your blow/draw alterations. To move to the next higher note from any blow note starting at the 7-hole, you must move up to the next draw hole. For example, if you're blowing a C on the 4-hole of your C-major diatonic harp and want to play a D, you simply draw the same 4-hole. If you're blowing a C on the 8-hole, you would have to move to the 9-hole draw to play a D, and so forth. Hole 10 is somewhat different from holes 8 and 9. The draw reed is A and the blow reed is C, which means that the B is left out. This probably makes no sense at all on the page, so just pick up your harp and try it. You'll immediately see what we mean.

High-Note Exercise Number 1

Practice playing high notes on your C-major diatonic harmonica. Play the 7- through 10-holes, both blow and draw. Play long notes, increasing and decreasing the volume. If you're having trouble getting a sound out of any hole, you probably are blowing or drawing too hard, or your airstream isn't focused enough. Or possibly your harp is simply not broken in for the higher notes. Keep practicing and concentrate on blowing "more lightly" and focusing (narrowing) your airflow.

High-Note Exercise Number 2

Practice the following high-note exercises, slowly at first, and then gradually increase the speed. Play them until you become comfortable with the ordering of notes starting at the 7-hole and with moving between them.

↑ ↑ ↓ ↓ ↑ ↑ ↓ ↓ ↑ ↓ ↓ ↑ ↓ ↓ ↑
4 5 4 5 5 6 5 6 6 7 6 7 7 8 7

↑ ↓ ↓ ↑ ↓ ↓ ↑ ↑ ↓ ↓ ↑ ↑ ↓ ↓ ↑
7 6 7 6 6 5 6 5 5 4 5 4 4 3 4

Now try this one:

↑ ↑ ↓ ↓ ↑ ↑ ↓ ↓ ↑ ↑ ↓ ↓ ↑ ↓ ↑
7 8 8 9 8 9 9 10 9 8 9 8 8 8 7

↑ ↑ ↓ ↓ ↑ ↑ ↓ ↓ ↑ ↑ ↓ ↓ ↑ ↓ ↑
10 9 10 9 9 8 9 9 10 9 10 9 8 7 7

Now learn the following familiar song, which is written for the higher octave on your harmonica.

🔴 Red River Valley

```
|   ↑  ↑ |↕  ↑  ↑ |↕  ↓  ↑ |↕  ↕ |   ↑  ↑ |
| R  6  7 | 8  8  8 | 8  8  8 | 8  7 | R  6  7 |

| ↑  ↕  ↑ |↕  ↓  ↑ |↕ |   ↑  ↓ |
| 8  8  7 | 7  7  7 | 8 | R  9  9 |

|↕  ↕ |↕  ↓  ↑ |↓  ↑  ↓  ↓ |↕  ↑  ↓ |
| 8  8 | 7  8  8 | 9  8  9  10 | 9  7  8 |

|↕  ↕ |↓  ↑  ↑  ↓ |↑ |
| 8  8 | 8  7  8  8 | 7 |
```

Blues Clues

It's easier to play high notes on the lower-key harps, such as the G-major diatonic harp. The reeds and slots are longer on this and other lower-key harmonicas. The C-major diatonic harmonica is a mid-range harmonica, so it shouldn't be too difficult to play the high notes on it. The F-major and high G-major are the most difficult harmonicas to successfully break in and play the 8- through 10-holes.

A note about playing high notes: they aren't played nearly enough. A surprising number of talented harpists rarely go above the 6-hole. This is a shame, because high notes can sound good and add variety to any style of music. Take the time to get familiar with and learn how to play the high end of your harmonica. When you're playing, whether set pieces or spontaneous jams, don't be afraid to go high.

That's Really Trilling

Trilling, warbling, and shaking are all different names for the same harp effect: moving your harp or your head (or both) while rapidly alternating between two adjacent blow or draw holes. The effect is very dynamic and commonly used in blues, rock, and country music.

There are several different techniques to accomplish this effect, and you should play whichever one you're most comfortable with. You should learn them all, however, because most likely you'll choose the style based on the playing situation.

- **Handshake.** A common trilling style is to (1) loosen the grip with your left hand, and (2) use the thumb and index finger of your right hand to shake the harmonica from side to side. You can get more "speed" using this method.

- **Headshake.** Many harpists prefer to keep the harp stationary and shake their head quickly from side to side. This is more difficult to control because you're not used to shaking your head this way. However, this method makes a lot more sense when you're playing through a microphone and you find it difficult (and cumbersome) to free up your right hand for a handshake. Also, a handshake could scrape against the microphone—not a pleasant sound.

- **They both shake.** It actually might be easier to shake both your hands and your head *a little bit.* This is probably the easiest method to control because you're moving both your head and hands the shortest distance when you alternate from one note to the other. (Besides, why take the chance that a pure headshake might dislodge your brain?) If you use this method, you don't need to use the thumb/forefinger technique (see the handshake description in the following figure) to move the harp. You can just cradle the harp in both hands and shake to your head's delight.

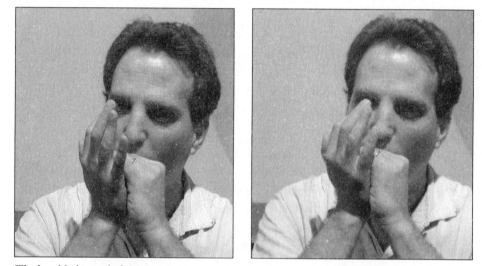

The handshake method (r.) is easier to control and makes it easier to develop speed. The head-shake (l.) is more difficult to control but is a better choice when using a microphone.

Regardless of the method you use, the following tips apply:

- The trill should be performed to the beat of the music. It needs to be smooth and even with a constant number of trills to each beat.

- Start slowly and build up speed, particularly for the headshake method.

- Always limit the alternation to the two intended notes so that you don't slop over into adjacent notes.

- The most common trills are between the 3- and 4-draw-holes and the 4- and 5-draw-holes, but trills are used all up and down the harp on both draw and blow notes.

- When you learn tongue-blocking octaves and bending in Chapter 11 and Chapter 12, you'll find it very effective to combine those techniques with trills.

tr ~~~~ *tr* ~~~~ *tr* ~~~~ *tr* ~~~~
4   5   6   5

The sign for a trill is placed above the harmonica tablature over the notes that should be trilled.

Blues Clues _____

You can also play a three-note trill, which sounds very good in certain types of music. It isn't technically a trill, but it's played with any of the same techniques as a trill is. It consists of a steady, even shake between three notes on your harmonica, stopping precisely at the top and bottom notes to reverse direction. All three notes must be played smoothly and evenly. It has the sound of cascading notes, and with practice you can move up and down the harmonica in a series of these cascading triple notes that produces an arpeggio effect.

Trill Exercise Number 1

1. Practice playing long trills between various sets of adjacent holes. Start with the 3- and 4-draw-holes and the 4- and 5-draw-holes. Work on keeping the trill smooth and even.

2. Try the same exercise on other holes, both blow and draw. Try your trills using the different techniques we've described. As you become more comfortable, move from your first set of adjacent holes to other sets of adjacent holes, moving up and down the harp without breaking the airflow. Try to make the transition to a new set of adjacent holes as smoothly as possible.

Trill Exercise Number 2

1. Now try the same exercises while alternating between three holes. Make sure you're cleanly hitting only three holes.

2. After you've practiced the exercises with three holes, try starting at the low end and "cascading" up the harp in three-note trills. Then cascade back down the harp, again using three-note trills. As you cascade, you should be moving one hole to the right or left (depending on whether you're cascading up or down) for the starting note of each three-note trill.

Practice the following songs, which all contain trills.

She'll Be Coming Around the Mountain

↑	↓	↑	↑	↑	↑	↓	↑	↑	↑	tr~ ↑		↑	↓
R	6	6	7	7	7	7	6	6	5	6	7	R	7	8

↑	↑	↑	↑	↑	↑	↓	↑	tr~ ↑		↑	↓
8	8	8	8	9	8	8	7	8	R	9	9

↑	↑	↑	↑	↓	↑	↑	↑	↓	↓	↓	↓	↓	↑	↓	↓
8	8	8	8	8	7	7	7	6	6	6	6	8	7	7	6

↑	↑	↑	↑	↑	↓	↑	↓	tr~ ↑	
6	6	6	6	8	8	7	7	7	

Oh, Susanna

```
| R 4 4 | 5 6 6 6 | 6 5 4 4 | 5 5 4 4 | 4    4 4 |
| 5 6 6 6 | 6 5 4 4 | 5 5 4 4 | 4    4 4 |
| 5 6 6 6 | 6 5 4 4 | 5 5 4 4 | 4    4 4 |
| 5 6 6 6 | 6 5 4 4 | 5 5 4 4 | 4 |
| 5 5 | 6 6 6 | 6 6 5 4 | 4    4 4 |
| 5 6 6 6 | 6 5 4 4 | 5 5 4 4 | 4 |
```

My Old Kentucky Home

```
| R 4 4 | 5 5 | 4 4 5 | 5 5 5 6 | 6 5 |
| 5 4 4 | 4 3 4 | 4 R 4 4 |
| 5 5 | 4 4 5 | 5 5 5 6 | 6 4 4 |
| 5 5 | 4 4 5 4 | 4 R 7 8 |
| 8 8 7 8 8 | 9 8 9 10 | 9 9 |
| 8 7 8 | 9 9 9 8 | 8 R 9 9 |
| 8 8 8 | 7 8 8 | 9 9 | R 6 |
| 6 7 7 | 8 7 8 | 7 |
```

Try doing the trills using each of the different techniques we've described. Also, try trilling with the holes both below and above the designated note. Each of them will give your song a different sound. Make sure you trill only between the designated note and the hole on either side. Don't slop over into a third note. These are good songs for mixing in chords with your single notes and trills to give them your own unique style.

Grace Notes

A grace note is an *ornament* played very quickly immediately before a melody note. On a harmonica you can easily play a grace note by blowing or drawing the hole just below the hole you want to play and then sliding quickly onto that hole. The grace note should be played *prior* to the beat: the main melody note that you slide into should be played *on* the beat.

def•i•ni•tion

An **ornament,** in music, is a note or technique used to embellish a melody line. It's also sometimes referred to as a "decoration." An ornament creates an effect or a special sound. Methods of ornamentation vary widely between musical styles and contribute greatly to their respective identities. For example, grace notes are very common in Celtic music and, together with the Celtic rhythm and tonal patterns, contribute to the "Celtic feel" of the music. Trills, slides, dropoffs, tongue blocking techniques, and bends are other techniques that can be used as ornaments.

A grace note is shown in our harmonica tablature by placing a dash between the hole numbers of the grace note and the melody note. Only the melody note has an arrow designating blow or draw. The grace note is always the same blow/draw direction as its melody note.

It also can be effective to play a *double* grace note, which is somewhat like a *single* trill. You play this ornamental effect exactly as you would play a single grace note except that you slide from the first grace note up to a second grace note and then back to the first note. The result is that your first grace note is the same note as your melody note. You also can think of it as a trill that stops after only one trill. As with the single grace note, *both* double grace notes must be played prior to the beat, with the melody note falling on the beat.

```
   ↑      ↑      ↓
 4 - 5   5 - 6   6 - 7
```

Harmonica tablature showing a grace note.

```
      ↑           ↑           ↓
 4 - 5 - 4    5 - 6 - 5    6 - 7 - 6
```

Harmonica tablature showing double grace notes.

Play the following song that includes both single and double grace notes.

🌑 **Moon Dance**

```
|     ↕|     ↕|   ↑ ↓ ↑ ↓ |  ↑    ↑    ↑    |
| 6-7-6 | 6-7-6 | 6-7-6 5 5 5 | 5-6  5-6  5-6  R |
```

```
|     ↕|     ↑|   ↑ ↓ ↑ ↓ |  ↓    ↓    ↓    |
| 6-7-6 | 6-7-6 | 6-7-6 5 5 5 | 4-5  4-5  4-5  R |
```

```
|     ↕|     ↕|   ↑ ↓ ↑ ↓ |  ↑    ↑    ↑    |
| 6-7-6 | 6-7-6 | 6-7-6 5 5 5 | 5-6  5-6  5-6  R |
```

```
|     ↕ |    ↕ |   ↑ ↓ ↑ ↓ |  ↑    ↓    ↕|
| 6-7-6 | 6-7-6 | 6-7-6 5 5 4 | 4-5  3-4  3-4 |
```

Slides and Dropoffs

Slides are two different varieties of a *glissando*. Actually, harmonica terminology has become far too complicated when trying to describe this relatively easy technique. You'll see glissandos referred to as slides, dropoffs, falloffs, whipups, whipdowns, and probably several other terms we haven't yet encountered. In this book, we try to keep it simple:

glissando   A sliding of the harmonica either right or left with the effect of rapidly sliding through notes while still blowing or drawing. It includes both *slides* and *dropoffs*.

slide   A glissando, moving either right or left, with a definite ending note. A slide may or may not start with a definite note, but it always ends with one.

dropoff   A glissando, moving either right or left, without a definite ending note. Dropoffs usually involve moving your harmonica quickly to the right in a descending direction. Thus, you "drop off" a definite starting note in a descending direction, but have no definite ending note. You generally continue to dropoff until you run out of notes at the low end.

When you do a slide or dropoff, remember to move your harp, not your head.

Glissando Exercise Number 1

Slides:
```
        ↑    ↑    ↑    ↓
   ~~4  ~~5  ~~6  ~~5
```

Dropoffs:
```
        ↑    ↑    ↑    ↓
   4~~  5~~  6~~  5~~
```

The glissando designation in harmonica tablature.

```
   ↑    ↓    ↑    ↓    ↑    ↓    ↓    ↑
~~4  ~~4  ~~5  ~~5  ~~6  ~~6  ~~7  ~~7
```

```
   ↑    ↓    ↓    ↑    ↓    ↑    ↓    ↑
~~7  ~~7  ~~6  ~~6  ~~5  ~~5  ~~4  ~~4
```

Harmonica tablature for ascending and descending slides.

Start each slide four holes ahead of the ending note. Make sure that you end each slide cleanly on the correct note. After you hit the ending note cleanly, break your airflow and go back to begin your next slide four holes ahead of the next ending note. Practice this exercise slowly at first, and then gradually speed up.

Now practice the following descending dropoffs.

Glissando Exercise Number 2

```
↑    ↓    ↑    ↓    ↑    ↓    ↓    ↑
4~~  4~~  5~~  5~~  6~~  6~~  7~~  7~~
```

```
↑    ↓    ↓    ↑    ↓    ↑    ↓    ↑
7~~  7~~  6~~  6~~  5~~  5~~  4~~  4~~
```

Harmonica tablature for descending dropoffs.

Play the following song, which contains both slides and dropoffs.

For He's A Jolly Good Fellow

```
|  ♪  ↑ | ↑  ↓  ↑ | ♪ ♪ |  ♪  ↓ | ↓  ↑  ↓ | ♪ ♪ |
 ~~5  5 | 5  4  5 | 5  5 |  ~~4  4 | 4  4  4 | 5  4 |
```

```
|  ♪  ↑ | ↑  ↓  ↑ | ♪ ♪ | ↓  ↑  ↓ | ↑  ↓ | ♪ | |
 ~~5  5 | 5  4  5 | 5  6 | 6  6  6 | 5  4 | 4~~ | R |
```

```
|  ↑  ↑  ↑ | ♪ ↓ | ♪ | |  ↑  ↑  ↑ | ♪ ↓ | ♪ | |
 ~~6  6  6 | 6  6 | 6~~ | R |  ~~5  5  5 | 5  5 | 5~~ | R |
```

```
|  ♪  ↑ | ↑  ↓  ↑ | ♪ ♪ |  ↓  ↓ | ↓  ↑  ↓ | ♪ ♪ |
 ~~5  5 | 5  4  5 | 5  5 |  ~~4  4 | 4  4  4 | 5  4 |
```

```
|  ♪  ↑ | ↑  ↓  ↑ | ♪ ♪ ↓ | ↑  ↓  ↑ | ♪ ↓ | ♪ |
 ~~5  5 | 5  4  5 | 5  6  6 | 6  6  6 | 5  4 | 4~~ |
```

Hanon for Harp

Sometime around 1873, a relatively obscure French composer named Charles-Louis Hanon published a collection of piano exercises called *The Virtuoso Pianist.* It received a modest amount of acclaim at the time, winning a silver medal for Hanon at the Exposition Universelle in 1878. Since that time, Hanon's book of exercises has become a standard practice tool for pianists aspiring to virtuoso status. The point of the exercises is to teach the pianist to use all five fingers on both hands with equal strength and dexterity. There are 60 exercises that focus on different areas of piano technique. The following are similar exercises for the harmonica. They are not the same exercises as composed by Hanon (what's good for the piano isn't necessarily good for the harp), but are instead *in the style* of Hanon.

The purpose of these exercises is to give you an opportunity to practice playing very fast notes on the harmonica. This skill will come in very handy in all styles of music. Obviously, you need to start slowly, and not start speeding up until you can hit all the notes correctly and cleanly. Again, *do not try to play these exercises any faster than you can play them cleanly.* Do not slide between the notes. Practice playing the notes short and unconnected. You do this by slightly breaking the airflow between each note.

> **Straight from the Harp**
>
> Hanon was a very religious man and devoted much of his life to church music. Although this music did not make him a wealthy man, it did earn him a congratulatory letter from the pope and appointment as an honorary maestro of the Accademia di Santa Cecilia in Rome.

Hanon for Harp Exercises

Hanon Harp #1

```
↑ ↓ ↑ ↑ ↓ ↓ ↑ ↓ ↓ ↑ ↓ ↑ ↑ ↓ ↑ ↓ ↓ ↑ ↓ ↓ ↑
4 4 5 4 4 5 5 4 5 5 6 5 5 6 6 5 6 6 7 6

↓ ↓ ↑ ↓ ↓ ↑ ↓ ↓ ↑ ↓ ↑ ↑ ↓ ↑ ↓ ↓ ↑ ↓ ↑ ↑
6 7 7 6 7 7 8 7 7 8 8 7 8 8 9 8 8 9 9 8

↓ ↑ ↓ ↓ 𝄾 ↓ ↑ ↓ ↓ ↑ ↓ ↑ ↑ ↓ ↑ ↓ ↓
9 9 10 9 10 10 9 9 10 9 9 8 9 9 8 8 9

↑ ↓ ↑ ↑ ↓ ↑ ↓ ↓ ↑ ↓ ↓ ↑ ↓ ↓ ↑ ↓ ↓ ↑ ↓ ↓
8 8 7 8 8 7 7 8 7 7 6 7 7 6 6 7 6 6 5 6

↑ ↓ ↑ ↑ ↓ ↑ ↓ ↓ ↓ ↑ ↓ ↑ ↑ ↓ ↑ ↓ ↓ ↑ ↑ ↑ 𝄾
6 5 5 6 5 5 4 5 5 4 4 5 4 4 3 4 4 3 2 1
```

Do you notice how the order of your blow and draw switches at the 7-hole? These are good exercises to practice to develop the ability to play single notes very fast. It will come in handy when you want to play Celtic jigs and reels. Go ahead and compose some of your own "Hanon for Harp" exercises. All you have to do is create a pattern and repeat it up and back down the harmonica.

By this point, you should be playing single notes and chords fairly cleanly on your harmonica. It's now time to move on to the cross-harp techniques commonly played in blues, country, and rock music. But first we're taking a break in the following chapter, "Music Break Number 1," and giving you an opportunity to become very comfortable with straight-harp playing before we move on to new techniques. By the time you get through the next chapter and can play all the songs included there, you'll be ready to wail.

🔵 **Hanon Harp #2**

↑ ↑ ↑ ↑ ↓ ↓ ↓ ↓ ↑ ↑ ↑ ↑ ↓ ↓ ↓ ↓ ↑ ↑ ↑ ↑
4 3 2 3 4 3 2 3 5 4 3 4 5 4 3 4 6 5 4 5

↓ ↓ ↓ ↓ ↑ ↑ ↑ ↑ ↓ ↓ ↓ ↓ ↓ ↑ ↓ ↓ ↑ ↑ ↓ ↑
6 5 4 5 7 6 5 6 7 6 5 6 8 7 6 7 8 7 6 7

↓ ↓ ↓ ↓ ↑ ↑ ↑ ↑ ↓ ↓ ↓ ↓ 𝄾 ↑ ↑ ↑ ↑
9 8 7 8 9 8 7 8 10 9 8 7 10 10 9 8 10

↓ ↓ ↓ ↓ ↑ ↑ ↑ ↑ ↓ ↓ ↓ ↓ ↓ ↑ ↑ ↓ ↑ ↓ ↓ ↑ ↓
10 9 8 10 9 8 7 9 9 8 7 9 8 7 6 8 8 7 6 8

↑ ↓ ↓ ↑ ↑ ↓ ↑ ↑ ↓ ↓ ↓ ↓ ↓ ↑ ↑ ↑ ↑
7 6 5 7 7 6 5 7 6 5 4 6 6 5 4 6

↓ ↓ ↓ ↓ ↑ ↑ ↑ ↑ ↓ ↓ ↓ ↓ ↑ ↑ ↑ 𝄾
5 4 3 5 5 4 3 5 4 3 2 4 4 3 2 1

The Least You Need to Know

◆ Play high notes cleanly by using less air but focusing the airflow more.

◆ Play trills, grace notes, and glissandos to add some additional style to your music.

◆ Play the Hanon for Harp exercises cleanly at a moderate speed to improve your skill.

Music Break Number 1

In This Chapter

- ◆ Applying what you've learned to real music
- ◆ Having fun
- ◆ Entertaining your friends and relatives

Now it's time to take what you've learned so far and play real music. This chapter includes 20 songs that you've most likely heard before, so it should be pretty easy to figure out what they're supposed to sound like. Remember, after you get familiar with each song, don't be afraid to experiment a little with your own ideas and style. The harmonica is supposed to be a spontaneous instrument played from your soul. You might as well start right now. Put your mark on each song and make it your own. And don't think you need to play each song the same way every time. Just go with your feelings at the moment.

Familiar Songs That Are Fun to Play

Before you get started, please do us a favor. Go back to Chapter 6 and Chapter 7. Page through them—no, don't go so fast—and refresh your memory as to the absolutely essential techniques introduced there (which happen to be all of them). Focus on your breathing technique, mouth and lip position, hand position, and posture. Be ready to use pucker *and* tongue-block single notes, full chords and partial chords, vibratos, and tonguing techniques. Remember the ten tips to top tone. Are all of them firmly implanted in your mind? *Now is the time to use them.*

Also, go back and review the harmonica tablature system in Chapter 5 one more time. Remember that we're using vertical lines to designate measures. As you tap your foot, each measure should have exactly the same number of taps, or beats. That will help you discern the correct rhythm of the notes designated in each measure.

Down in the Valley

```
↑  ↑  ↓ ↗↗ ↗↗ |↑  ↑  ↓  ↗↗|↓  ↓  ↓  ↗↗ ↗↗|↓  ↑  ↓ ↗↗
3  4  4  5  4  R |5  4  4  4 |2  3  4  5  4  R |5  6  5  5
                  4  3  3  3                    4  5  4  4
                  3  2  2  2                    3  4  3  3
```

```
↑  ↑  ↓ ↗↗ ↗↗ |↑  ↑  ↓  ↗↗|↓  ↓  ↓  ↗↗ ↗↗|↓  ↓  ↓ ↗↗
3  4  4  5  4  R |5  4  4  4 |2  3  4  5  4  R |5  4  3  4
                  4  3  3  3                    4  3  2  3
                  3  2  2  2                    3  2  1  2
```

Blues Clues

Practice your tone tips, vibratos in particular, as you play the notes in the slower songs.

You'll notice a 2-hole draw in "Down in the Valley." This can be a contentious note. Concentrate on your tone tips for this note. You can also play the same note on the 3-hole blow. Try it both ways. See how a good tone is more difficult to achieve with the 2-hole draw than with the 3-hole blow?

Swanee River

```
↗↗ ↓  ↑  ↑  ↓ |↑  ↑  ↓  ↗↗|↗↗ ↑  ↑  ↗↗
5  4  4  5  4 |4  7  6  7 |6  5  4  4  R
```

```
↗↗ ↓  ↑  ↑  ↓ |↑  ↑  ↓  ↗↗|↑  ↑  ↑  ↓  ↓ ↗↗
5  4  4  5  4 |4  7  6  7 |6  5  4  4  3  4  R
```

```
↗↗ ↑  ↓  ↑ ↗↗|↓  ↑  ↑  ↑|↑  ↓  ↓  ↓ ↗↗
7  7  8  6  6 |6  6  7  7 |6  5  7  6  R
```

```
↗↗ ↓  ↑  ↑  ↓ |↑  ↑  ↓  ↗↗|↑  ↑  ↑  ↓  ↓ ↗↗
5  4  4  5  4 |4  7  6  7 |6  5  4  4  3  4
4  3  3  4  3               5  4  3  3  2  3
3  2  2  3  2               4  3  2  2  1  2
```

Notice that the following song combines full chords and partial chords (only two notes). The full chords should be played firmly, while the partial chords should be played very lightly, with the lower note being almost an afterthought. Play this song once through, playing only the top note as single notes, and add the chords and partial chords the second time through. Don't hurry with "Shenandoah." Take a meaningful pause at the rests before moving on. Play with emotion. This is a song about a river, and a river is an emotional thing.

Shenandoah

```
↑ |↑  ↑  ↗↗ ↓  ↑  ↓ |↓  ↗↗    ↑  ↓|↗↗ ↑  ↓  ↑|↑  ↗↗    ↑
3 |4  4  4  4  5  5 |6  5  R |7  7 |6  6  6  6 |5  6  R  6
   3  3  3  3  4  4  5  4           5  5  5  5  4  5
   2  2  2  2                                   3  4
```

```
↗↗ ↓  ↑  ↑ |↓  ↗↗    ↑ ↗↗    ↑  ↑  ↓ ↗↗     ↑  ↓ ↗↗ ↑  ↓ ↗↗
6  5  6  5 |4  4  R  3 |4  R  3  4  6 |6  R  4  4 |5  4  4  4
5  4  5  4            3             5           4  3  3
                       2             5           3  2  2
```

The following song picks up the pace a little. It's about Texas. It's not an emotional song—unless you're from Texas.

The Yellow Rose of Texas

↑ ↓ | ↑ ↑ ↑ ↑ | ↓ ↯ ↓ | ↑ ↑ ↑ ↓ | ↯ ↑ |
6 5 | 5 6 6 6 | 6 6 5 | 5 6 7 8 | 8 6 |

| ↑ ↑ ↑ ↑ | ↑ ↯ ↑ | ↓ ↑ ↓ ↑ | ↯ ↑ ↓ |
| 6 8 8 8 | 8 8 7 | 7 7 8 8 | 8 6 5 |

| ↑ ↑ ↑ ↑ | ↓ ↯ ↓ | ↑ ↑ ↑ ↑ | ↯ ↑ |
| 5 6 6 6 | 6 6 5 | 5 6 7 8 | 8 6 |

| ↑ ↓ ↓ ↓ | ↓ ↑ ↯ ↑ | ↑ ↑ ↑ ↓ | ↯ |
| 6 9 9 9 | 9 8 8 7 | 7 6 8 8 | 7 |

Blues Clues

Starting with "The Yellow Rose of Texas," as far as playing chords is concerned, you're on your own for the rest of this chapter. You've had enough practice playing them to determine where you should play chords and where you shouldn't in songs such as these. They often sound good when you play them the first time with single notes and then add chords on subsequent verses, or when you play single notes on the verses and add chords in the chorus. Don't worry about the music theory of chords right now. Just go with what sounds good on your C-major harmonica. We leave you with only one thought: beware of playing the 6- and 7-draw-holes together.

Aura Lee

| ↑ ↑ ↓ ↑ | ↓ ↓ ↯ | ↑ ↓ ↓ ↓ | ↯ |
| 6 7 7 7 | 8 6 8 | 7 7 6 7 | 8 R |

| ↑ ↑ ↓ ↑ | ↓ ↓ ↯ | ↑ ↓ ↓ ↓ | ↯ |
| 6 7 7 7 | 8 6 8 | 7 7 6 7 | 7 R |

| ↑ ↑ ↯ | ↑ ↑ ↯ | ↑ ↓ ↑ ↓ | ↯ |
| 8 8 8 R | 8 8 8 R | 8 8 7 8 | 8 R |

| ↑ ↑ ↓ ↑ | ↓ ↓ ↯ | ↑ ↓ ↓ ↓ | ↯ |
| 8 8 9 8 | 8 6 8 | 7 7 8 8 | 7 |

Yes, the above song sounds so familiar. It's on the tip of your tongue, isn't it?

Spancil Hill

```
↓ | ↕ ↓ | ↕ ↓ | ↕ ↕ | ↑ ↕ | ↓ ↑ ↑ | ↑ ↕ | ↑ ↕ |   ↓
6 |  6  4 |  6  6 |  6  5 |  4  4 |  5  6  5 |  4  4 | 4 R  6

| ↕ ↓ | ↕ ↑ | ↕ ↑ | ↕ ↓ | ↕ ↓ | ↑ ↓ ↓ | ↕ |  ↓
|  6  8 |  8  8 |  8  7 |  6  7 |  7  8 |  7  7  6 | 6 R | 6

| ↕ ↓ | ↕ ↑ | ↕ ↑ | ↕ ↓ | ↕ ↓ | ↑ ↓ ↓ | ↕ |  ↑ ↓
|  6  8 |  8  8 |  8  7 |  6  7 |  7  8 |  7  7  6 | 6 R |  7  7

| ↕ ↓ | ↕ ↓ | ↕ ↑ | ↑ ↓ | ↑ ↑ ↑ | ↕ ↑ | ↕ |
|  6  4 |  6  6 |  6  5 |  4  4 |  5  6  5 |  4  4 | 4
```

Don't try to play chords on "Spancil Hill." Although you can play it using only single notes on a C-major diatonic harmonica, it actually is written in a different key, and the chords on your harmonica don't fit the music. More on this later.

Silent Night

```
| ↕ ↓ ↑ ↕ | ↕ ↓ ↑ ↕ | ↕ ↓ ↕ ↕ ↑ ↕ |
|  6  6  6  5 R |  6  6  6  5 R |  8  8  7  7  7  6 R

| ↕ ↓ ↕ ↓ ↓ ↕ ↓ ↑ ↕ | ↕ ↓ ↕ ↓ ↓ ↕ ↓ ↑ ↕ |
|  6  6  7  7  6  6  6  6  5 R |  6  6  7  7  6  6  6  6  5 R

| ↕ ↕ ↕ ↓ ↓ ↕ ↕ | ↑ ↑ ↑ ↑ ↓ ↓ ↕ |
|  8  8  9  8  7  7  8 R |  7  6  5  6  5  4  4
```

William Tell Overture

```
↑ ↑ | ↑ ↑ ↑ ↑ ↑ ↑ | ↑ ↓ ↑ ↑ ↑ | ↑ ↑ ↑ ↑ ↑ | ↓ ↓ ↑ ↑ ↑ |
3 3 | 3 3 3 3 3 3 | 4 4 5 3 3 | 3 3 3 4 5 | 4 3 3 3 3

| ↑ ↑ ↑ ↑ ↑ ↑ | ↑ ↓ ↑ ↑ ↑ | ↕ ↓ ↑ ↓ | ↑ ↑ ↑ |
| 3 3 3 3 3 3 | 4 4 5 4 5 | 6 5 5 4 | 4 5 4
```

The above song is good for practicing the tonguing techniques you learned in Chapter 7.

🔘 Red River Valley

```
|   ↑ ↑ |↕ ↑ ↑ |↕ ↓ ↑ |↕ ↕ |  ↑ ↑ |
| R 6 7 | 8 8 8 | 8 8 8 | 8 7 | R 6 7 |

|↑ ↕ ↑ |↕ ↓ ↑ |↕   ↑ ↓ |
|8 8 7 |7 7 7 |8 R 9 9 |

|↕ ↕ |↕ ↓ ↑ |↓ ↑ ↓ ↓ |↕ ↑ ↓ |
|8 8 |7 8 8 |9 8 9 10 |9 7 8 |

|↕ ↕ |↓ ↑ ↑ ↓ |↑ |
|8 8 |8 7 8 8 |7 |
```

🔘 Michael, Row the Boat Ashore

```
|   ↑ ↑ |↕ ↑ ↑ ↓ |↕ ↑ ↑ |↕ ↕ ↑ ↑ |
| R 4 5 | 6 5 6 6 | 6 5 6 | 6 6 5 6 |

|↕ ↑ ↓ ↑ |↕ ↑ ↓ |↕ ↕ |↕ |
|6 5 5 5 |4 4 4 |5 4 |4 |
```

Repeat the above tune as many times as you like.

⚷ Blues Clues

Some of the songs you're learning in this chapter you'll learn again in the following chapters, just in a lower octave on your harmonica, using note bends. They'll sound totally different to you.

🔘 Over There

```
|   ↑ ↑ |↕   ↑ ↑ |↕   ↑ ↑ |↑ ↑ ↑ ↑ ↑ ↑ |↕   ↓ ↑ |
| R 8 6 |7 R 8 6 |7 R 8 6 |7 8 6 7 8 6 |7 R 8 8 |

|↓ ↑ ↓ ↕ ↓ |↑ ↓ ↑ ↕ ↑ |↓ ↓ ↑ ↓ ↓ ↑ |↕   ↑ ↑ |
|9 8 8 9 9 |8 8 7 8 7 |7 6 7 6 7 7 |8 R 8 6 |

|↕   ↑ ↑ |↕   ↑ ↑ |↑ ↑ ↑ ↑ ↑ ↑ |↕   ↑ ↓ |
|7 R 8 6 |7 R 8 6 |7 8 6 7 8 6 |7 R 8 8 |

|↕ ↑ ↑ ↓ ↑ |↕ ↑ ↓ ↓ |↑ ↑ ↑ ↑ ↓ |↑ ↓ ↓ ↑ ↕ |
|7 6 8 8 7 |8 6 6 7 |7 7 7 7 8 |7 7 6 7 7 |
```

The Irish Washerwoman

	↑	↓	↑	↑	↑	↑	↑	↑	↑	↑	↑	↑	↓	↑
R	6	5	5	4	4	3	4	4	5	4	5	6	5	5

↓	↓	↓	↓	↓	↓	↓	↓	↓	↓	↑	↓
5	4	4	3	4	4	5	4	5	6	6	5

↑	↑	↑	↑	↑	↑	↑	↑	↑	↑	↓	↑
5	4	4	3	4	4	5	4	5	6	5	4

↓	↑	↓	↓	↑	↓	↑	↑	↑	↑	↑	↓
5	5	5	4	6	5	5	4	4	4	4	4

↑	↑	↑	↑	↑	↑	↑	↑	↑	↑	↓	↑
5	4	4	3	4	4	5	4	5	5	4	4

↓	↓	↓	↓	↓	↓	↓	↓	↓	↓	↑	↓
4	3	3	2	3	3	4	3	4	4	4	3

↓	↑	↑	↑	↑	↑	↓	↑	↑	↑	↑	↑	↓	↑	↓	↓	↑	↓	↑	↑	↑	↑
6	7	7	6	7	7	5	7	7	4	7	7	5	5	5	5	4	6	5	5	4	4	4

The above song is good for working on your single notes using both puckering and tongue-blocking techniques. Then mix in chords where they sound good. This song has some good jumps in it. Don't be in a hurry; concentrate on hitting the notes cleanly with full tone. Speed will come with practice.

House of the Rising Sun

	↓	↕	↑	↕	↓	↨	↓	↕	↓	↕	↓	↕	↓	↑	↕		↓
R	4	4	5	5	6	6	4	4	6	8	6	7	6	6	6	R	4

↕	↑	↕	↓	↨	↓	↕	↓	↕	↓	↨	↓	↑	↕		↓
4	5	5	6	6	4	5	4	5	4	5	4	4	4	R	4

↕	↑	↕	↓	↨	↓	↕	↓	↕	↓	↨	↓	↑	↕		↓
4	5	5	6	6	4	4	6	8	6	7	6	6	6	R	4

↕	↑	↕	↓	↨	↓	↕	↓	↕	↓	↨	↑	↕
4	5	5	6	6	4	5	4	5	1	1	2	1

"House of the Rising Sun" is another song you can play on your C-major diatonic harmonica in single notes, but the chords on your harp don't fit the music because it's written in a different key.

🎵 **Dixie**

```
|   ↑ ↑ | ↑ ↑ ↑ ↓ ↑ ↓ | ↑ ↑ ↑ ↑ |
| R 6 5 | 4 4 4 4 5 5 | 6 6 6 5 |
```

```
| ↓ ↓ ↯ ↑ | ↯ ↑ ↓ ↓ ↑ ↓ | ↯ ↑ ↑ | ↯ ↑ ↑ | ↯ ↓ ↑ | ↯ ↑ ↑ |
| 6 6 6 6 | 6 6 6 7 7 8 | 9 8 7 | 8 6 5 | 6 4 5 | 4 6 5 |
```

```
| ↑ ↑ ↑ ↓ ↑ ↓ | ↑ ↑ ↑ ↑ |
| 4 4 4 4 5 5 | 6 6 6 5 |
```

```
| ↓ ↓ ↯ ↑ | ↯ ↑ ↓ ↑ ↓ ↑ | ↯ ↑ ↑ | ↯ ↑ ↑ | ↯ ↓ ↑ | ↯ ↑ |
| 6 6 6 6 | 6 6 6 7 7 8 | 9 8 7 | 8 6 5 | 6 4 5 | 4 6 |
```

```
| ↑ ↑ ↓ ↑ | ↓ ↯ ↓ | ↯ ↓ ↯ ↑ |
| 7 8 8 7 | 6 7 6 | 8 6 8 6 |
```

```
| ↑ ↑ ↓ ↑ | ↓ ↓ ↑ ↓ | ↑ ↑ ↑ ↑ ↑ ↯ ↑ |
| 7 8 8 7 | 6 7 7 6 | 6 5 7 5 5 4 5 |
```

```
| ↯ ↑ | ↯ ↓ | ↑ ↑ ↯ ↑ | ↑ ↯ |
| 4 5 | 4 6 | 6 5 8 7 | 8 7 |
```

The following tune was actually imported from England (called "The Unfortunate Rake") and turned into one of the great cowboy songs of all time.

🎵 **The Streets of Laredo**

```
|   ↑ ↓ | ↯ ↓ ↑ | ↓ ↑ ↓ | ↑ ↓ ↑ | ↓ ↑ ↑ |
| R 5 5 | 6 5 5 | 5 6 5 | 5 4 4 | 3 3 3 |
```

```
| ↯ ↓ ↑ | ↓ ↑ ↓ | ↑ ↓ ↑ | ↯ ↑ ↓ |
| 4 3 4 | 4 5 5 | 5 4 4 | 4 5 5 |
```

```
| ↯ ↓ ↑ | ↓ ↑ ↓ | ↑ ↓ ↑ | ↓ ↑ ↑ |
| 6 5 5 | 5 6 5 | 5 4 4 | 3 3 3 |
```

```
| ↯ ↓ ↑ | ↓ ↑ ↓ | ↑ ↓ ↓ | ↯ |
| 4 3 4 | 4 5 5 | 5 3 4 | 4 |
```

🔘 Drunken Sailor

```
| ↓ ↓ ↓ ↓ ↓ ↓ | ↓ ↓ ↓ ↓ | ↑ ↑ ↑ ↑ ↑ ↑ | ↑ ↑ ↑ ↑ |
| 6 6 6 6 6 6 | 6 4 5 6 | 6 6 6 6 6 6 | 6 4 5 6 |

| ↓ ↓ ↓ ↓ ↓ ↓ | ↓ ↓ ↑ ↓ | ↑ ↓ ↑ ↑ | ↕ ↕ |
| 6 6 6 6 6 6 | 6 7 7 8 | 7 6 6 5 | 4 4 |

| ↓ ↓ ↓ ↓ ↓ ↓ | ↓ ↓ ↓ ↓ | ↑ ↑ ↑ ↑ ↑ ↑ | ↑ ↑ ↑ ↑ |
| 6 6 6 6 6 6 | 6 4 5 6 | 6 6 6 6 6 6 | 6 4 5 6 |

| ↓ ↓ ↓ ↓ ↓ ↓ | ↓ ↓ ↑ ↓ | ↑ ↓ ↑ ↑ | ↕ ↕ |
| 6 6 6 6 6 6 | 6 7 7 8 | 7 6 6 5 | 4 4 |
```

Guess what the above song is good for practicing? Keep at it until you can do it cleanly at a good speed.

🔘 Wildwood Flower

```
|   ↑ ↓ | ↕ ↓ ↑ | ↕ ↓ ↑ | ↕ ↑ ↓ | ↕ ↑ ↓ |
| R 5 5 | 6 6 7 | 5 5 5 | 4 5 4 | 4 5 5 |

| ↕ ↓ ↑ | ↕ ↓ ↑ | ↕ ↑ ↓ | ↕ ↑ ↑ |
| 6 6 7 | 5 5 5 | 4 5 4 | 4 6 7 |

| ↑ ↕ ↓ | ↕ ↑ ↑ | ↓ ↕ ↓ | ↕ ↑ ↑ |
| 8 8 8 | 7 6 6 | 6 7 6 | 6 4 4 |

| ↑ ↕ ↓ | ↕ ↑ ↑ | ↕ ↑ ↓ | ↕ |
| 5 6 6 | 6 5 4 | 4 5 4 | 4 |
```

🔘 Wabash Cannonball

```
|   ↑ | ↑ ↑ ↑ ↓ | ↑ ↕ ↑ | ↑ ↑ ↓ ↑ | ↕ ↓ |
| R 6 | 6 6 7 8 | 8 9 9 | 8 8 8 7 | 5 6 |

| ↑ ↑ ↓ ↓ | ↑ ↕ ↑ | ↓ ↑ ↓ ↓ | ↕ ↑ |
| 6 6 7 8 | 8 8 7 | 7 7 7 6 | 6 6 |

| ↑ ↑ ↑ ↓ | ↑ ↕ ↑ | ↑ ↑ ↓ ↑ | ↕ ↓ |
| 6 6 7 8 | 8 9 9 | 8 8 8 7 | 5 6 |

| ↑ ↑ ↓ ↓ | ↑ ↕ ↑ | ↓ ↑ ↓ ↓ | ↕ |
| 6 6 7 8 | 8 8 7 | 7 6 6 7 | 7 |
```

Scotland the Brave

```
| ↕ ↑ ↓ | ↑ ↓ ↑ ↑ | ↕ ↑ ↓ | ↑ ↑ ↑ ↑ |
  4 4 4   5 4 5 6   7 7 7   7 6 5 4

| ↕ ↓ ↓ | ↕ ↑ ↑ | ↕ ↑ ↓ | ↑ ↓ ↑ ↓ ↑ ↓ |
  5 6 5   5 6 5   4 6 6   6 6 6 5 5 4

| ↕ ↑ ↓ | ↑ ↓ ↑ ↑ | ↕ ↑ ↓ | ↑ ↑ ↑ ↑ |
  4 4 4   5 4 5 6   7 7 7   7 6 5 4

| ↕ ↓ ↓ | ↕ ↑ ↑ | ↕ ↑ ↓ ↓ | ↕ ↑ ↑ |
  5 6 5   5 6 5   4 5 5 3   4 5 6

| ↕ ↑ ↓ | ↑ ↑ ↑ ↑ | ↕ ↑ ↓ | ↑ ↑ ↑ ↑ |
  7 7 7   7 6 5 6   7 7 7   7 6 5 6

| ↕ ↓ ↓ | ↕ ↑ ↑ | ↕ ↑ ↓ | ↑ ↓ ↑ ↓ ↑ ↓ |
  5 6 5   5 6 5   4 6 6   6 6 6 5 5 4

| ↕ ↑ ↓ | ↑ ↓ ↑ ↑ | ↕ ↑ ↓ | ↑ ↑ ↑ ↑ |
  4 4 4   5 4 5 6   7 7 7   7 6 5 4

| ↕ ↓ ↓ | ↕ ↑ ↑ | ↕ ↑ ↓ ↓ | ↕ |
  5 6 5   5 6 5   4 5 5 3   4
```

Waltzing Matilda

```
| ↕ ↑ ↑ | ↕ ↕ | ↕ ↑ ↑ | ↕ ↕ | ↕ ↑ ↑ | ↕ ↑ ↓ | ↕ ↓ ↑ | ↕ ↑ ↓ |
  6 6 6   6 5   7 7 7   7 6   6 6 6   6 6 6   6 5 5   4 7 8

| ↕ ↑ | ↕ ↕ | ↑ ↓ ↑ ↑ | ↓ ↓ ↑ ↓ |
  8 8   8 8   7 8 8 7   6 7 7 6

| ↕ ↑ ↑ | ↕ ↓ ↑ | ↓ ↓ ↓ | ↕ |
  6 7 8   9 9 8   8 8 7   7
```

You changed octaves in the middle of "Waltzing Matilda." That's because not all the notes you need to play it in straight harp are available on the lower octave. Did you notice how the articulation between blow- and draw-holes reversed when you went to the higher octave?

The songs you've played in this chapter are all in straight-harp style, which is the style generally used for folk, traditional, and Celtic music. In the upcoming chapters, you'll be learning the more challenging cross-harp techniques used in blues, rock, and country music. It's important that you know how to play both styles and that you can move from one to the other comfortably. This gives your harp music more variety and personality.

The Least You Need to Know

- ◆ Your breathing technique, mouth and lip position, hand position, and posture should start feeling fairly natural to you.
- ◆ You should have no problem playing full or partial chords.
- ◆ You should be able to do an effective hand and tongue vibrato; throat and diaphragm vibratos will take longer.
- ◆ You should be able to articulate the tonguing techniques described in Chapter 7 with reasonable speed.
- ◆ Your tone should be starting to sound clear, clean, rich, and full (you pick the adjectives that mean the most to you and strive for that sound).
- ◆ You should be impressing the heck out of your family and friends.

Part 3

Steppin' Up

While it's certainly not necessary to be able to read music in order to become a very good harmonica player, the ability to read music will open up a whole new world to you and make your music experience that much more enjoyable. Chapter 10 explains the basic fundamentals of music and teaches you what you need to know to play the harmonica from traditional sheet music. When you get comfortable with reading notes, beats, signs, and keys, you'll be reading music as naturally as you're reading this book.

You can then learn some more amazing techniques—tongue blocking and note bending—probably the most important techniques you *must* master to play the diatonic harmonica as it's meant to be played.

We get really serious in this part, where you can learn all about harp positions and the distinct tonal and harmonic qualities of the harmonica's seven musical modes.

Reading and 'Riting and 'Rhythmatic

In This Chapter

- ◆ Why it's important to learn to read music
- ◆ The four basic concepts: notes, beats, signs, and keys
- ◆ Practice exercises and songs written in both music notation and harmonica tablature systems

If you've gotten this far into the book, you already can *play* music without necessarily knowing how to *read* music. Yes, it's a good idea to learn to read music, but it's not a requirement for learning from the rest of the chapters in this book and becoming an accomplished harpist.

In this chapter, we explore some of the reasons why you should learn to read music, and then teach you how to do it. We break music notation down into its four basic elements: notes, beats, signs, and keys. And we explain how to read, understand, and play each of them. We also provide numerous musical exercises and songs so that you can practice and get familiar with music notation concepts before moving on to more difficult harmonica pieces.

Why Read Music?

The reasons for learning to read music are both clear and compelling. If you *don't* read music, you either have to hope the songs you want to play are written in harp tablature, or have someone else play the songs first so you can pick them up by ear. A mere fraction of the world's music has been written in harp tablature. Whether or not you can speak the language of a foreign country, however, you can play its music if you can read music notation. An orchestra full of different nationalities all speaking different languages can read the same music and play together.

Reading music also enables you to learn complex embellishments and styles more quickly, particularly those of musicians playing different instruments. By reading their music, you can more easily comprehend what they are playing and figure out how to transpose it to the harp.

Finally, harmonica tablature of any variety is severely limited in scope. It simply is not possible to convey all the messages, instructions, and other information found in standard music notation through a bunch of arrows and circles.

However, having made the case for reading music, it's equally important that you never allow written music to become a straightjacket over your own style. At its core, written music is nothing more than someone else's interpretation of what a song should sound like. Use music notation to understand the elements and structure of a song, but don't hesitate to develop your own interpretation of the music that reflects *your* feelings and moods.

Music, whether played by ear, from sheet music, or created spontaneously, should always be a personal expression by the particular musician playing it at that time. So by all means read your sheet music, but don't take it too seriously.

Notes

The first concept of reading music you need to understand is "notes." Notes are the symbols used to indicate which hole or holes (blow or draw) you need to play on the harmonica to achieve a particular sound.

Note Names

All notes are named after the initial seven letters of the English alphabet:

    A-B-C-D-E-F-G

Each note has a *pitch*, the sound associated with a particular note. On a piano keyboard, the notes are laid out as follows:

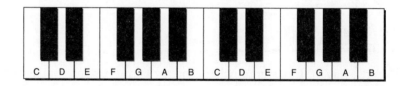

def•i•ni•tion

Pitch is the sound of a note that identifies it as a specific note. The pitch of a note is determined by the speed of the vibrations that are creating it. For example, the pitch of a note on a harmonica is determined by the speed of the cyclic sound wave patterns produced by the reed vibrations. Pitch is expressed as "vibrations or cycles per second," such as A = 440 Hz. Hz stands for hertz, and hertz is shorthand for cycles per second.

On your C-major diatonic harmonica, these same notes are laid out as follows:

How Notes Are Written

Notes are written on staves, which are sets of five lines and four spaces ordinarily identified as a treble clef staff or bass clef staff. To keep this as simple as possible, we disregard the bass clef staff in this book, as you almost always read harmonica music from a treble clef staff. The treble clef staff is written like this:

The notes that you're supposed to play are indicated on the treble clef staff as follows:

The notes that you're supposed to play are indicated on the treble clef staff as follows:

Try playing this song just by looking at the notes on the treble clef staff. If you have problems, use the harmonica tablature to get you started.

Sharps, Flats, and Naturals

The notes you've learned thus far are all naturals, meaning they correspond to the white notes on a piano keyboard and the notes on your C-major diatonic harmonica.

The black keys on the piano keyboard are called sharps and flats:

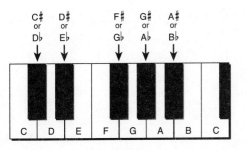

 (Blues Clues sidebar)

🔑 **Blues Clues**

Before you play the songs and exercises in this chapter, try vocalizing them first, focusing on the rhythm patterns and the pitches of the different notes. This is obviously much easier to do with familiar songs, so we use songs that you've probably heard before. As you vocalize them, visualize the holes and breathing directions for each note.

Note that each black key has both a sharp name and a flat name. Both of these names are used in music, but, fortunately, not usually in the same song. G sharp is a half step higher than G. A flat (which is the same note as G sharp) is a half step lower than A.

Sharps, flats, and naturals are indicated in music as follows:

What Note Shapes Mean

Notes come in a variety of different shapes, but each shape tells you something about how long the note is to be played. Shapes are roughly equivalent to the stem lengths in harmonica tablature, but much more precise. The following are the most common notes you're likely to encounter:

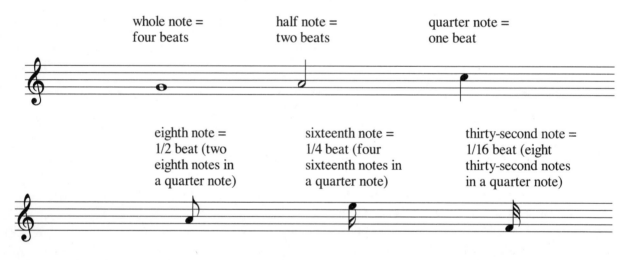

Now would be a good time to practice a song that demonstrates the different notes and their lengths:

● Note Exercise Number 1

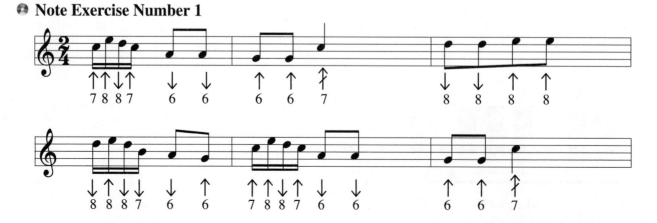

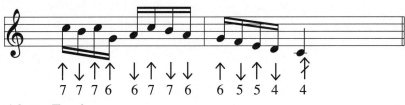

Arkansas Traveler

Notes often go above or below the staff, and the lines that the notes are written on are called ledger lines. Following are the names of notes above and below the staff that you may encounter on your diatonic harps:

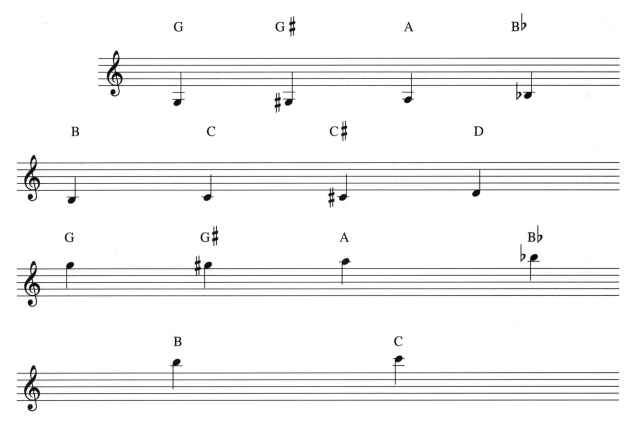

Generally, the 4-hole blow note on your C-major diatonic harmonica corresponds to the C on the first ledger line below the staff, so your 9-hole blow note is the G in the first space above the staff. However, this is not set in stone, and harmonica music written primarily for the 1- through 4-holes often is moved up an octave into the staff so that it's easier to read.

The Unnotes

You don't play on every beat. The interludes of silence are called *rests,* and look like the following.

whole note rest:
rest for four beats
(or entire bar)

half note rest:
rest for two beats

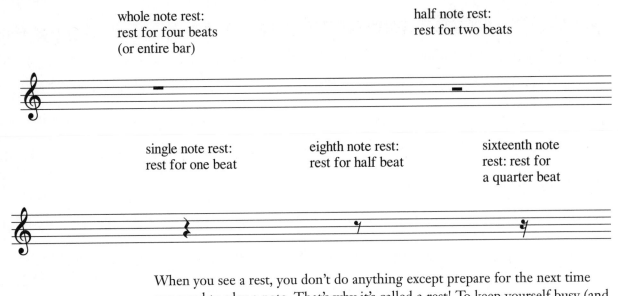

single note rest:
rest for one beat

eighth note rest:
rest for half beat

sixteenth note
rest: rest for
a quarter beat

When you see a rest, you don't do anything except prepare for the next time you need to play a note. That's why it's called a rest! To keep yourself busy (and to make sure you start again in the right place), you should count the beats while resting.

Notes with Lines and Dots

Lines and dots are used to indicate that notes are to be held longer or connected to other notes, as follows:

Dotted half note:
hold three beats
instead of two

Dotted quarter note:
hold 1 1/2 beats
instead of one

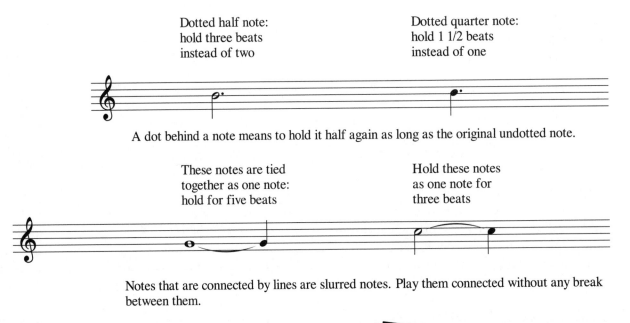

A dot behind a note means to hold it half again as long as the original undotted note.

These notes are tied
together as one note:
hold for five beats

Hold these notes
as one note for
three beats

Notes that are connected by lines are slurred notes. Play them connected without any break between them.

Now play the following exercises that use dotted notes, tied notes, and slurs:

Note Exercise Number 2

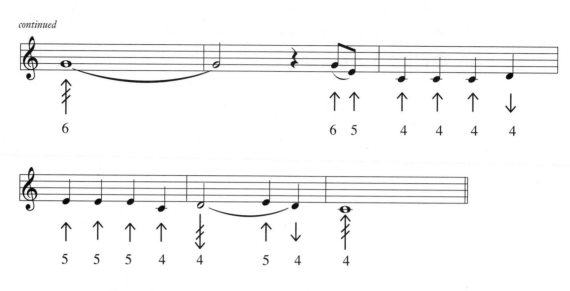

Chords

For now, we'll stick with our working definition of a chord: a group of notes that sound good together and are often strummed by a guitar or played by a piano as accompaniment to a lead melody. Go back to the drawing of the C-major diatonic harmonica at the beginning of this chapter and match the notes on your harmonica to the following chords:

Treble clef staff showing all the different chords that can be played on the C-major diatonic harmonica.

If you have access to a piano, use the drawing of a piano keyboard at the front of this chapter to identify and play each of the chords that can be played on your C-major diatonic harmonica.

You often see chords represented by a chord symbol above the staff, with only the melody line notated as notes on the staff, as follows.

This kind of notation is particularly useful for harmonica players. It gives you the option of playing either chords or single-note melodies, or you can alternate between them as you deem appropriate.

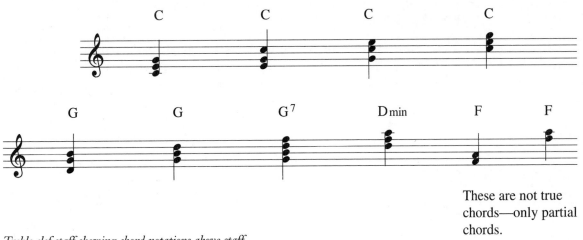

These are not true chords—only partial chords.

Treble clef staff showing chord notations above staff.

Minor Chords

Most of the chords you can play on your C-major diatonic harmonica are major chords. The other principal chords you'll encounter are minor chords. The best way to describe the difference between major and minor chords is that major chords sound bright and happy, while minor chords sound sad and melancholy. Minor chords are often used to create a "somber" mood. You also find minor chords quite often in particular styles of music, such as East European or Celtic tunes.

You can play only one minor chord on your C-major diatonic harmonica, and that's probably more by accident than by design. If you draw on the 4-5-6 or 8-9-10 holes, you'll play a D-minor chord (D, F, A).

What follows is a table that provides the notes for several important major and minor chords. If you have access to a piano, find and play each of them on the keyboard (playing the major chord first and then the corresponding minor chord).

> **Straight from the Harp**
>
> There are numerous other chords in addition to major and minor chords: seventh, diminished, augmented, and more. We explore other chords you're likely to encounter when we start playing different harmonica positions in Chapter 13.

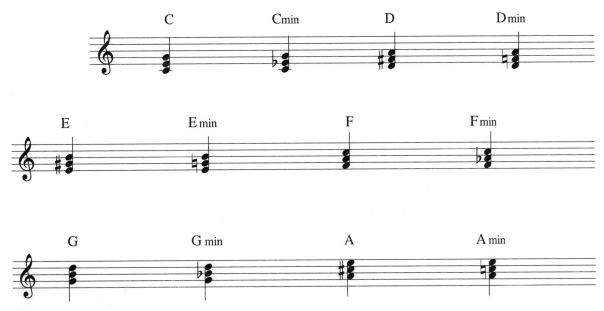

Table of major and minor chords.

Broken Chords

The notes of a chord are not always played simultaneously; they're often played quickly, one after the other, starting with the lowest note of the chord. This is called a broken chord, or arpeggio. You continue to play each of the notes as the new ones are added, so the final effect is a full chord. Broken chords are indicated like this:

played like this:

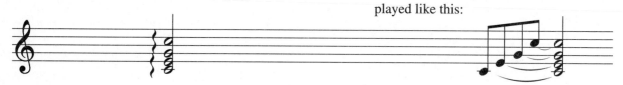

Treble clef staff showing C-major chords with arpeggio symbol, indicating that a broken chord should be played.

This arpeggio effect is often used on the harmonica. It can be achieved by starting the chord as a single note, and then quickly widening your lip opening first to a two-note chord followed by a three-note chord and so on.

Note Exercise Number 3

Try playing a series of chords, first as regular full chords and then as arpeggios or broken chords. Start with the 1-hole blow and move up the harmonica all the way to the 7-hole blow. Play a series of three-note chords as you move up the harmonica, first as a regular chord, and then as a broken chord. Do the same thing with draw notes, starting at the 1-hole and moving up to the 7-hole. This exercise helps you hear the chords better and helps you understand their structure and harmonic interrelationships better.

Beats

You've already learned that music is divided into measures or bars, which provide a rhythm and accent pattern for the notes. Measures are marked by bar lines. You've seen them in the harmonica tablature used throughout this book and in the music examples in this chapter.

Note that the end of a song is always marked with a double bar line. Double bars are also used to separate different sections of a song.

At the beginning of a piece of music, you always find a set of two numbers, one on top of the other. This is the time signature, which tells you how many beats per measure and the value of each beat. For example, a typical time signature would look like one of the following.

In each of the time signatures, the top number tells you how many beats per measure, and the bottom number tells you the value of each beat. For example, 4/4 means there are four beats per measure and each beat is a quarter note. 3/4 means there are three quarter-note beats per measure; 6/8 means there are six eighth-note beats per measure, and so forth. Bear in mind that the time signature tells you how many beats per measure, not how many notes per measure.

A measure in 4/4 time could have any number of notes, but it would have only four beats. Some of the notes could be quarter notes, but some could also be half notes, eighth notes, sixteenth notes, or any combination of notes with different values.

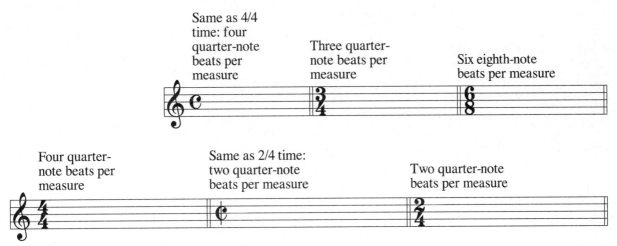

Staves with several different time signatures: 4/4, 3/4, 2/4, and so on.

Beat Exercise Number 1

Play the following songs to become familiar with different time signatures. Note the natural accent that you give to the first beat of each measure. In songs with four beats to a measure, the third beat is also slightly accented (but not as much as the first beat). We don't include the harmonica tablature for the rest of the songs in this chapter. What's the point of trying to learn to read music if you always have the crutch of harp tablature to rely on? We'll go back to a combination of music notation and harmonica tablature in subsequent chapters so you'll have the choice of which system to read.

Finally, beats are sometimes missing at the beginning of a song. It's very common for the initial lead-in measure to be only a partial measure. Several of the songs in this chapter start with partial measures. (Actually, the beats aren't missing. If you look at the end of a song, you'll almost always find them there, so all the measures end up being complete.)

Sweet Betsy from Pike

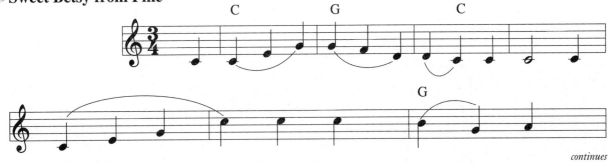

continues

continued

Joy to the World

Gary Owen

Songs written in different time signatures.

Beat Exercise Number 2

You'll also encounter special groupings of notes, such as triplets. Triplets are very common in all time signatures and are indicated as follows:

The notes are to be played evenly, with each note given the same value or length. The first note of each triplet should be slightly accented. Play the preceding exercises while you count the beats in your head, and make sure the triplets are all played evenly and within a single beat.

 **Sir William's Hornpipe**

Signs

A multitude of signs are used in music notation to give you a message or instruction as to how a particular song, passage, or note should be played (at least in the opinion of the composer, for what that's worth). Sometimes these signs are written in English, and sometimes in Italian. Other signs are nontextual symbols that have a special meaning.

Blues Clues

When a sharp or flat symbol is used in a measure or bar for a particular note, that note is played as a sharp or flat every time it appears subsequently in that measure. For measures that follow, the note is played as a natural unless it is sharpened or flattened again. A natural sign is used if a note that previously has been sharpened or flattened in a measure should be played as a natural later in the same measure.

What Speed to Play

One important set of signs informs you as to the speed, or tempo, of the music. When written in English, their meanings are rather obvious. When written in Italian, their meanings are not quite so clear, unless you happen to speak Italian.

Tempo Signs

English Signs	Italian Signs
Very slowly	*Largo:* very slow
Moderate	*Allegro:* fast
Brightly	*Presto:* very fast
Light waltz	*Andante:* slowly, at a walking pace
With spirit	*Moderato:* moderately
Broad and dignified	*Adagio:* leisurely
	Vivace: lively
	Ritardando: slow down gradually
	Accelerando: speed up gradually
	A tempo: return to the original tempo

Note that many of these signs specify not only the speed of a song, but also an indication of the "feeling" the music should be played with.

How Loud to Play

Another very important set of signs tells you the volume at which a song should be played. These signs also come in a mixture of English and Italian words, as well as in symbols. The following are the more common volume signs you'll encounter:

pp (*pianissimo*): very softly

p (*piano*): softly

mp (*mezzo-piano*): moderately softly

m (*mezzo*): medium

mf (*mezzo-forte*): moderately loudly

f (*forte*): loudly

ff (*fortissimo*): very loudly

crescendo (<): gradually get louder

diminuendo (>): gradually get softer

Other Important Signs

There are enough music signs to fill a huge music dictionary, and you should purchase one if you find yourself constantly running up against signs you don't understand. Following are some of the more important signs that are likely to be used regularly in your music:

Table of symbols, Italian names, and English meanings for miscellaneous music signs.

Keys

Your harmonica is tuned to the key of C-major, and you already know that harmonicas are available that are specially tuned to almost every major and minor key.

So Just What Is a Key?

When we say that music, or a harmonica, is in a particular key, all we mean is that its notes are based on the scale that starts with the note of the same name. For example, the key of C-major is based on the C-major scale, which starts at C and consists of all the white notes on a piano. As we noted earlier, a major scale consists of a series of alternating steps and half steps. The half steps occur between the third and fourth notes and the seventh and eighth notes. Recall that a C-major scale is C-D-E-F-G-A-B-C. The half steps are between E-F and B-C. A C-major diatonic harmonica is tuned to play all the same notes.

A G-major scale starts with G and ascends at the same *intervals* as a C-major scale. A G-major scale is G-A-B-C-D-E-F sharp-G. There are half-step intervals between the third and fourth notes and the seventh and eighth notes, just as in the C-major scale. The key of G thus has an F sharp in it.

The key of F-major starts with an F and must ascend at the same intervals as a C-major scale, so it is F-G-A-B flat-C-D-E-F. The key of F-major thus has a B flat in it.

Likewise, a G-major diatonic harp is tuned to play an F sharp (instead of an F), and an F-major diatonic harp is tuned to play a B flat (instead of a B).

def•i•ni•tion

> An **interval** is the distance between two notes. The interval between every note on a piano keyboard is a half step. The intervals between the notes of a major scale are always as follows: whole step—whole step—half step—whole step—whole step—whole step—half step. For a C-major scale, this translates as C, D, E, F, G, A, B, C. The intervals for every other major scale, regardless of the note it starts on, are identical.

Now look at the following G-major and F-major harmonicas: these two harmonicas enable you to play all the notes you need for the keys of F-major and G-major.

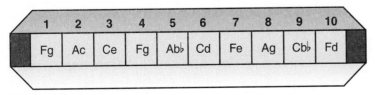

Blow and draw notes of an F-major diatonic harmonica.

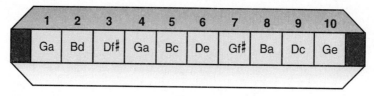

Blow and draw notes of a G-major diatonic harmonica.

Key Signatures

A key signature is a sign at the front of a song (or a new section of a song) that tells you which notes are always sharpened or flattened. For example, a key signature of C-major has no flats or sharps, so you know that all notes are played as naturals. A key signature of F-major has a B flat, so all Bs that appear in the music are flattened. A key signature of G-major has an F sharp, so all Fs that appear in the music are sharpened. Key signatures are written as follows:

G-major key signature and scale.

D-major key signature and scale.

A-major key signature and scale.

E-major key signature and scale.

B-major key signature and scale.

F-major key signature and scale.

B♭-major key signature and scale.

E♭-major key signature and scale.

A♭-major key signature and scale.

D♭-major key signature and scale.

The notes that are "permanently" sharpened or flattened are indicated by a sharp or flat sign located on the line for that note. Note that *all* notes with the same note name are affected by the key signature, *even those appearing on different lines than the flat or sharp sign in the key signature.*

Key signatures often change in a song. A change in key signature is indicated by a double bar line and a new key signature. The new key signature cancels out the previous one. Also, watch for *accidental* sharps, flats, and naturals. They are sharp, flat, or natural signs that don't appear in the key signature but appear in a measure. When you see an accidental, it's effective for the entire measure but does not extend to subsequent measures.

Minor Keys

We've already told you about minor chords, which are composed of the first, third, and fifth notes of the corresponding minor key. Minor keys often are used to set a somber, mournful feeling or mood. The most common minor keys you're likely to encounter are A-minor, D-minor, G-minor, E-minor, and B-minor:

A-minor key signature and scale.

D-minor key signature and scale.

G-minor key signature and scale.

E-minor key signature and scale.

B-minor key signature and scale.

Songs written in the preceding keys are based on the notes found in the scales for each of the keys. *Please note one very important anomaly between a minor key signature and its corresponding scale:* the seventh note of a minor scale is usually sharpened even though the sharpened note does not appear in the key signature. This sharpened seventh note is instead sharpened throughout the music by using an accidental sharp. Thus, even though an A-minor key signature does not contain a G sharp, the G is usually sharpened both in the A-minor scale and in music written in the key of A-minor.

Note how the intervals for these scales are different from the intervals for the major scales spelled out earlier in the chapter. Can you compare the intervals for a major scale with the intervals for these harmonic minor scales and define the differences? If you play these scales, you'll undoubtedly notice that they make you feel just a little sad.

Blues Clues

When you get to the point of purchasing minor-tuned harmonicas, you'll find two differently tuned models: natural minor and harmonic minor. The natural minor model has the same notes in cross-harp position as found in the corresponding minor key signature. The harmonic minor model has the same notes in straight-harp position as used in the minor scale (the seventh note is sharpened). Thus, an A-natural minor harmonica does not have any sharps or flats, and the A-harmonic minor harmonica has a G sharp.

When a minor key and a major key have the same key signature, they are said to be *relative* to each other. Thus, A-minor is the relative minor to C-major (and C-major is the relative major to A-minor), because neither of them has any sharps or flats in their key signatures.

Identifying the Key

It isn't all that difficult to tell what key a song is in. First of all, if there's music (and you've read this chapter), just look at the key signature. There are only two choices: either the major or minor key corresponds to that key signature. You can tell if it's in the minor key or major key by examining some of the chords, particularly the last chord. For example, if the key signature has no sharps or flats, you know it's played in C-major or A-minor, and you can tell which one it is from the chords. A song written in C-major obviously has a lot of C-major chords, and a song written in A-minor has a lot of A-minor chords. With luck, the chord symbols will be written above the staff. If they aren't, use what you learned in this chapter to figure it out. Then choose the right key for your harp accordingly.

If there's no music, the first thing you should do to find out the key is to raise your hand and ask one of the other musicians (anyone but the drummer). If no one knows, you might consider finding a different band to play with. Alternatively, just ask the musicians to play a few bars while you experiment with a couple of different harps. You'll figure it out pretty quickly. Most songs start or end (or both) with the same chord as the key the song is written in. If you don't want to fumble around with harmonicas, buy a *pitch pipe*, a relatively inexpensive, small device you can use to pinpoint the key of a song.

Checklist for Reading Music

As you get comfortable reading music, it will become second nature to you. But to get started, we suggest you go through the following checklist each time you are reading a new song:

1. Check the beginning of the music for the clef sign, time signature, key signature, and tempo. Make sure you understand these structural characteristics of the song.

2. Check for any changes in tempo, time signature, or key signature so that you won't be surprised when they occur.

3. Look for any repeats and figure out what's repeated and what jumps you have to make in the music. Get a feeling for the flow of the song.

4. Look for any other signs you're not familiar with so that you can look them up before you start playing.

5. If you're not familiar with the song, sing or hum parts of the melody so that you have an idea of what it's supposed to sound like. Better yet, if you have a piano, play the melody line on the keyboard.

6. Go through the song several times without getting bogged down. If you encounter a difficult section, get through it as best you can and move on. It's important to develop a "total picture" of the song in your mind.

7. If you encounter signs, symbols, or words you don't understand, just keep playing. You can look them up later—and don't forget to do it. If someone took the trouble to include a sign in the music, it's worth understanding what it means.

8. Identify the sections giving you trouble and practice them separately.

9. Alternate between playing the entire song all the way through and practicing specific difficult sections. This method keeps you from getting discouraged, and speeds up your learning process.

10. As you get better at the song, start playing more and more of it without the music. You don't want to be reading music when you perform it. Admittedly, this is easier said than done, particularly for difficult pieces, but reading music while you perform has a dulling effect on your innovation and showmanship. Break away from the sheet music as much as you can.

11. Practice sight-reading. Learn to read music on the fly. It's a good skill to have when you start jamming and performing impromptu with other musicians.

12. When you buy sheet music, start out with music written especially for the harmonica. Then branch out and buy music written for other instruments. Piano and fiddle music are particularly adaptable to harp playing. You'll find that music written for other instruments often is more developed, robust, and challenging than a lot of the music written for the harmonica. You'll then have music you can use when you want to play with other musicians, too.

The Least You Need to Know

- If you're serious about reading music, you really need to know everything in this chapter. You can't stop in the middle of a song to look something up.

- The only way to learn to read music is to *practice* reading music using the tips in the checklist.

- Don't fret. Just get comfortable with the basic concepts for now, and then move on. By the time you finish this book, reading music will be very natural and easy for you.

Chapter 11

Tongue-Blocking Tricks

In This Chapter

♦ Octave tongue-blocking techniques and exercises

♦ Tongue-blocking chords

♦ Techniques and exercises for slaps, lifts, and tremolos

In Chapter 7, we explained the tongue-blocking method of playing single notes. If you didn't pay much attention to that technique, go back and practice it some more. You need to be able to play tongue-block single notes to learn the more difficult tongue-blocking techniques in this chapter.

Here you can learn an extension of tongue-blocking that enables you to play octaves, chords, and tremolos simply by varying the position and timing of your tongue-block. Actually, we should not use the word *simply* when describing these techniques. They are not simple at all. You'll need to practice these techniques for months to master them, so you shouldn't get bogged down here. We're introducing them so that you can understand how they're done, get reasonably comfortable with them, and then move on. As you go through the subsequent exercises and songs, you should spontaneously interject these techniques into the music where they feel right. Come back to the exercises in this chapter periodically, and you'll discover that you can play them better each time.

Tongue-Block Octaves

You can play single notes through both the right and left sides of your mouth by using your tongue to block the airflow to the two or three holes between these notes. The two notes you play when using this tongue-blocking technique are separated by an interval called an octave. As mentioned earlier, an octave is where the scale starts over in a higher-frequency range. Consequently, both notes played when using this technique are in a sense the same notes. This technique adds fullness to your sound. The following diagram demonstrates the positioning of your lips and tongue on the harmonica.

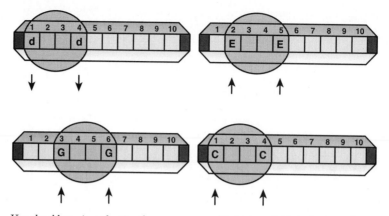

You should use just the tip of your tongue to block the middle holes (but if you're trying to block three holes, you'll need a really big tongue to do it). Press your tongue lightly against the harmonica.

Tongue-Block Octave Exercise Number 1

1. Place the harmonica in your mouth, in the tongue-blocking position.

2. Play several tongue-block single notes to reacquaint yourself with the technique.

3. Now move your tongue to the right and allow the air to flow on both sides of your tongue. This is where it gets a little tricky. You need to control both your tongue and your lips so that you're playing only one note on each side of your tongue.

4. Try this on the 4-hole blow note, blocking the 2- and 3-holes with your tongue and playing the 4- and 1-holes by blowing through the right and left sides of your tongue. This is a C octave, meaning that both holes are playing the same note but an octave apart.

5. Try the same thing blocking the 5- and 6-holes and blowing through the 4- and 7-holes. This is also a C octave, but one octave higher than your previous one. Practice this exercise until you can play both of these octaves cleanly—only one note being played on each side of your tongue.

In this next exercise, you use the same tongue-blocking technique, but you use it to play intervals other than the octave. Due to the layout of the diatonic harmonica, the same physical technique does not produce the same musical intervals as you move through the range of the instrument.

Tongue-Block Octave Exercise Number 2

1. Start again at the 1- and 4-holes (blocking the 2- and 3-holes).

2. Play your way all the way up the harmonica, starting at the 1- and 4-blow holes, followed by the 1- and 4-draw-holes.

3. Then move to the 2- and 5-holes (blocking the 3- and 4-holes) and so forth.

4. Move all the way up the harp until you're blocking the 8- and 9-holes while playing the 7- and 10-holes, and then move back down the harp in the same manner. Focus on playing only one note on each side of your tongue.

You probably noticed two things while playing this exercise. First, you were producing a very full-bodied sound. That's good. Second, some of the notes you played clearly weren't octaves. That's good or bad, depending on the style of music you're playing. Look at the following harmonica drawing to see the notes you were actually playing in the various blow and draw positions.

1	2	3	4	5	6	7	8	9	10
Cd	Eg	Gb	Cd	Ef	Ga	bC	dE	fG	aC

You can see that by blocking two holes with your tongue, sometimes you're playing an octave and sometimes you are playing something else. When you're playing straight harp, these "nonoctave" draw notes often don't fit with the music, so tongue-block octaves should be used with care. When you play blues or rock on cross harp, these same notes often sound great. They give the music an edgy, *dirty* sound that can be very effective. The 2- and 5-hole draw notes are a particularly common combination in blues and rock music.

As you're learning to play these intervals, it would be a good idea to associate their technical names with their sound quality to help register their distinct color. The following chart shows the different intervals while drawing in all positions:

Holes	Interval
1-4	octave
2-5	minor seventh
3-6	minor seventh
4-7	major sixth
5-8	major sixth
6-9	minor sixth
7-10	minor seventh

Can you hear that the intervals starting in positions 2-5, 3-6, and 7-10 are somehow the same as the intervals in the 4-7 and 5-8 positions?

We don't use any special symbol in harmonica tablature for tongue-block octaves. It's designated like a chord, except that the middle note is missing.

Practice the following song, which includes tongue-block octaves.

Blues Clues

It's possible to play more pure draw octaves by blocking three holes with your tongue. Look at the preceding harmonica drawing, and you'll see the various draw combinations that produce pure octaves. This is a difficult, but not impossible, technique. It kind of depends on how big your mouth and tongue are.

● **Alouette**

↓ ↑ ↑	↓ ↑ ↓ ↑ ↑ ↑	↓ ↑ ↑	↓ ↑ ↓ ↑	
4 4 5 5	4 4 4 5 4 3	4 4 5 5	4 4 4 5	4
1 1 2 2	1 1 1 2 1	1 1 2 2	1 1 1 2	1

↓ ↑ ↑	↓ ↑ ↓ ↑ ↑ ↑	↓ ↑ ↑	↓ ↑ ↓ ↑	
4 4 5 5	4 4 4 5 4 3	4 4 5 5	4 4 4 5	4
1 1 2 2	1 1 1 2 1	1 1 2 2	1 1 1 2	1

↑ ↑ ↑ ↑ ↑ ↑ ↑	↑ ↓ ↑ ↓ ↑ ↓ ↑	↑ ↑ ↑ ↑ ↑ ↑	
4 4 4 5 6 6 6	6 6 6 5 5 4 4	6 6 6 3 3 3	6
1 1 1 2 3 3 3		3 3 3	3

↓ ↑ ↑	↓ ↑ ↓ ↑ ↑ ↑	↓ ↑ ↑	↓ ↑ ↓ ↑	
4 4 5 5	4 4 4 5 4 3	4 4 5 5	4 4 4 5	4
1 1 2 2	1 1 1 2 1	1 1 2 2	1 1 1 2	1

Tongue-Block Chords

Tongue-block chords are difficult techniques that take a while to master. Learning to play them will help you hear how they're used, which will give you the incentive you need to gain proficiency as well as provide guidance on how to apply them.

There are two different styles to playing tongue-block chords, both easy to describe but difficult to master.

♦ **Tongue slap.** With this technique, you play a chord first, and then a tongue-block single note. This technique is commonly used in blues-harp playing. The idea is to play a "fat" chord and then *slap* your tongue on the harmonica to block all the notes except one. When you perfect it, you'll play the chord to single-note transition so fast that it sounds like one note.

♦ **Tongue lift.** This is the opposite technique of the tongue slap. You play a tongue-block single note first, and then lift your tongue in a rhythmic *la-la* pattern. The effect is like playing a melody line and rhythm chords simultaneously, and it often sounds like two harmonicas.

Tongue-Block Chords Exercise Number 1

1. Play a 2-3-4 blow chord on your harmonica. Then slap your tongue on the harmonica and block the 2- and 3-holes. Do not try to go too fast at first. Concentrate on playing a full, fat chord, and then slap the tip of your tongue (or just below the tip) on the 2- and 3-hole.

2. Keep repeating this on the same hole nice and slow until you can slap your tongue on the harp and cleanly block the 2- and 3-holes, leaving just a clean, single-note 4-hole.

3. When you can do this slowly, gradually start speeding up. Don't break the airflow between your chord and single note. As you get faster, you'll notice that you're starting to play the chord and the single note as one note, and that's how a tongue slap is supposed to sound.

Tongue-Block Chords Exercise Number 2

Now do the exact same thing as in Exercise Number 1, but draw instead of blow. This is more difficult than tongue-slap blowing, but you'll get comfortable with it. There's a tendency on the tongue-block draw to let the airflow through on both sides of your tongue after the block, thus creating an octave. Actually, moving from a draw chord to a draw tongue-block octave is a very effective technique for blues and rock music. However, concentrate for now on slapping your tongue tightly against the left side of your mouth so that you produce a clean tongue-block single note on the 4-hole only.

Tongue-Block Chords Exercise Number 3

Practice both the blow and draw tongue slaps, moving from the 1-2-3 holes up to the 5-6-7 holes and then back down to the 1-2-3 holes. Do the blow series first and then the draw series. Play five repetitions of each tongue slap before moving on to the next hole. This might not sound very musical, but it gets you comfortable with the technique and helps you develop control over your tongue.

Tongue-Block Chords Exercise Number 4

1. Take a deep breath. Play a tongue-block 4-hole single note, and make an effort to regulate your airflow so that you don't exhale all at once. Then lift your tongue and place it back on the harmonica in a *la-la* pattern. By creating the *la-la* effect, you'll find that the tongue-block is actually done with the bottom of your tongue, just slightly below the tip. After every lift, place your tongue back on the harmonica in its tongue-block position to create tongue-lift chords.

2. Try doing this while playing the chords in a syncopated rhythm. Then try it in a waltz (or "oomp-pah-pah") rhythm. Don't break the airflow on your single note. Although it may seem a bit unnatural at first, you have to place your tongue back on the harmonica after each lift without breaking the airflow. For now, concentrate on playing a clean single note with the 4-hole only (do not let your airflow through on the left side of your mouth during the tongue-block single notes).

3. You can also practice coordinating your breathing and tongue technique without the instrument. Again, take a deep breath. Move your tongue into the tongue-block position. As you start to

smoothly and slowly exhale, rhythmically move your tongue back and forth between the front of your lips and the inside of your mouth. You should hear a steady hiss of air periodically augmented by the flopping sound of your tongue as it moves back and forth between your lips and the interior of your mouth, up until you completely expel the air in your lungs.

Tongue-Block Chords Exercise Number 5

Play the exact same exercise as Exercise Number 4, but this time do it on the 4-hole draw.

Tongue-Block Chords Exercise Number 6

1. Play a series of blow tongue lifts starting with the 3-hole (blocking and lifting from the 1- and 2-holes) and moving up to the 7-hole (blocking and lifting from the 5- and 6-holes), and then move back down the harmonica to the 3-hole.

2. Do the same thing, starting with the 3-hole and moving up to the 7-hole and back again while drawing. Do not try to go too fast. Concentrate on playing clean single notes and on not breaking the airflow on the single notes. Play several different rhythms on each hole before moving on to the next hole.

We don't use any special symbols in our harmonica tablature for these tongue-block chord techniques. You may see a chord designation that immediately transforms to a single note (tongue slap) or a chord rhythm interspersed with a single-note melody (tongue lift). Mostly, however, you should just interject these techniques when they feel right. Now play the following songs, which will give you a feel for how these techniques can be used in music.

Don't Harp On It

You're learning a lot of different techniques in this chapter and elsewhere in this book. Don't expect to find symbols for most of them anywhere in the music you're playing, whether harmonica tablature or traditional music. The whole idea is to mix and match these techniques spontaneously wherever and whenever they feel good. Remember, you're playing the harp, not the French horn.

🔘 **German Waltz**

The lower two sets of notes are tongue-lift chords that should be played as a rhythm to the single-note melody line.

The following version of "The Irish Washerwoman" is a slightly different version of the one you played in Chapter 9. Don't try to play this too fast at first.

● **The Irish Washerwoman**

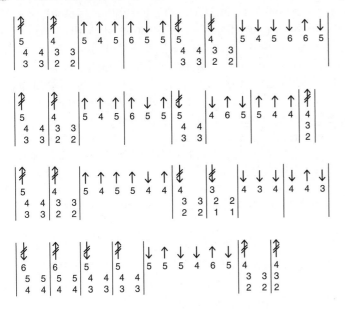

You should be playing tongue-block technique on all notes and holding the top single note all the way through the tongue-block chords. Don't break your airflow on the single note when you blow or draw the chords. Make sure you don't have any air leaking on the left side of your mouth.

Tongue-Block Tremolos

This technique is similar to the tongue lift. You start with a clean, tongue-block single note and lift your tongue in a *la-la* motion, but you play your *la-la*s very rapidly. This creates a tremolo effect.

Tongue-Block Tremolo Exercise Number 1

1. Play a 4-blow tongue-block single note. Then lift your tongue rapidly in a *la-la* motion. You may want to do the tongue-block with the underside of your tongue, just below the tip, to get a *la-la* instead of *da-da* effect.

2. Then play a 4-draw in the same fashion. Make sure you play a clean single note on the 4-blow and 4-draw without any air leaking through on the left side of your tongue. Do not break your airflow on the single note. A steady flow of air is an essential component of this technique.

Tongue-Block Tremolo Exercise Number 2

Now play tongue-block tremolo notes on both blow and draw holes from the 3-hole up to the 7-hole and back to the 3-hole, much like the preceding tongue-block exercises. Go nice and slow. Make sure that your single note on the right side of your tongue is clean and that you don't break the airflow for this note.

Your tongue is probably a little worn out by now, but hopefully you can feel progress in playing these tongue-block techniques. These techniques won't take place overnight or feel natural to you immediately. They'll take practice, but they're very important to learn if you want to get that great, "fat" blues sound that in all likelihood prompted you to buy this book in the first place. Insert these techniques where they feel right, both in the exercises and songs included in this book and, *more important*, when you play along with CDs. Periodically, we suggest that you come back to this chapter and go through the exercises again. Each time you do, your tongue-block technique will get a little better.

The Least You Need to Know

- Some of these exercises are difficult, but you can get through all of them, at least slowly.
- If you keep returning to the practice exercises in this chapter, you can get to feel very comfortable playing tongue-block octaves and tremolos.
- Eventually, with enough practice, you'll be able to play slow tongue-lift and tongue-slap chords in various rhythms.

The Art of Bending

In This Chapter

- ◆ The basics of draw and blow bends
- ◆ Bending techniques and exercises
- ◆ Songs with ornamental and target note bends
- ◆ The overbending art

In this chapter, we teach you some of the more advanced techniques that will turn your diatonic *harmonica* into a *harp.* You'll be able to pick up on some of them very quickly; others will take months of practice. Some, such as overbends, you might never master. Don't get discouraged. Just practice the more difficult techniques that you can't learn fairly quickly until you feel some solid progress. Then move on. The chapters that follow this one are designed to give you the opportunity to practice these techniques and build on your initial progress. Come back to this chapter periodically and go over the exercises again. You'll improve your abilities and gain more confidence every time you do, and the better you sound, the more motivated you'll be to master these techniques. And for those of you who choose to rush through this chapter to get to the "good stuff," we expect to see you back here again real soon.

Draw and Blow Bends

Now we're going to venture into the most important technique you'll learn on the diatonic harmonica if you want to play blues, country, or rock music: bending notes. Bending notes to play pitches that are not designed into the harmonica is the very essence of blues, rock, and country-harp playing. It's what gives the harmonica its unique personality in these styles of music. It's what turns a harmonica into a harp.

What is bending? Bending notes on a harmonica is the lowering (and sometimes raising) of the pitch of a note by altering the direction of the airflow and the shape of your vocal cavity. Through the traditional bending technique, you can play 32 notes on your 10-hole major diatonic harmonica, as opposed to the

20 that are available in its design. By adding the much more difficult technique of overblowing and overdrawing described later in the chapter, you can play 10 additional notes, giving you a full chromatic scale on a diatonic harmonica.

The Basics of Bending

The notes available on a C-major diatonic harmonica through bending are shown in the following drawing.

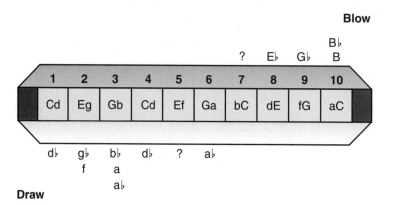

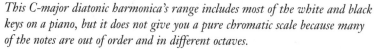

This C-major diatonic harmonica's range includes most of the white and black keys on a piano, but it does not give you a pure chromatic scale because many of the notes are out of order and in different octaves.

There are a few important things to observe in this drawing:

- There are five draw notes and three blow notes that can be bent on a major diatonic harmonica.

- Five of the notes can be bent a half step down in pitch (the 1-4-6 draw holes and 8-9 blow holes). Two of the notes can be bent down two half steps in pitch (the 2-draw-hole and 10-blow-hole), and one of them can be bent down three half steps in pitch (the 3-draw-hole).

- On any one hole, you can bend only the higher of the two notes available on that hole. For example, you can play a blow C and a draw D on the 4-hole. The D is higher than the C, so you can bend only the draw D. On the 8-hole, you can play a blow G (higher) and a draw F (lower). You can bend only the blow G on this hole.

- The larger the interval between the two notes available on any hole, the greater the bend you can achieve. For example, the interval between the blow and draw notes on the 4-hole is one full step, and you can bend the higher of these notes a half step. The interval between the blow and draw notes on the 3-hole is two full steps, and you can bend the higher of these notes three half steps.

- You can bend the higher note on any hole down to a pitch that is approximately one half step higher than the lower note on that hole. For example, the draw D on the 4-hole can be bent down to a D flat, which is one half step higher than the blow C on the 4-hole. You can bend the draw B on the 3-hole down to an A flat, which is one half step higher than the blow G on the 3-hole.

Blues Clues

The bending patterns for differently tuned diatonic harmonicas are different from those for the major diatonic harmonica, because the intervals between the high and low notes on any hole can vary from the major diatonic harmonica's. For example, the 5-blow is E flat and the 5-draw is F on a C-minor diatonic harmonica. Therefore, you can bend the 5-draw down to an E, whereas the 5-draw on a major diatonic harmonica cannot be bent a half step.

♦ Note that the 5-draw and 7-blow are designated as question marks. You cannot achieve a pure bend on either of these holes. You can bend the pitch down somewhere between the draw and blow notes available for that hole, but you can't achieve a half-step bend. That's because the blow and draw notes on these holes are already *only a half step apart*. Remember that you only can bend down to a pitch one half step higher than the lower note on the hole. For these holes, the high note is only one half step higher than the low note to begin with, so there isn't room to bend a half step.

The Physics of Bending

The flattened pitches you can achieve through bending notes on any hole actually are created by the interaction of that hole's draw *and* blow reeds. As the higher reed (in pitch) is bent, the lower reed begins to vibrate as well. This is caused by the alterations to your airflow and vocal cavity that result from your bending technique. The farther the higher reed is bent down, the more the lower reed vibrates until the higher reed eventually stops vibrating altogether. At this point, the lower-pitched reed is almost entirely creating the bent note. For example, if you bend the draw D on the 4-hole of a C-major diatonic harmonica, the reed for the blow C on that hole begins to vibrate. It will vibrate more as you increase your bend until eventually the draw reed stops vibrating, and your resulting bent note is being mostly produced by the blow C reed. For a detailed explanation of this phenomenon, you should read Steve Baker's *The Harp Handbook* (Wise Publications, 1999). Actually, you should read Baker's book whether you're interested in note-bending physics or not; it's one of the best harmonica books available.

The Technique of Bending

The technique for bending notes is not an easy thing to describe in a way that's understandable for anyone who hasn't done it before. Part of the problem is that bending is a somewhat "subjective" technique in that each person might approach it somewhat differently to get the same result. In addition, we're describing things you have to do with your mouth, tongue, and vocal cavity that normal humans just don't do. The following tips are for producing draw bends on the major diatonic harmonica. For now, use only the 4-hole draw, as it's the easiest to get started on. Remember, the goal is to change your airflow and the shape of your vocal cavity so that you change the flow of air over the reeds, thus changing the way that they vibrate. Keep these tips in mind as you go through the exercises.

Ten Tips for Bending Draw Notes

1. *Think your notes lower.* Much of the success of your note bends will come from your brain in addition to your mouth. *Think* the notes lower by focusing on opening your throat, enlarging your vocal cavity, and playing the flattened note in your head.

2. Try whistling a high note and then a low note. Then sing a high note followed by a low note. Do you feel what happens to your vocal cavity and airflow? You want to get that same feeling to bend your draw notes.

3. All the important techniques we introduced in Chapter 3 still apply. Stay relaxed. Place the harp deep into your mouth. Maintain a controlled, focused airflow.

4. For starters, play a 4-draw on your harmonica. Without doing anything else, tilt the harmonica downward slowly to an angle and then bring it back up. You'll hear the pitch flatten. You do not want to do this when bending a draw note. As you probably noticed, the tone became thin and pinched in addition to lower. Now you know the effect that changing the direction of your airflow has on the reed's pitch.

5. When playing a draw bend, focus on dropping your tongue flat against the bottom of your mouth, lowering your jaw, and opening your throat wide. All this creates the right shape for your vocal cavity. A side effect of this will be that, as you drop everything lower, you'll feel your nose pinch shut. That's good. You don't want any air up there. The idea is to change the shape of your vocal cavity by lowering it.

6. You should *purse*, or pinch, your lips slightly to help achieve the bend. You should feel your upper lip tighten slightly downward at the corners and your lower lip raise just slightly. Don't overdo this, because you're not trying to cut off the airflow. Pursing your lips merely helps you control and change the direction of the airflow.

7. Use *vowels* to help you lower the pitch. Mouth a "weeeh" sound while drawing the note and then switch to an "aauh" sound. This will naturally cause you to lower your jaw, drop your tongue, and enlarge your vocal cavity.

8. Just think about sticking your jaw out there like Popeye the Sailor Man. Stick it out and be proud. If you can get the right jaw action, your tongue, throat, and lip positioning will fall into place naturally.

Blues Clues

Harps in the *same key* from different vendors have different bending characteristics because of differences in materials and design. Harps in *different keys* likewise have different bending characteristics because the reeds are different lengths. For example, a G-major diatonic harmonica is lower pitched than a C-major diatonic harmonica, so its reeds are longer.

9. To bend single notes, it's much easier to use the pucker technique than the tongue-block technique. However, it's good to learn both techniques because tongue-block bends create a different effect than pucker bends and are preferable for some styles.

10. Do *not* breathe air any harder. Creating a draw (or blow) bend does not require more air. Blowing or drawing harder only makes your bends more difficult. The reason you alter the shape of your mouth cavity is to increase air pressure on the two participating reeds.

Note Bend Exercise Number 1

1. Practice bending the 4-draw using the preceding techniques. This will not come to you immediately. You'll have to work at it. Keep going back to the tips on bending notes to keep them firmly in mind. Eventually, they'll become second nature, and you'll follow them without even realizing it.

2. After you feel somewhat comfortable with the 4-draw bend, practice the 1-draw bend. Use exactly the same technique as with the 4-draw bend, but everything will be "deeper" in your mouth, meaning that you'll need to exaggerate your tongue-dropping, jaw-lowering, and throat-opening techniques. Make them even more pronounced with lower notes.

When you start playing bends on diatonic harmonicas in different keys, you'll notice two things. First, it will take a while for some of the holes, particularly the 2- and 3-draw-holes, to break in sufficiently for a solid bend. Second, your technique will vary slightly from harp to harp, key to key, and note to note.

You'll find that bends on certain holes are easier or more difficult than on those same holes on a different harmonica. For all of them, however, the technique is exactly as described in this chapter. You merely have to experiment with airflow and the shape of your vocal cavity to get the right sound for that particular harp.

You can bend draw holes 1-6 on a major diatonic harmonica, but the 2-, 3-, and 4-draw bends clearly are the most important and most used, particularly in blues and rock music. You've practiced the 4-draw bend already, so let's turn to the more difficult 2- and 3-draw bends. They are more difficult, both because the 2- and 3-draw-holes are problematic in any event, and because more than one note can be played through bending on both of these holes. This raises the issue of controlling which note you're playing with your bend.

Note Bend Exercise Number 2

1. Play a 2-draw on your harmonica. Bend the note downward using your proper bending technique. You'll notice that the range of the bend is longer because you're covering two half steps instead of just one. Start out by hitting the lowest possible note, two half steps

below the starting note. You'll be trying to play an F on a hole designed to play a G. If possible, sit at a piano and play a middle F while trying to hit the F bend on your 2-hole (you can also use a pitch pipe to test your pitch). When you can hit the F, practice this bend until you can slide all the way down to it comfortably.

2. Now try bending all the way down to the F, and then raise your jaw and tongue slightly while still drawing. You'll hear the pitch raise slightly. Go back to your whistling or singing exercise and go from a high note to a low note and then to a note midway in between. See how your tongue and jaw raise slightly on the third note. You're adjusting your airflow and vocal cavity to hit the higher note, and the same thing happens when you go from a deep draw bend to a middle draw bend on the harmonica.

3. Go back to the piano and play a middle G, followed by an F, F sharp, and G while you play the following notes on your 2-hole: G (normal draw), F (deep draw bend), F sharp (middle draw bend). Use the pitch pipe to check your notes if you don't have a piano. Repeat this exercise again and again, concentrating on hitting the correct notes squarely.

4. Then switch it around, playing the G first, then bending down first to the F sharp middle draw bend, and then the F deep draw bend and back up again. On both of these exercises, start out very slowly. Speed is not important right now.

5. Remember that we use B^2 in our harp tablature to designate the double bend down to the F.

Note Bend Exercise Number 3

1. Now on to the very difficult 3-draw bend. The range on this bend is the deepest of any on your diatonic major harp. The interval between the draw hole (B) and the blow hole (G) is two full steps, so you can achieve three different draw bend notes (B flat, A, and A flat). Approach this exactly as you did the 2-draw bend in Exercise Number 2. First get comfortable hitting the deep bend all the way down to the A flat. Then practice raising your jaw and tongue slowly so that you hear the pitch raising all the way back to the original B. This is very difficult, and it will take much practice to be able to control these notes. By starting with the deepest bend, you'll find you gain control over your middle bends more quickly.

2. Practice the same exercises as in Exercise Number 2, going first from B all the way down to A flat and then back up through A and B flat. Then start with the B and go down to B flat, B, A flat, and back up again. Check your pitch with a piano or pitch pipe. Repeat the exercise many times, trying to hit the notes squarely. Do not be discouraged that this does not happen immediately or that your

bends might sound like a foghorn. It will take months of practice to perfect the 3-draw bends. Get started now and then keep coming back to it.

3. Remember that we use B^3 in our harp tablature to designate the triple bend down to the A flat.

On all these exercises, make sure you practice both hitting the bent notes squarely and also sliding down to the bent note and then sliding back up to the normally occurring pitch. We want to reemphasize here that it can take a while to become proficient at these techniques.

The following are some more note bend exercises to help you develop control over your draw bends. It would be a good idea to take a week or so of your practice and focus almost exclusively on bending exercises, as boring as that may seem. Then move on, but keep coming back to them periodically

Note Bend Exercise Number 4

Play your full range of draw bends on each hole, starting with the 1-draw and going up to the 6-draw, and then back again. Go ahead and play the 5-hole bend, such as it is. Play each hole five times before moving on to the next hole. Play all the notes that can be hit through bending for each hole. Concentrate on hitting them squarely. On each hole, slide through the bends without breaking the air-flow. This will give your bends a "curving" effect.

Note Bend Exercise Number 5

Play the exact same exercise as Exercise Number 4, but break the airflow between the bends. That means you'll be trying to hit each note bend squarely without sliding into it (think of stair steps instead of a slide). Use your piano or pitch pipe to check your pitches.

Note Bend Exercise Number 6

Repeat Exercises Number 4 and 5, but this time, when you get to the deepest draw bend note for any hole, play the blow note for that hole before going back up to the original note. For example, on the 4-draw you would play these notes: D draw—D flat draw bend—C blow—D flat draw bend—D draw. This will give you practice moving from draw bends to blow notes and vice versa.

Note Bend Exercise Number 7

Practice playing the 1- through 6-draw-holes *by starting at the deepest note bend and sliding up to the normal draw note.* This means you must position your airflow and vocal cavity for a note bend before you hit the note. Start at the deepest note bend for each hole, slide up to the normal draw note, and then slide back down to the deep note bend you started with. On the 2- and 3-draws, start by just doing a slide from the deep note bend up to the normal draw note and back. Then try to hit the middle note bends squarely.

Playing blow bends on the high notes is pretty much like playing draw bends on the lower notes, with a few subtle differences. The idea still is to alter the airflow and the shape of the vocal cavity, just as with the draw bends. All the 10 tips for bending earlier in the chapter apply to blow bends as well as draw bends, particularly the warning against blowing too hard. The following five additional tips may be helpful in producing blow bends on the 8-10 holes of your diatonic major harp:

1. You might want to purse your lips even a little more for the high-note blow bends than you did for the low-note draw bends.

2. Visualize *blowing down* into the hole on blow bends.

3. It's okay to slightly (very slightly) tilt your harmonica downward to help you play the blow bends, at least to get you started. You won't need to do it after you get comfortable with the technique of playing blow bends.

4. Some harpists slightly puff their cheeks when playing blow bends, which seems to help them control the airflow better.

5. It's very difficult to hit both notes that are available through bending on the 10-hole blow, particularly on a C-major diatonic harp (or any higher key harp). If you haven't purchased a G-major diatonic harp yet, just skip the 10-blow bends for now.

Now try the following high-note blow bend exercises.

Note Bend Exercise Number 8

1. Play an 8-blow note on your harp. Try to bend the note downward using the techniques described previously. You eventually will be able to bend it one half step lower. *Do not blow too hard.* Puff your cheeks slightly and tilt the harp downward very slightly (in addition to all the tongue-dropping, jaw-lowering, and throat-opening that you were doing for your draw bends).

2. Then try the 9-hole the same way and, if you have a G-major diatonic harp, the 10-hole. On the 10-hole, you'll be able to play two notes by bending, each a half step apart. The deepest bend will come most quickly to you. The middle bend on the 10-blow will come only after much practice. (We haven't mentioned the 7-hole because you can't play a pure half-step bend on this hole).

The Music of Bending

Note bends are used in almost every style of music, but they predominate in cross-harp blues, country, and rock. They're often used in cross harp as ornaments—that is, to add an embellishment or effect to a note. You may play a note and then bend down to a lower note, or play a note starting in the bend position and slide up to the normal "nonbent" note. Long notes often are flattened through bending for a wavering, slow-tremolo effect. Long trills can be bent, resulting in a very effective "dirty" sound.

The better you get at bending notes, the more you'll be able to interject them spontaneously as ornaments to give your music a style and personality all your own. The best way to get ideas for effectively using bends to enhance your music is to listen to the masters on CD, particularly blues and rock artists. Some good harp CDs to listen to (and play along with) are listed in Appendix B. We'll refer to recorded examples of many bending techniques in the upcoming chapters.

Equally important, particularly for cross-harp blues and rock playing, is the ability to play a note bend as the target note. This involves playing a note bend as the intended note, not as an ornament, because the note you need to play is not otherwise available on your harp. You therefore must have your airflow and vocal cavity adjusted for the bend prior to playing it. This technique is particularly important for playing a song at the low end of the harp that otherwise would have to be played at the high end (which often sounds "too bright" for the style of music being played). Playing a note bend as the target note is more difficult and takes more practice to perfect than playing one as an ornament. The notes probably will sound like a foghorn at first (although this isn't necessarily so bad for a heavy blues sound) and initially will be hard to play at the correct pitch.

The following songs demonstrate using bends both as ornaments and target notes. Don't be too concerned if your ornamental bends are not as smooth and deep as you would like and/or your target note bends are off pitch and "foghornesque." Note bends are going to take a lot of practice on your part.

Don't Harp On It

The C-major diatonic harp is not a particularly good choice for learning 3-draw bends because it's quite a contentious note on the C-major harp. If you're enjoying your harp and are ready to spend a little more money, this is a good time to buy a G-major diatonic harp, which gives you much more control on the 3-draw bend.

Blues Clues

In subsequent chapters, we usually don't designate tongue-block techniques, trills, ornamental note bends, and other purely ornamental music elements with any special symbols or instructions (we do designate note bends as target notes). Ornaments should be your personal expression. Insert them where they feel right to you. As you listen to CDs, you'll get ideas about where and how to use ornaments to make your music sound better.

In the following song, you're trying to hit a double bend in the 3-draw. It's in the middle of the three bent notes that are possible on that hole. In this song, slide from note to note with feeling. Use your vibrato. Go ahead and bend into the draw notes as you move into them, starting with a slightly flattened (bent) tone and sliding up into the note.

Amazing Grace

$$
\begin{array}{cc|ccc|ccc|cc}
 & \downarrow & \updownarrow & \downarrow & \downarrow & \updownarrow & \downarrow & \uparrow & \uparrow & \updownarrow & \downarrow \\
R & 1 & 2 & 3 & 2 & 3 & 3B^2 & 3 & 2 & 1 & 1
\end{array}
$$

$$
\begin{array}{ccc|ccc|c|cc}
\updownarrow & \downarrow & \downarrow & \updownarrow & \downarrow & \downarrow & \updownarrow & & \downarrow \\
2 & 3 & 2 & 3 & 4 & 5 & 4 & R & 3
\end{array}
$$

$$
\begin{array}{cc|cc|cc|cc}
\updownarrow & \downarrow & \updownarrow & \downarrow & \uparrow & \uparrow & \updownarrow & \downarrow \\
4 & 4 & 3 & 3B^2 & 3 & 2 & 1 & 1
\end{array}
$$

$$
\begin{array}{ccc|cc|c}
\updownarrow & \downarrow & \downarrow & \updownarrow & \downarrow & \updownarrow \\
2 & 3 & 2 & 3 & 3B^2 & 3
\end{array}
$$

The 3-hole bend in this song probably would be easier to hit on a G-major diatonic harp, if you have one.

I Saw the Light

$$
\begin{array}{ccccc|cccc|ccccc|ccc}
\downarrow & \updownarrow & \uparrow & \downarrow & \downarrow & \downarrow & \updownarrow & \uparrow & \updownarrow & \downarrow & \updownarrow & \uparrow & \downarrow & \downarrow & \downarrow & \updownarrow & \uparrow & \updownarrow \\
1 & 1 & 2 & 2 & 3 & 1 & 1 & 2 & 3 & 3B^2 & 2 & 2 & 2 & 2 & 3B^2 & 2 & 2 & 1
\end{array}
$$

$$
\begin{array}{ccccc|cccc|ccccc|ccc}
\downarrow & \updownarrow & \uparrow & \downarrow & \downarrow & \downarrow & \updownarrow & \uparrow & \updownarrow & \downarrow & \updownarrow & \uparrow & \downarrow & \downarrow & \uparrow & \downarrow & \updownarrow & \downarrow & \updownarrow \\
1 & 1 & 2 & 2 & 3 & 1 & 1 & 2 & 3 & 3 & 4 & 5 & 4 & 3 & 3 & 3 & 3 & 3B^2 & 3
\end{array}
$$

The Art of Overbends and Harp Valves

In addition to bending notes, you can play additional notes that are not designed into your diatonic harmonica by *over*bending (*overblowing* and *overdrawing*) certain holes. Overbending enables you to play the following 10 additional notes on a major diatonic harmonica:

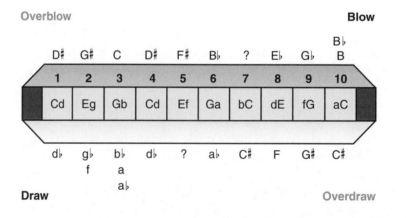

Successfully using this technique involves "cracking" the note into an overbend by simultaneously tightening your upper lip and opening your throat. Extreme control over your airflow and lip positioning is required. It also usually requires regapping your reeds closer to the reed plate than they are normally set by the manufacturer. As with a normal bend, the note created by this technique is the product of both reeds working together.

Overbending is an extremely difficult technique to master and is beyond the scope of this book. You are years away from even attempting to overblow or overdraw notes on your diatonic harmonica. When you're ready, Baker's *The Harp HandBook* has an excellent description of how to overbend notes. You can also find comprehensive instructions on overbending on various websites, such as Mike Will's www.angelfire.com/tx/myquill.

An alternative method for playing most of these same notes is to "valve" your diatonic harmonica. This involves placing windsaver valves on some of the slots of your diatonic harmonica. By doing this on the inside draw reed plate for the 1- through 6-holes and the outside of the blow reed plates for the 7- through 10-holes, you essentially create a harmonica with both the traditional note bends and the same additional notes you can play through overbending. By doing this, you're preventing the opposite reed from vibrating when you blow on holes 1-6 and draw on holes 7-10. The bend is derived from lowering the pitch of the blow reeds on holes 1-6. On holes 7-10, the pitch of the draw reeds is lowered. This is how bending works on the chromatic harmonica as well.

It's possible to valve your reed plates yourself, and the valves can be obtained from Hohner as well as other manufacturers. When you feel you're at the stage where you want to try this, refer to Baker's *The Harp Handbook* or Mike Will's Angelfire website for good information on how to do it. Suzuki also offers a harmonica, ProMaster, already valved in this manner. You'll surely notice that the bends available on a valved diatonic are very different from those on a nonvalved diatonic and closely resemble the sound of bent notes on a chromatic harp.

The Least You Need to Know

- By note bending, you can get 12 more notes from your major diatonic harp than it was designed to play.
- Note bends are typically used in cross-harp blues, country, and rock, but they're found in every style of music.
- It takes a great deal of practice to become proficient at note bending.
- Overbending is an extremely difficult technique that takes years to master.

Harp Positions and Musical Modes

In This Chapter

- ◆ The circle of fifths related to harmonica positions
- ◆ More positions than the *Kama Sutra:* harp positions 1 through 6, and 12!
- ◆ Sample songs to practice in each position
- ◆ Modes and chord progressions

If you think that a diatonic harmonica can only be played in the key it's tuned to, guess again! Blues and country-harp players often play a harp that's not tuned to the key of the song—a C harmonica, for example, when the band is in G major. A country, blues, or rock player could even use the same harp when the band is in D minor or E minor.

The Circle of Fifths and Harmonica Positions

A diatonic harp player frequently thinks of the different keys on the harmonica as different "positions." In more general musical terms, each of these positions is called a "mode." The interesting thing about these modes or positions is that even though they all use the same set of notes, each achieves a distinct character by switching around the functional roles of each of the notes in the scale.

There's a straightforward system for describing the positions on a diatonic harp: the circle of fifths. This circle played a significant role in early Greek philosophy, ancient Egyptian mathematics, and the evolution of classical music, but we're not going to talk about any of that right now. Instead, we'll describe how it works.

Let's begin with the seven notes of the C-major scale, which we described back in Chapter 10. Get out a piece of paper and a pencil and write it down in letters as follows.

C D E F G A B

Now, repeat it three more times, making a total of four repetitions of the letter names of the scale, and then add one C at the end for good measure:

C D E F G A B C D E F G A B C D E F G A B C D E F G A B C

Starting with C, draw an arrow to the letter four steps to the right of C, that is, to G. Your chart should look like this:

C D E F G A B C D E F G A B C D E F G A B C D E F G A B C

Recall from our discussion in Chapter 10 that the distance between C and G is an interval of a fifth? Now let's repeat the process, starting from G, D, A, E, B, and F. Circle all those letters, as well as the Cs at the beginning and the end. Your chart should end up looking like this:

C D E F G A B C D E F G A B C D E F G A B C D E F G A B C

Notice how the arrow from F points forward to C, forming a closed circuit of relationships. Next, draw a circle and start placing the letters at equidistant points, clockwise, around the circle. Start with the C at the top, and then place the other circled letters in succession. Now your chart should look like this:

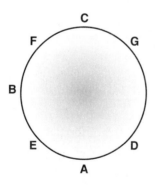

A harmonica player describes these points on the circle as various "positions" in a numerically ascending order, starting clockwise from C. C is called first position. G is called the second position, and so on. Let's add these position names to our circle.

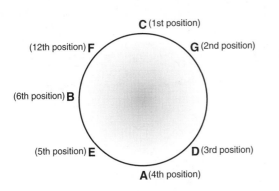

I'm sure you're wondering why the position for F is numbered 12. Read on ...

And You Thought the Kama Sutra Had a Lot

As we pointed out, positions correspond with what music theorists call modes. Related sets of modes all use the same group of notes, but organize them differently to create unique musical effects. The names of our modes derive from ancient Greek modes, which accounts for their exotic names. We use them, as they're the most conventional system for labeling the modes.

Familiarizing yourself with modes will make you aware of the possibilities that each position on the harmonica offers. It can also be helpful in blues, rock, jazz, or salsa jams when you're improvising over a short, repetitive accompaniment, or "vamp."

The following gives you an opportunity to familiarize yourself with the distinct tonal and harmonic qualities of the seven modes most accessible on a diatonic harmonica. The best way to understand the character of each mode is to play melodies that use it. We wrote an eight-bar étude for each mode to illustrate its signature in a very condensed form. The rhythms are deliberately kept simple so you can concentrate on mastering playing the various note sequences, which are designed to further cultivate your growing instrumental facility. Take them slowly. You could even learn them two bars at a time. When you're comfortable with a sequence, try playing it with different rhythms.

In the following whirlwind tour of the modes, we use a C-major harmonica.

Ionian Mode (First Position)

Let's begin at the top of our circle with C. The mode available from here is technically known as the "Ionian" mode. Harp players call it "first position." It's also known as a C-major scale, which you've worked with a lot in earlier chapters. Its root note is C. The basic root chord is a C-major triad, and it's basically got a major-key feel. Facility in this mode will help you play a wide variety of folk and pop tunes. Our étude "Ionian Breeze" exhibits its mild, comfortable quality.

Pay particular attention to how this melody repeatedly winds back to the root note C. There are seven instances where the melody skips from B up to D and then resolves on C. It also moves to E and G frequently, to emphasize the major triad that constitutes its core harmonic flavor.

Ionian Breeze

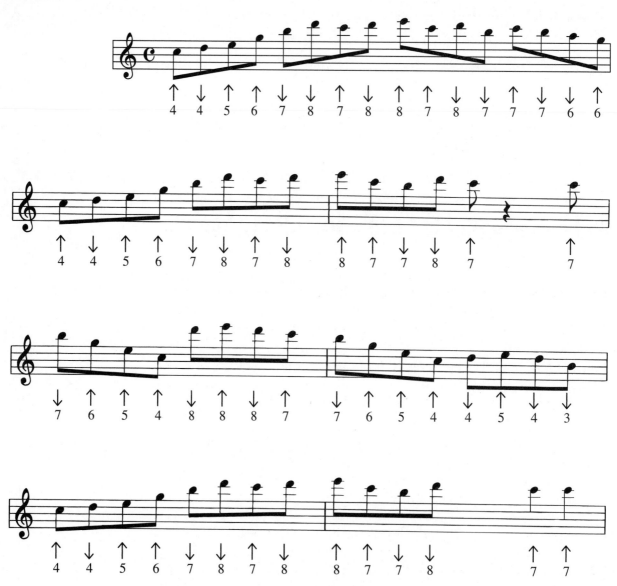

Mixolydian Mode (Second Position)

Moving one step clockwise on the circle, we come to G, which harp players call "second position." You'll find the tonic for this mode on holes 2-draw, 3-blow, 6-blow, and 9-blow. This gives us the Mixolydian mode. Mixolydian has an edge you don't typically get with first position. Our second position étude "Mixolydian Meltdown" demonstrates its driving, unsettled quality. You'll have to bend to get one of the notes in the lowest octave.

As in the prior etude, the melody repeatedly resolves on its root note, which is G in Mixolydian. Again, we frequently precede the root with the seventh note in the mode, which is F. Unlike Ionian, in which the seventh is a half step lower than the root, in this mode, it's a whole step lower. This "flatted seventh" contributes to Mixolydian's angular quality: it's got an itch that it can't scratch. Pay particular attention to the quality of the interval between F and B. This interval is called a *tritone*, and is considered the most tense and unstable interval in Western music.

def•i•ni•tion

A **tritone** is a musical interval spanning a distance of three whole tones. It is considered by many to be the most dissonant of all musical intervals. The medieval church claimed that the tritone came from the devil. Most jazz and blues players believe it's pure heaven. Not surprising, second position is used frequently in blues, rock, and country.

Mixolydian Meltdown

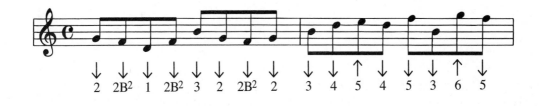

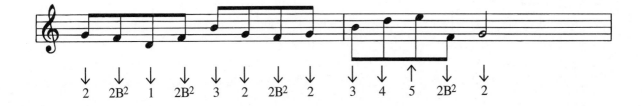

Dorian Mode (Third Position)

The next stop on the circle brings us to D, the Dorian mode, "third position." It has a moody, contemplative quality. Notice that the seventh note is flatted as in Mixolydian, and that the third note is a half step lower than the corresponding note in both Ionian and Mixolydian. This "flatted third" gives Dorian a minor quality and contributes greatly to its melancholy, wistful quality. It's well suited to minor-key folk tunes but can also be used to good effect in blues. "Dorian Dawn to Dusk" is reminiscent of a doleful English ballad with a few bluesy twists.

Dorian Dawn to Dusk

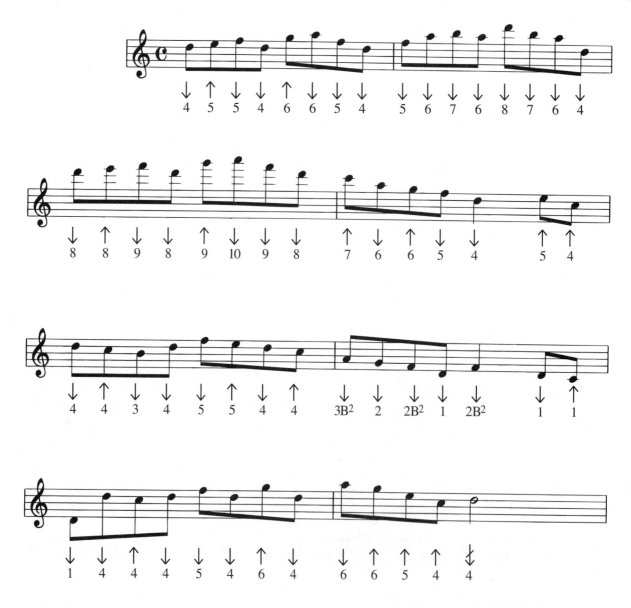

Aeolian Mode (Fourth Position)

Aeolian is our next stop, following Dorian. It starts on A. Harp players call this "fourth position." It can be a bit tricky to get this one started in the lower range of the harp, as it starts on a 3-draw bend.

Aeolian shares a lot of the qualities of Dorian. It features an A-minor triad and has a flatted seventh as well. What distinguishes it from Dorian is the sixth degree, which is lowered a half step in Aeolian. This flatted sixth makes it sound a bit more stately and austere than Dorian. Nevertheless, it works well with a number of minor folk ballads. The demonstration melody "Aeolian Lament" features this flatted sixth.

Aeolian Lament

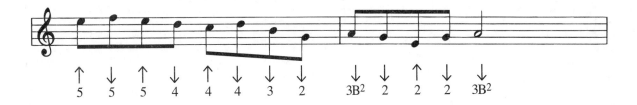

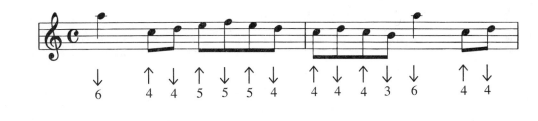

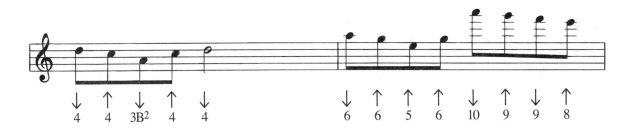

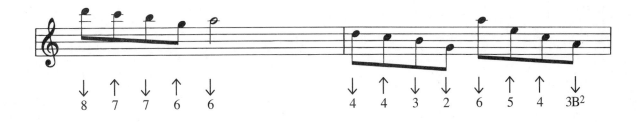

Phrygian Mode (Fifth Position)

These modes seem to get a little more exotic as we move farther clockwise, and the next one is no exception. The Phrygian mode starts on E and is called "fifth position."

Its backbone is an E-minor chord. Like Aeolian, it has a flatted sixth. The lower octave has three bends and is somewhat difficult to play accurately.

Some consider Phrygian to have a Mediterranean or "flamenco" quality. In addition to a flatted third, sixth, and seventh, it also has a flatted second. Emphasizing the flatted second brings out its characteristic mood. Note how often "The Phrygian Bull-Air-O," our next étude, wavers between the flatted second and the root note.

The Phrygian Bull-Air-O

Locrian Mode (Sixth Position)

Our "sixth position" on the circle features a Locrian mode starting on B. This one is plain weird. Its weirdness derives from its principal triad, B-D-F, which is played on draw holes 3, 4, and 5 on the lower end of the harp. It's a diminished triad, which makes the aforementioned Mixolydian sound as calm as a placid pond. Notice that the outer notes of this triad are a tritone interval. Though we like Locrian, it never sounds like it wants to retain its identity. It is perhaps the most unstable mode of all. The following étude, "Locrian Asylum," is our best shot at keeping Locrian under sedation.

Locrian Asylum

Lydian Mode (Twelfth Position)

After the unsettling quality of Locrian, our next and last mode, Lydian, sounds familiar, but with a twist. It's also called "twelfth position." The reason we skip from sixth to twelfth position is that positions seven through eleven are comparatively difficult to play due to a high proportion of bends, overdraws, and overblows. Starting on F, Lydian involves a lot of bends in the first octave, but plays easily in the second and third octaves. It's similar to our first mode, Ionian.

Lydian's foundation is an F-major triad, and it's the only mode other than Ionian with a natural seventh. What distinguishes this mode is its fourth scale note, B: it's a raised fourth, which forms a tritone with the tonic note F. If Ionian is bright, Lydian is brilliant. You might want to put on your sunglasses before attempting "The Lydian Lights." Notice how the core major triad of the mode is emphasized in the latter part of the melody just to steal a bit of the spotlight from that showy raised fourth note.

The Lydian Lights

Of course, these same modes can be played on any major diatonic harp. You can make circles for the other keys using the method we described in this chapter as a model.

The best way to deepen your understanding of the different modes is to improvise your own tunes on them. This will work particularly well if you can continually sound the root note and/or the basic chord within each mode as you play it. You could use a piano for this, or better yet, tape down the key of the tonic note on a keyboard synthesizer with a sustained patch, like an organ. If you have a sequencer, you could create a MIDI file composed of nothing but a droning tonic and/or principal chord. You might even experiment with starting in one mode and moving into another while maintaining the sustained tonic of the first mode. Two good combinations are Mixolydian (second position) to Locrian (sixth position), and Ionian (first position) to Aeolian (fourth position).

Of course, minor-tuned harmonicas have their own distinct modes. Many of them are gorgeous and exotic. The method we outline here for exploring modes applies to them as well.

Modes and Chord Progressions

Whole musical traditions are based on modal composition and improvisation. Indian classical music, for example, proves that the possibilities for beauty and invention are endless when you improvise melodies within a mode accompanied by a tonic drone.

Most of the music we hear, however, is not modal. Instead of establishing one tonal center and sounding it throughout a piece of music, most European and American musical compositions move through a series of related tonal centers, each of which is typically supplemented with related notes, thereby creating a series of chords. These chord series are commonly known as chord progressions.

There are two basic types of chord progressions:

- Those in which all chords belong to the same key
- Those in which subsets of chords belong to different keys

The next few chapters explore playing over typical chord progressions of the former type, found in blues, country, and folk styles.

The Least You Need to Know

- You can play in keys other than the one a harmonica is tuned to.
- Harmonica players use the circle of fifths to numerically identify different keys on the harmonica.
- Harmonica players refer to different keys on the harmonica as different positions.
- Positions are equivalent to modes in common musical terminology.

◆ Each mode has its own characteristic flavor.

◆ The harmonic structure of a song can either be based on a single unchanging tonal center or a series of different tonal centers. The former type of harmony is called "modal," while the latter indicates a chord progression, which could be either diatonic or chromatic.

Chapter 14

Alternate Tunings

In This Chapter

- The basics of alternate tunings
- Setting the mood and style with alternate tunings
- Sample tunes for the principal alternate tunings

In this chapter, we'll learn the basics of alternate tunings for the diatonic harmonica and explore the three principal alternate tunings: harmonic minor, natural minor, and the Melody Maker. The former two are manufactured by both Hohner and Lee Oskar, while the latter is made exclusively by Lee Oskar.

Why Differently Tuned Harmonicas?

The richter-tuned diatonic harmonica is a special-purpose instrument by design. As we've seen and heard, the standard major diatonic harmonica is laid out so that major triads are very easy to play: just wrap your lips around a few holes and blow. You'll sound some inversion of a major triad. You can play the second most important chord, the dominant, by breathing in on those same selected notes. This layout makes it pretty easy to embellish melodies with appropriate chords. Small wonder that the instrument is sometimes called the mouth organ!

And you aren't restricted to playing major melodies on the major harp. We've discussed how different positions open up different melodic possibilities. Blues and country players strongly favor second position because it fits the expressive characteristics of those playing styles. Another significant advantage of second position is that it's very easy to play a major triad or a dominant seventh chord. Major tuning also can be great for playing minor melodies in third, fourth, or fifth position. However, chording opportunities in these positions become progressively more limited. Finally, it can be challenging trying to remember what notes to play when, in order to make it sound like you're not playing in first or second position.

Alternate tunings remove some of these limitations. Natural minor and harmonic minor tunings make it very easy to sound minor triads: just wrap your lips around a few holes, blow, and you'll sound some inversion of a minor triad (sound familiar?). Each layout also makes it pretty easy to embellish minor melodies with appropriate chords but with some important differences.

Harmonic Minor Tuning

Let's begin with the harmonic minor. As discussed in Chapter 3, the harmonic minor is well suited to a wide variety of Eastern European folk melodies and minor-key American spirituals. The opening measures of the spiritual "Let My People Go" could be played on major diatonic, but you wouldn't be able to add the chord embellishments found below. This example is in G minor and is played on a G harmonic minor harmonica.

⦿ Let My People Go

Harmonic Minor Example

The next-to-last chord is identical to the chord available on a major diatonic on the same holes when inhaling. This is because harmonies to many minor melodies use a dominant for the five chord. The harmonic minor tuning is therefore ideal for playing minor tunes in first position where the five chord is dominant. Be sure to check out "The Silver Wedding" in Chapter 19 to get familiar with playing first position in this tuning. Other positions on the harmonic minor offer interesting possibilities but they're pretty esoteric.

Natural Minor Tuning

By contrast, the natural minor tuning is equally useful in first and second position. Either one enables you to easily play minor triads. And second position is great for playing minor blues. Draw bending on the 4-hole produces the same effect as on a major-tuned instrument—that wailing bluesy fifth. The 3-hole draw on the other hand gives you a minor third instead of a major third, and this is exactly what we want in a minor blues song. Check out the following bluesy phrase played on a G natural minor harmonica.

⦿ Natural Minor Example 1

First position on the natural minor is particularly nice for playing reggae-type accompaniment patterns.

● Natural Minor Example 2

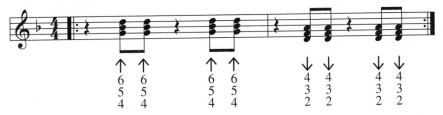

One reason it works is because you get minor chords on both the draw and blow notes, which is just what this style of music often requires. Afro Reel in Chapter 19 demonstrates this principal in action, but over an Afro-Cuban 6/8 rhythm. You can hear a convincing example of how to use natural minor harps (in a duet, in fact!) in a reggae context on the song "Yesterday Morning" from the Hazmat Modine CD *Bahamut*.

Melody Maker Tuning

Unlike the natural minor and harmonic minor tunings, the principal advantage of the Melody Maker tuning has nothing to do with available chords. Rather, its key benefit is that it makes it easy to play major melodies in second position, which is the preferred position of many blues, country, and rock players. This tuning makes it easy to really wail on even the "Star Spangled Banner."

● Star Spangled Banner

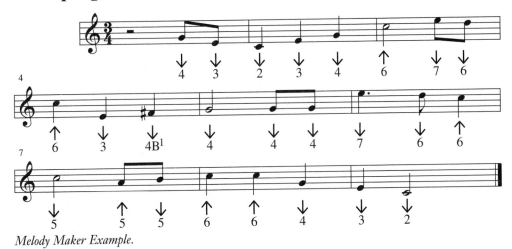

Melody Maker Example.

In Chapter 19, "Porgianna" demonstrates an original melody played on the Melody Maker, which closely follows a chord progression similar to a chestnut standard tune.

Blues Clues

Both Huang and Hohner produce harmonicas that make it easy to play major melodies in second position, but they are laid out differently than the Lee Oskar Melody Maker. All three tune the 5-hole draw to play the major seventh of the second position key. But the Hohner Country Tuned Marine Band and the Huang Jazz Harp are otherwise tuned exactly like a standard major diatonic. Additionally, the Lee Oskar Melody Maker tunes the 9-hole draw up a half step and the 3-hole blow up a whole step.

But Wait ... There's More!

In addition to these factory tunings, there are literally hundreds of alternate tunings that have been designed and explored. Steve Baker presents many possible tunings in his book *The Harp Handbook*.

There are also tunings that conform to the basic standard factory tunings but provide subtle nuances of intonation. For example, the Hering company's 1923 Vintage Harp Harmonica follows major tuning but employs a form of "just intonation" that makes the first position and second position triads sound very smooth. Conversely, the Hohner Golden Melody, though laid out like a standard major diatonic harp, is tuned to "equal temperament," which is what's used for most conventional instruments. This tuning is great for single-note playing but the chords sound really harsh.

Whatever your custom tuning interests, don't think you have to special-order it from the factory. Our earlier chapter on harmonica repair gives you the basic information you need to reproduce or invent any tuning imaginable.

The Least You Need to Know

- The harmonicas discussed in this book are designed to facilitate playing both melodies and simple chord embellishments in specific keys.
- Though the major diatonic is by far the most common tuning, there are different tunings provided by manufacturers that are good for playing minor key songs or for playing major key songs in second position.
- You can create your own tunings using repair techniques described earlier.

Part 4

It's Showtime!

By now you ought to be sounding pretty good, and it's time to start putting it all together. This is where you start sounding like a real harpist. We teach you blues-playing techniques and important musical techniques like call-and-response, riffs and licks, improvisation, and jamming.

But there's got to be more than the blues in your harmonica life. We demonstrate other styles of music in which the harmonica is a popular instrument: rock, country, Celtic, and Appalachian. We explain the key characteristics of these music styles and how to successfully play them with the harmonica.

Armed with all this new knowledge and talent, don't you think you ought to get out of the house and introduce yourself to the music world? You can get the lowdown on playing well with other musicians (while keeping your day job), forming a band, getting gigs, playing through amplifiers, and putting on a successful show.

We close this part, and the book, not with something new to learn, but a last chance for you to make some music and have some fun before you move on.

Chapter 15

Ready for the Blues (and Improvisation)

In This Chapter

◆ Getting introduced to blues harmonica

◆ Learning to improvise with spontaneity and still tell a story

◆ Sustaining a rhythmic groove

◆ Learning about basic riffs and how to play them

◆ Practicing call-and-response phrases between repetitions of riffs

◆ Learning your licks: blue notes, rhythmic placement, and melodic ornaments

If you love playing diatonic harp, it's hard not to love the blues. No other music has favored our chosen instrument for such a long period and in so many different ways.

Blues synthesized antecedent black musical genres such as spirituals, work songs, and hollers, in which the voice played the principal role. The harmonica's ability to imitate the voice—in particular an emotionally charged, distinctly African American voice—made it a natural choice for the blues.

We are fortunate that a huge, chronologically complete and stylistically varied discography of virtuoso blues-harp performances exists (a few of the many essential recordings are listed in Appendix B). And we are even more fortunate that blues harp is a living tradition with many excellent players still barnstorming the planet and recording their music for posterity.

This chapter provides a starting point for the blues. Because improvisation, also known as "spontaneous composition," plays such a critical role in the blues, we explore both by looking at ways to improvise blues songs.

Improvisation: Making Your Story Make Sense

It's rare for a blues player to play anything exactly the same way twice. Spontaneous embellishment or improvisation is an essential feature of blues performance. Musical improvisation is often described as just playing whatever comes to mind in the moment. While spontaneity is key to effective musical improvisation, so is the ability to tell a story, and effective narrative—musical or otherwise—requires continuity in the story line.

We've got a joke for you that illustrates a common problem we have when improvising:

"I'm eating peas. My mother-in-law used to drive a Cadillac. Then, the elephant will stand up and shout … RADAR!!!!"

Get it (nudge, nudge)? We don't. The vocabulary is familiar, and the grammar is okay. There's only one minor problem: it doesn't make any sense! There's no meaningful connection between the three sentences. Sometimes musical improvisers have a tendency to play a lot of right notes and sequences of correct musical phrases, but they don't seem to be meaningfully connected. This kind of playing is more accurately described as "noodling" than improvising.

Two common ways to achieve connectedness in blues improvisation are as follows:

- Using repeated melodic themes or "riffs."
- Alternating a repeated theme with new melodic phrases.

Legendary bluesmen Lightnin' Hopkins and John Lee Hooker frequently created songs that had compelling, coherent statements by spontaneously sequencing series of traditional and personal blues lyrics. We do something analogous to that process in the following exercises. Although using such techniques may seem limiting, we're confident you'll find that they'll lead to greater improvisational freedom in the long run than just blowing with abandon.

Don't Harp On It

If you think that being able to set up and sustain a rhythmic feel is something only beginners do, consider this: much of traditional West African music is built around a characteristic fundamental rhythm played with a bell or rattle. Playing this part well is so crucial to the successful performance of the ensemble that only master drummers are allowed to play it!

Riffing up a Groove: Simple Ain't Easy

The foundation for playing convincing music on the harp, blues or otherwise, is solid rhythm. To have solid rhythm, you need to maintain a constant tempo and keep a good "feel" happening. A metronome can help with the first objective. Listening to good blues-harp players helps with the second. It's tough to create and sustain a groove when playing unaccompanied. Learning to do it will strengthen your rhythmic sense and help internalize a sense of musical structure. For now, you *are* the band. Blues-harp master Sonny Terry sustained a long career on solo performances that rivaled the groove of any dance band.

We'll start out by learning a few two-bar melodic phrases or "riffs" in second, third, and first position on a C harp. Refer to Chapter 13 if you've forgotten which keys correspond to these positions. These are the three principal positions that blues-harp players use.

We present second position first, because it's the one you'll likely use most. Third position is presented before first, because it's easier to get a blues flavor in third than in first. We present a basic riff and an intermediate riff in each position. Intermediate riffs require you to bend some notes, while basic riffs don't.

The "Straight Eight" and the "Shuffle" Rhythms

The notes are as indicated for each riff, but you should play the rhythms with two distinct feels—"the straight-eight" feel and the "shuffle" feel. The straight-eight feel is basically a double rhythm while the shuffle is based on a triple rhythm.

- In a straight-eight rhythm, all eighth notes have equal duration. The straight-eight feel is heard frequently in old rock-'n'-roll and New Orleans R&B. It has a driving, aggressive quality. An outstanding example of the straight-eight feel is Chuck Berry's classic "Johnny B. Goode."
- In a shuffle rhythm, eighth notes on downbeats are twice as long as eighth notes on upbeats. In contrast to the straight-eight feel, the shuffle feel has a relaxed, loping quality. Check out Bobby Blue Bland's original version of "Further on up the Road" for a masterful example.

The key objective with all these riffs is to play them repeatedly at a fixed tempo in both straight-eight and shuffle feel. Pick a comfortable tempo for each riff and stick with it! Play it until it starts to feel like it's playing itself.

Six Basic Riffs

Here's our basic riff in second position:

Second Position Riff 1 (Basic)

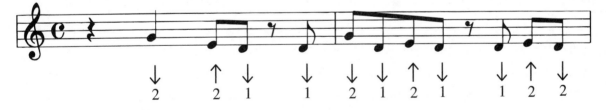

Notice how the end of the phrase leads into the top of the phrase, creating a kind of closed loop. Take care not to shorten or extend the rest on the first beat of the phrase. We'll be occupying this vacancy in later sections.

Second Position Riff 2 (Intermediate)

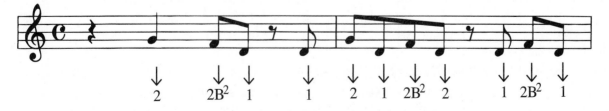

The intermediate second position riff requires a bend on the 2-hole. This produces the flatted seventh, which makes the phrase sound bluesier than the basic riff.

● Third Position Riff 1 (Basic)

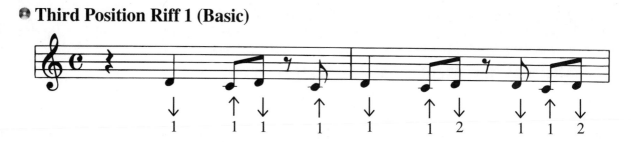

The basic riff in third position provides the flatted seventh on the 4-blow.

● Third Position Riff 2 (Intermediate)

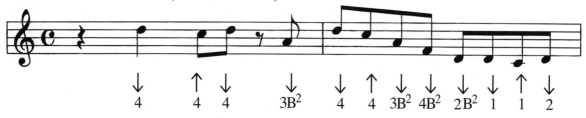

The intermediate third position riff requires two bends. The bend on the 3-hole is the "middle" bend, and the one on the 2-hole is the lowest bend. This riff really brings out the minor-key character of third position.

● First Position Riff 1 (Basic)

The basic riff for first position could work in any music.

● First Position Riff 2 (Intermediate)

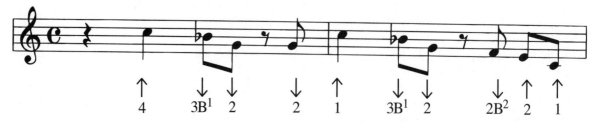

The interval between the two notes is wider than in the other basic riffs (a perfect fifth), but it's only one hole below the starting note, so it's easy to play. The key challenge in playing the intermediate first-position riff is playing the shallow bend on the 3-hole accurately. Doing so produces the flatted seventh.

When you've mastered these six riffs, invent some of your own. Try to create short phrases that sound good over and over again.

Call-and-Response

Playing a repeated riff creates a great musical foundation. Inserting new musical phrases between repetitions of a riff builds on that foundation. This technique is often referred to as "call-and-response" playing. It's heard not only in blues but also in antecedent styles such as spirituals and work songs. A good example of call-and-response is the venerable spiritual "Let My People Go":

When Israel was in Egypt's Land (call)

Let My People Go! (response)

Oppressed So Hard They Could Not Stand (call)

Let My People Go! (response)

Go Down, Moses (call)

Way Down in Egypt's Land

Tell Old Pharaoh

Let My People Go! (response)

We presented six "responses" in the last section. Now we're going to associate them with several different "calls." We'll again present examples in all three positions in basic and intermediate forms. Remember to try playing them with both shuffle and straight-eight feels. Like the responses, the calls are two bars long.

Here are two basic second-position calls and two intermediate second-position calls:

Second Position Call 1 (Basic)

Second Position Call 2 (Basic)

Second Position Call 3 (Intermediate)

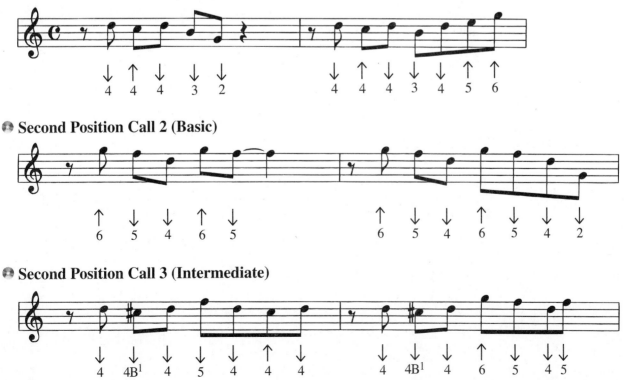

● Second Position Call 4 (Intermediate)

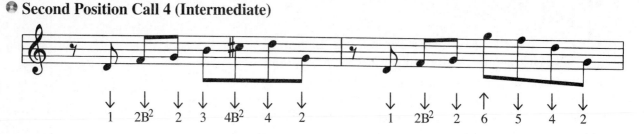

When you're comfortable playing them, try playing each one and following it with one of the second-position riffs from the previous section. For example, here's the basic second-position Call 1, followed by the basic second-position riff:

Call

Response

This is just one of eight possible combinations.

Practice playing calls and responses until you can spontaneously play any of the calls and follow it with one response. Maintain a steady tempo in your chosen feel and don't add or subtract any beats! It's particularly easy to lose the beat when you get to the rests.

Repeat the preceding practice procedure with the following sets of third- and first-position calls, and the third- and first-position riffs from the preceding section:

● Third Position Call 1 (Basic)

Third Position Call 2 (Basic)

Third Position Call 3 (Intermediate)

Third Position Call 4 (Intermediate)

First Position Call 1 (Basic)

First Position Call 2 (Basic)

First Position Call 3 (Intermediate)

● **First Position Call 4 (Intermediate)**

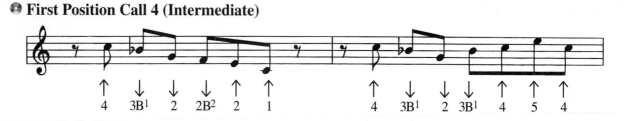

When you're comfortable with these calls, make up some of your own. As a final step, try improvising a call on the spot but commit yourself to playing the response at the right time, so that you don't bust the groove! Your improvised calls can be dirt simple to begin with; you can even make a repeated note sound good if you put the right rhythm to it.

Twelve-Bar Blues Techniques

It's common for blues players to use the call-and-response form by itself, but it's even more common for them to use the technique within a 12-bar structure. Blues is primarily a vocal music, and the song form most commonly used in the blues supports a series of three-phrase stanzas, where the first phrase introduces a theme, the second phrase repeats it with slight variations, and the third phrase completes the idea introduced in the first phrase. Musicians tend to refer to a stanza as a "chorus." Here's a traditional chorus that's been sung by both Albert King and Carl Perkins:

> Sometimes I wonder, will a matchbox hold my clothes?
>
> Sometimes I wonder, will a matchbox hold my clothes?
>
> I don't have so many, but I've got so far to go.

Each phrase occupies two measures and is followed by a two-bar instrumental phrase that complements, or answers it, creating a composite four-bar vocal/instrumental phrase. Four bars multiplied three times makes twelve bars.

Sequencing Call-and-Response Units

The call-and-response technique is implied in a 12-bar blues chorus in both the lyrical form and the alternation of lyrical "calls" with instrumental "responses." The responses are frequently repeated riffs similar to those in the preceding section. If you've been practicing the call-and-response exercises in that section, you shouldn't have a problem creating a basic 12-bar blues chorus by sequencing three 4-bar call-and-response units together.

Creating an Ending

The only element you're missing is an ending musical phrase. The ending phrase provides closure for the 12-bar chorus. Here's a basic 2-bar ending phrase in second position to get you started:

● Second Position Ending 1 (Basic)

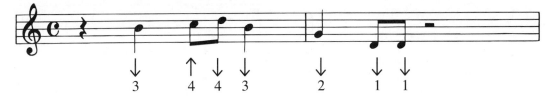

The following is an example of a second-position blues chorus using basic second-position Call 1 three times (bars 1-2, 5-6, 9-10), basic second-position riff two times (bars 3-4, 7-8), and the basic ending just introduced (bars 11-12). Try playing it with both a straight eight and a shuffle feel.

● Second Position Blues Chorus

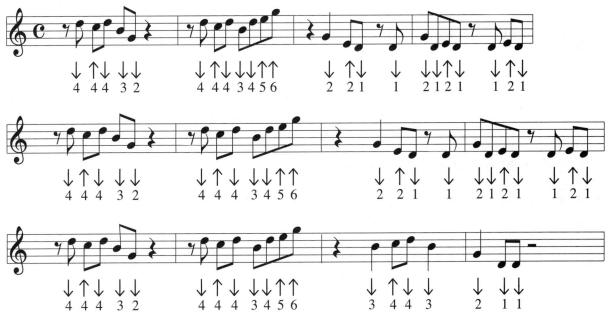

Play this chorus until you can do it effortlessly. The phrases are easy, but recalling their sequence without faltering may be challenging. When you've got this chorus working, try using two different calls, and alternate them with one response. Finish the chorus with the basic ending.

The following are an intermediate second-position ending phrase as well as basic and intermediate endings in third and first position:

● Second Position Ending 2 (Intermediate)

🔵 **Third Position Ending 1 (Basic)**

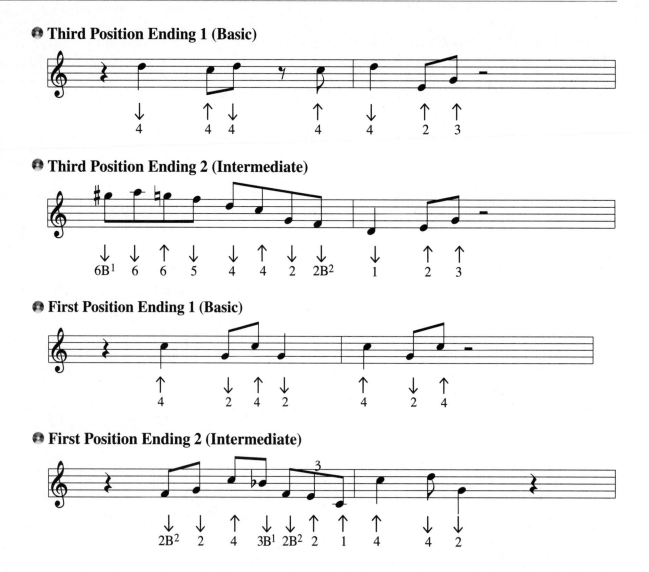

🔵 **Third Position Ending 2 (Intermediate)**

🔵 **First Position Ending 1 (Basic)**

🔵 **First Position Ending 2 (Intermediate)**

You can create many unique blues choruses using the calls, responses, and endings provided. And you'll be able to fashion many more by adding your own inventions and spontaneous improvisations. As we said earlier, improvisation and spontaneity are key ingredients in blues performance but so is achieving a balance between novelty and repetition.

The call-and-response technique detailed here is not the only way to tell a story in a blues chorus. We illustrate other approaches to shaping blues choruses in Chapter 18.

Licks: Spicing up the Meat

Preceding sections of this chapter are geared toward instilling a sense of musical form while allowing room for improvisation. It's the meat-and-potatoes stuff. Now we look at ways to gain facility with tonal, rhythmic, and ornamental practices characteristic of blues by presenting a series of musical phrases, or "licks."

Blues tonality is perhaps the most conspicuous feature of blues. The "blues sound" has a wailing, moaning quality often said to connote great melancholy and anguish. But as we all know, some of the best things in life are accompanied by a chorus of wails and moans!

Blue Notes

Musicians refer to three specific tones, collectively called "blue notes," as primary carriers of the blues sound. These notes are sometimes equated with the minor third, the flatted fifth, and the minor seventh, but they're actually distinct notes, each of which is slightly lower than the minor tones they are commonly confused with.

The only way to gain familiarity with blue notes is to hear them. For our purposes, the best recordings to listen to are those by blues-harp giants such as Little Walter. Before we tell you how to produce the three blue notes in second position, please consider listening to Little Walter's brilliant instrumental "Blue Midnight," which is currently available on the two-CD set *The Essential Little Walter* (see Appendix B for details). Believe me, this recording will tell you *all* you need to know about blue notes! The choruses are composed of series of long tones that glide between beautifully intoned blue notes that resolve to the related natural third, fifth, or root.

In the first chorus, Little Walter slowly slides back and forth between a blue fifth and the natural fifth in the first four bars of the chorus. To do so, he bends the 4-draw and then sinuously slides into a straight 4-draw. Bars five and six find him smoothly coaxing a blue seventh and then sliding up to the root. This is done by starting with a 2-hole deep draw bend and slurring all the way up to the 2-draw. The second chorus starts with a blue third, which sounds uncannily like a throaty tenor saxophone but even more voice-like and soulful. You'll need to play a shallow draw bend on the 3-hole to get the blue third.

> **Straight from the Harp**
>
> Although there aren't a lot of notes in these choruses, approximating Little Walter's sound and the subtle way he weaves in and out of the blue notes (not to mention his liquid phrasing) could be as challenging as anything else you ever try to do on the harp.

The following is a four-bar second-position call for practicing blue notes in second position. Those wavy lines connecting the notes indicate that you should slur into the natural notes from the blue notes in one unbroken swoop.

● Blue Notes 1

The song "Bent by the Blues" in Chapter 18 provides further practice on second-position bends.

In third position, the blue third is played nearly the same way as the blue seventh in second position, that is, a deep bend on the 2-draw in the first octave and a very slightly bent 5-draw in the second octave. You produce the blue fifth in this position by playing the deepest bend on the 3-draw in the first octave and a bent

6-draw in the second octave. This latter blue fifth really sings, and it's one of the easier bends to play. The seventh is a 1-blow in the first octave and 4-blow in the second octave. It's hard to do much with these. Here's an advanced call in third position.

Blue Notes 2

The song "Son of Bent by the Blues" in Chapter 18 provides further practice on third position bends.

The most accessible blue notes in first position in the first octave are the blue fifth produced by playing a shallow bend on the 2-draw, and the blue seventh produced by playing a shallow bend on the 3-draw. You have to skip up to the top octave to get the juiciest blue notes in first position. A blow bend on hole 8 gives you the blue third; a blow bend on hole 9 produces the blue fifth, and the deep blow bend on hole 10 provides the blue seventh. As we told you in Chapter 12, these blow bends play easier on the lower key harps such as A and G.

Blue Notes 3

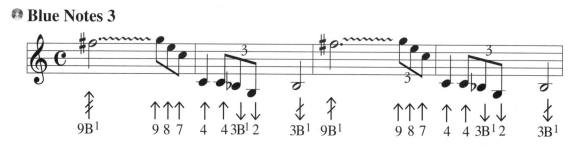

Bluesmen Jimmy Reed and George "Harmonica" Smith played extensively in first position with great finesse. Check out Reed's "Honest I Do" to hear how to make those high-note bends cry. The song "Bent Bluebird" in Chapter 18 provides further practice in first-position bends.

Rhythmic Placement and Phrasing

In addition to getting a blues sound, you also want to work on rhythmic placement and phrasing. Like a lot of African-derived music, blues relies heavily on syncopation for its rhythmic energy. It's common for blues players to start phrases on upbeats rather than downbeats. Review the calls and responses, and note how many don't start on a downbeat. Syncopation is one rhythmic device among many used in blues to create the impression that the player is incisively weaving around the rhythm—playing with it rather than on it. Little Walter arguably had the most versatile rhythmic vocabulary of any blues-harp player past or present. (That's the last pitch, we promise.) The song "Offbeat and Blue" in Chapter 18 provides a catalog of syncopated melodic rhythms.

Melodic Ornaments

Besides tonality and rhythm, here are also some melodic ornaments that blues-harp players favor:

- **The shake, or warble.** Involves a rapid alternation between two adjacent notes on the harp's keyboard. Common second-position shakes are between draw holes 4 and 5, draw holes 3 and 4, and draw holes 5 and 6. Shakes are frequently used at the top of an instrumental chorus or as an instrumental fill between vocal lines. It's also common to do shakes between nonadjacent holes, such as 3 and 5, by rapidly switching the position of the tongue to opposite sides of the mouth. Advanced players often insert one or more brief shakes in a melody. The song "Shakin' and Stirred" in Chapter 18 explores the shake in vigorous detail.

- **Double-stop.** Playing two notes at once on nonadjacent holes is a kind of ornament called a double-stop. The octave double-stop is the most popular, but other combinations can be used to great effect. "Double Stop 'Til You Drop" in Chapter 18 explores this technique.

- **The slide.** Slides occur when moving from nonadjacent holes on the harp. For example, when a blues-harp player goes from a 4-draw to a 2-draw, he or she will often slide through the 3-hole as well. These slides help give melodic lines on the harp a smooth legato feel.

We've covered a lot in this chapter, but we've just scratched the surface of the possibilities for playing blues on the harp. While the musical scores provided here and in Chapter 18 are helpful, they're just a start, kind of like a bike with training wheels. To go for a real ride, you'll need to check out some of the many great blues-harp players past and present. Happy travels!

The Least You Need to Know

- It is essential to listen to blues-harp masters to learn the unique qualities of blues tonality and blues rhythm.
- Convincing improvisation involves telling a story. An effective musical storytelling technique is alternating between a repeated group of musical patterns and spontaneously improvised ones.
- "Blue notes" are not minor thirds, fifths, and sevenths but distinct notes, slightly flat, of the adjacent minor thirds, fifths, and sevenths.
- Straight-eight and shuffle rhythmic feels are common in blues.
- Blues-harp players most commonly use second, third, and first positions.
- Like blues lyrics, blues improvisation is frequently based on a call-and-response model, which is often encapsulated within a 12-bar musical form.

Chapter 16

You Got More Than the Blues

In This Chapter

- ◆ The harp's extensive use in rock, country, Celtic, and other styles of music
- ◆ Special techniques for playing these musical styles
- ◆ Sample songs to practice in each style

The harmonica's popularity is not limited to folk and blues music. It's a very versatile instrument that has found widespread popularity across a broad range of musical styles. In this chapter, you learn how to play some of these other styles of music on your harp.

Country Harping

Country music encompasses styles known as Western swing, Nashville sound, honky-tonk, outlaw country, country rock, and new country. Its development has been influenced at various times by folk, gospel, rhythm-and-blues, and rock music (and country music in turn has influenced the direction of these styles).

Country music is one of the simpler styles of music from a structural and technical standpoint (and a very pleasant, nonintimidating style to listen to). It is lyrics oriented, in the sense that the primary role of the musical elements often is to highlight the lyrics. As with blues, country music generally relies on a repeated selection of three chords. It usually is written in 4/4 time with heavy accents on the first and third beats.

From the harmonica standpoint, many of the techniques used in blues and folk music also can be effectively used when playing country music. Both straight harp (first position) and cross harp (second position) can be used in country music, depending on the type of sound you want to create. Country music tends to be more "major" in tonality than blues, which contributes to the popularity of the straight-harp style. Generally, you would not use as much of the vibrato and heavy blues techniques (such as the tongue-blocking techniques described in Chapter 11) in country-harp playing. In short, country harping is a more melodic (sometimes even more "acoustic") style than blues harp.

The most distinguishing characteristic of country music, from the standpoint of the harmonica, is its scale structure. Country music often is built around the "major pentatonic" scale, which consists of all the notes of the major scale except the fourth and seventh notes. A C-major pentatonic scale thus would include C-D-E-G-A, but not F or B. This is not to say that F and B can't be played in a country tune, but they most likely will not be dominant tones. This scale structure is so prevalent in country music that it often is referred to as the "country scale." Take a look at the drawing of a C-major harmonica at the beginning of Chapter 3 to get a better understanding of how this relates to your harmonica. If you were to play a country song in straight harp (key of C), you could build your playing predominantly on the 4-blow, 4-draw, 5-blow, 6-blow, and 6-draw holes. If playing cross harp on the same harmonica (key of G), you could focus on the 2-draw, 2-blow, 3-draw, 4-draw, and 5-blow holes. This will give you G-B-D-E, which are four of the five notes of the G-major country scale (the second note, A, is missing at the low end of your major diatonic harp).

If you have a country-music CD, try this experiment. Find songs in the key of C and G (preferably slow ones, so you can concentrate on your notes). Play the C-major song in straight harp using only the five straight-harp blow and draw holes specified in the preceding paragraph. Do not play any other notes. Do you hear how you can build a very acceptable melody or harmony accompaniment without needing to play any other notes? Now play the G-major song in cross harp using only the five cross-harp blow and draw holes we specified. Again, these are all the notes you need. That's because the songs you're playing very likely are built around the C-major pentatonic (country) scale, which consists of these same notes.

One particularly troublesome note for playing country music on a major diatonic harp (when playing cross harp) is the 5-draw, which is an F on your C-major diatonic harmonica. The note sounds great when you play blues, but often sounds out of place in the more "major" oriented tonality of country music.

Straight from the Harp

Because the 5-draw on a major diatonic harp doesn't sound quite right for country music, many harpists use country-tuned harmonicas such as the Hohner Special 20 Country-Tuned diatonic when playing country music. This tuning raises the 5-draw hole from an F to an F sharp (on the C-major harp), thus giving you a major seventh on that hole when you play in cross harp. You can still hit the F through bending the 5-draw hole.

Practice the preceding style and technique points on the following country tunes.

My Dog Done Died
Country Waltz Tempo

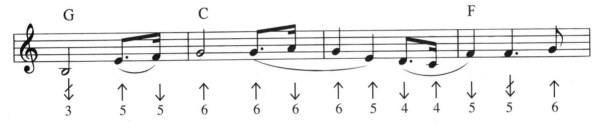

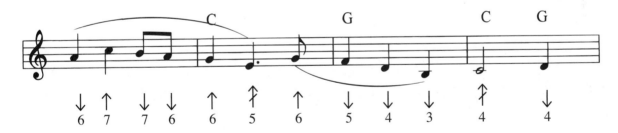

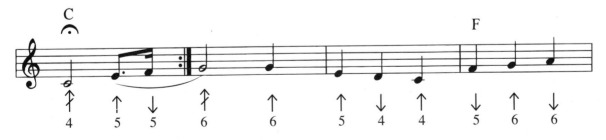

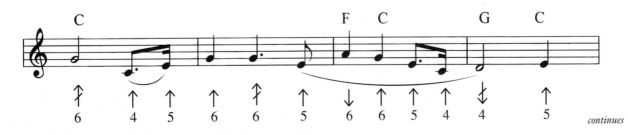

continues

continued

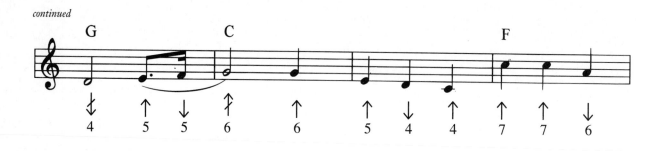

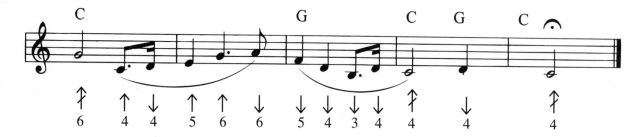

⚫ *Better Him, Than a Hog, Any Day*
Moderately, with much feeling

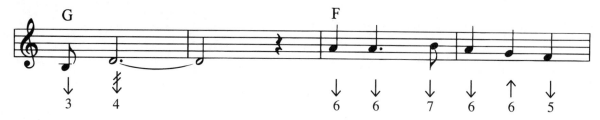

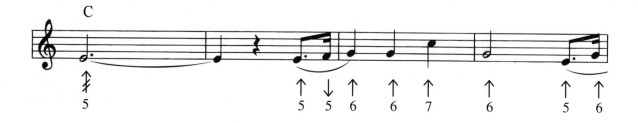

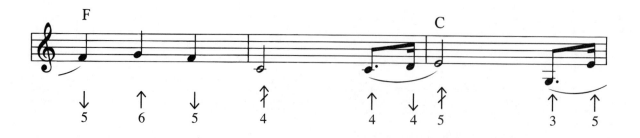

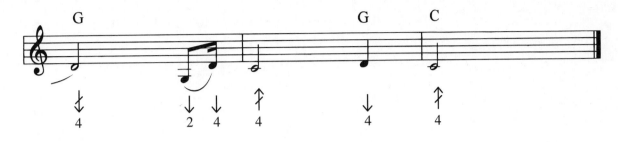

Rock Harp

It's somewhat difficult to narrowly define rock music, as it's been shaped by such a wide range of cultures and musical styles, including blues, country, and folk. Perhaps the single-most defining characteristic of rock music is that it has tended to be closely tied to developments in electronic technology. Amplification of instruments, innovative studio-recording techniques, and high-tech stage effects all play a strong role in most rock. So perhaps the best way to distinguish rock music as a "style" is to say that it invariably is loud.

The primary instruments played in rock music are the electric guitar, electric bass, keyboard, and drums. Other instruments that have found a special place include the saxophone and, of course, the harmonica.

Insofar as the harp is concerned, the musical elements of rock are very similar to those of blues and country music. Rock generally has a faster, less syncopated (more driving) beat and is a little more "major" in tonality than blues. Its beat is also distinguishable from, and much more frenetic than, a country-music beat. Nevertheless, you'll use most of the same techniques that you've already learned in this book when you play rock music (usually, but not exclusively, cross-harp techniques), though you probably will have to play them much louder.

The following is a harp rock tune, to give you an idea of the sound:

Rocker

continues

continued

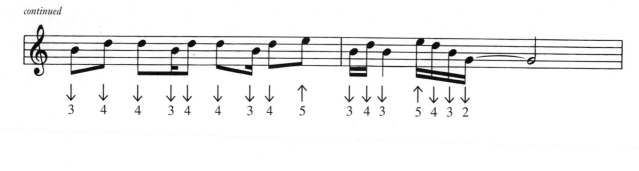

Erin Go Harp

The harmonica has become very popular in Celtic styles of music (primarily the music of Ireland, Scotland, and Wales, but also that of Brittany and the Canadian Maritime Provinces). This music was brought to America with the waves of Irish and Scottish immigrants during the eighteenth and nineteenth centuries, and provided the roots for much of America's traditional music. Celtic music traditionally was played on instruments such as fiddles, wooden flutes, and accordions (another free-reed instrument), so the harmonica was a natural fit with this sound.

Celtic music can be divided into four major types: reels, jigs, hornpipes, and waltzes.

◆ **Reels**   Tend to be played very fast and usually consist of continuous eighth notes written in 4/4 time.

◆ **Jigs**   Also feature eighth notes but usually are written in 6/8 time with accents falling on the first and fourth beats. Jigs are generally played much slower than reels.

◆ **Hornpipes**   Usually are written in 4/4 time and often are played without accents. They are similar to reels but usually are played more slowly.

◆ **Waltzes**   Are written in 3/4 time and are played at a nice "waltz pace" (obviously). Triple rhythms are common in all these styles.

Other key characteristics of Celtic music are the following:

◆ Celtic songs usually are written in key signatures with one or two sharps, so you need G-major and D-major diatonic harps (or one of the other specially tuned harmonicas discussed in the following section that can be played in these keys) to play most Celtic songs.

◆ Celtic music is "melody oriented," as opposed to being chord or harmony driven.

♦ Celtic music generally uses a high degree of ornamentation, particularly grace notes, triplets, and *rolls*.

♦ Bent notes are not all that common in traditional Celtic harp music.

Another very important characteristic of Celtic music is that it often tends to be played in alternative "modes" of the root major key. The four most common modes in which Celtic music is played are Ionian, Mixolydian, Dorian, and Aeolian. These are not all that complicated, and correspond to the first, second, third, and fourth positions, respectively, on your diatonic harmonica (described in Chapter 13). The scales for all these modes start on different notes but contain the same exact notes as their root scale; that is, the Ionian, Mixolydian, Dorian, and Aeolian scales for the key of C-major start on C, G, D, and A, respectively, and do not contain any sharps or flats. You thus can play Celtic songs written in C-major Ionian, Mixolydian, Dorian, and Aeolian modes on your C-major diatonic harp. These four modes are at the heart of Celtic music's distinctive sound—a mixture of minor and major tonal combinations.

So you have all the notes on your Richter-tuned major diatonic harmonica that you need to play in these four modes, but the problem is that they aren't very conveniently situated. You don't have enough of the right notes at the low end, so you end up jumping back to the high end. Many harpists use a variety of harmonicas to get around this problem: chromatic, tremolo, solo-tuned, Lee Oskar Melody Maker, and 12-hole diatonic harmonicas all are used to play Celtic music. All of them have the advantage of giving you additional notes where you need them.

The best way to get the notes where you need them is to either make or purchase a Paddy Richter–tuned diatonic harmonica as developed by Brendan Power. You can make this special tuning yourself by simply sharpening the 3-blow note a full step (this changes the G to an A on your C-major harp). You can immediately see that this change in one note opens up almost another full octave of the notes needed to play the four common modes of Celtic music. You can accomplish the same thing by combining the top reed plate of a Melody Maker harmonica and the bottom reed plate of a Lee Oskar standard-tuned major diatonic harp in the same key. However, we recommend that you visit Brendan Power's website, www.brendan-power.com, where you can purchase Paddy Richter–tuned harmonicas, a wide variety of other specially tuned harps, and a wealth of instructional materials and other Celtic paraphernalia. If you want to play Celtic music, you should become familiar with Brendan's site. Other good resources and instruction books on playing Celtic music are listed in Appendix B.

The following are Celtic songs in the Mixolydian, Dorian, and Aeolian modes. "Dance of the Naked Druid Maidens" should be played as fast as you can play it cleanly. For an example of a song in C-major Ionian mode (which is based simply on the root C-major scale), see "Sir William's Reel" in Chapter 9.

def•i•ni•tion

A **roll** is a five-note ornament that is played very quickly, and centers around a melody note; that is, melody note/note one step higher/melody note again/note one step lower/end on melody note. Rolls are very popular in Celtic music.

Dance of the Naked Druid Maidens
To be played as fast as you can play it cleanly

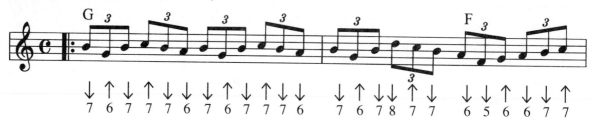

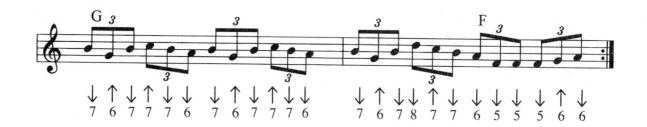

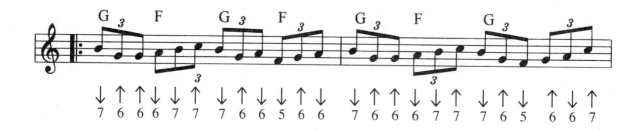

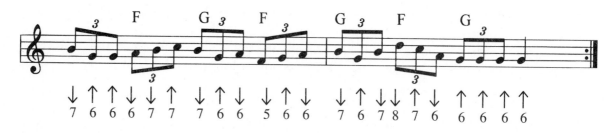

Star of County Down

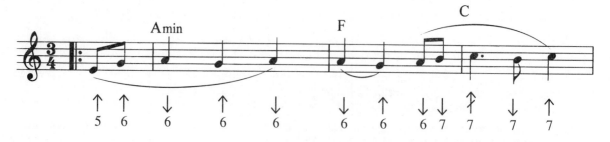

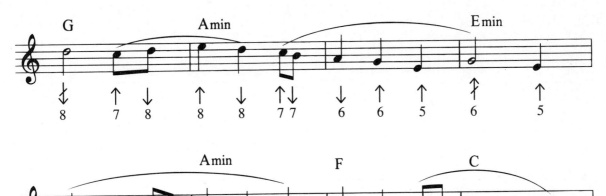

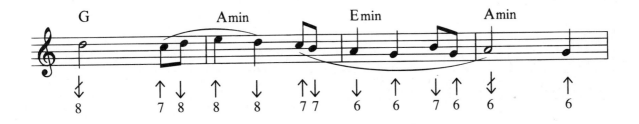

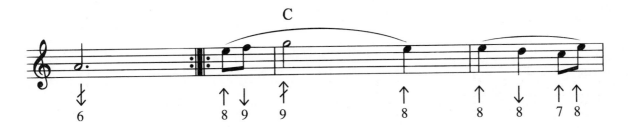

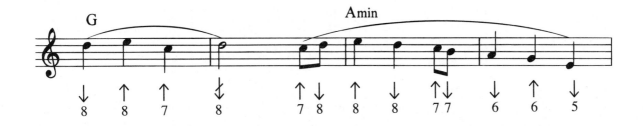

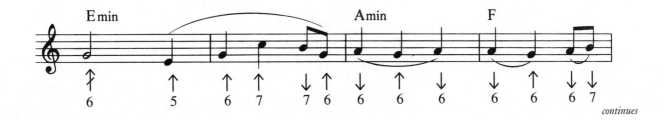

continues

continued

♩ *Óró 'Sé Do Bheatha 'Bhaile*

Fiddling on the Harp: Appalachian Fiddle Tunes

Appalachian fiddle tunes are so named because they evolved in several communities nestled in the Appalachian mountain range, which extends from Maine to Georgia. These communities were settled starting in the late sixteenth century by immigrants from Ireland, Scotland, England, and Africa. While Appalachian fiddle tunes are based on Anglo-Celtic instrumental dance tunes, they also incorporate the influence of African rhythms. Appalachian folk music is also referred to as "old-timey music." This name was coined in the early twentieth century and was used as a descriptor in the catalogs of several recording companies.

A lot of Appalachian fiddle music has a syncopated "two-beat feel," with accents placed on both upbeats. Here's an exercise to help you hear and play this rhythm. First, repeat saying "one-eee-and-uh two-eee-and-uh" at a steady tempo, making sure to give each syllable equal emphasis and rhythmic duration. Next, say the first syllable louder so that you're repeating "ONE-eee-and-uh TWO-eee-and-uh." You're now emphasizing what are known as the downbeats. Make sure these emphasized downbeats still have the same rhythmic duration as the other syllables, and keep your tempo steady. When you feel comfortable doing this:

1. Tap your foot on the downbeats while repeating "ONE-eee-and-uh TWO-eee-and-uh."

2. Now change the emphasis on the syllables from the first syllable to the third, so that you're repeating "one-eee-AND-uh two-eee-AND-uh" while tapping the downbeats with your foot as you've already been doing. You are now accenting the upbeats with your voice while using your foot to maintain the basic two-beat pulse.

Accenting the upbeat creates a sense of anticipation that is resolved by the downbeat that follows, creating a sustained sense of forward momentum without accelerating the tempo.

Now that you've got a basic understanding of this rhythm, let's learn a couple of tunes that use it. "Whisky Before Breakfast" is a good way to start your collection of Appalachian tunes for a number of reasons: (1) It's a favorite of "old-timey" players from West Virginia to the West Village of Manhattan, (2) you can get all the notes in first position, (3) and last but not least, the melody incorporates the syncopated two-beat feel in a simple, compelling manner.

Try to nail all the accents indicated using whatever technique is most comfortable for you, but don't exaggerate the accents: you want the tune to flow, and overemphasizing accents makes the music sound choppy. Pay particular attention to bars 3, 11, 21, 23, 29, and 31; hear how closely the rhythm of these musical phrases matches the earlier exercise. The tune basically consists of two distinct melodies, each repeated twice in a row. This is a very common tune structure in Appalachian music and is referred to as "AABB form."

Whisky Before Breakfast

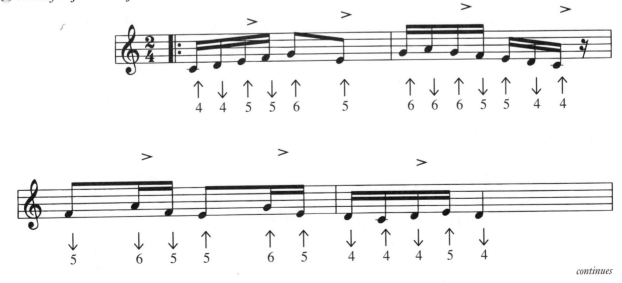

continues

continued

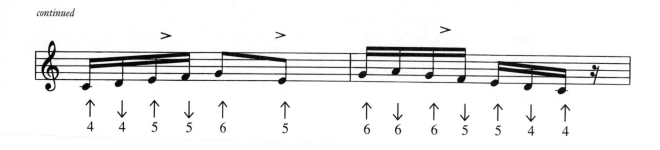

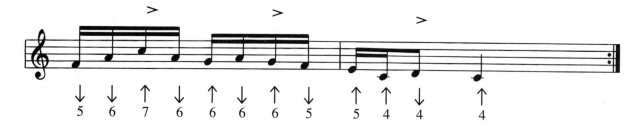

Our second tune, "Boatmen," can also be played in first position. Its melody is also a composite of melodic phrases repeated twice consecutively. However, it does this with three phrases rather than two, making it an "AABBCC form." The A and B sections are four bars long while the C section contains eight. This tune introduces another characteristic rhythmic feature of many Appalachian fiddle tunes: anticipation, which adds another level of rhythmic vitality to this piece.

Notice how the last note in several bars falls on the last sixteenth note of the measure and then extends into the next measure. With such rhythmic figures, it's the "uh" of "one-eee-and-uh" that gets accented rather than the "and." You can practice the feel of this rhythm by tapping out the basic two-beat pulse with your foot, while saying "one-eee-and-UH" and prolonging the "UH" until you reach the upbeat of the second beat, which you can emphasize using the "AND-uh" phrase. You end up with this: "one-eee-and-UH-hhh-hhh-AND-uh." What's happening is that these notes actually start phrases just slightly ahead of where you expect them to. Extending their duration lets the rhythm relax back into a more settled state.

🎵 *Boatmen*

continues

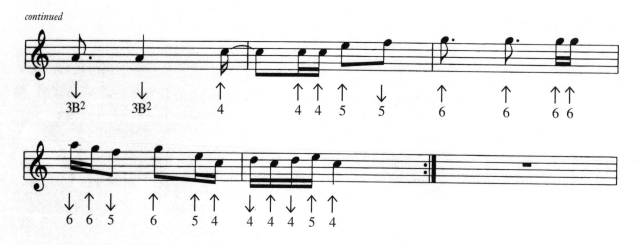

Like Celtic music, Appalachian fiddle tunes are part of a rich musical tradition with a subtle, highly nuanced rhythmic and melodic vocabulary. Some excellent recordings featuring Appalachian harmonica stylists are listed in Appendix B. In addition to listening to Appalachian harp masters such as Mark Graham, you'll be richly rewarded by listening to the repertoire performed on other instruments, particular the fiddle. I think you'll find that many aspects of the various fiddle-bowing patterns translate well to breathing patterns on the harp.

The Least You Need to Know

♦ The harmonica is a great instrument for many styles of music, so don't get in a rut playing only the blues.

♦ To play different styles of music well, you'll need to purchase specially tuned harmonicas or change the tuning on one or more of your Richter-tuned ones.

♦ Remember that the best way to learn a new style of music is to listen to and play along with CDs, copying and adding your own interpretation to the harmonica artist's style and technique.

Chapter 17

Keep Your Day Job

In This Chapter

- ◆ Playing in informal jam sessions
- ◆ Learning how to play well with others
- ◆ Putting together a band that gets paid to play
- ◆ Playing amplified so that people can hear you
- ◆ Marketing your group to club owners and the community
- ◆ Stage and performance tips

If you've gotten this far (and practiced), you're probably a pretty good harp player. Now it's time to announce yourself to the music world. The fun you've been having so far pales in comparison to the exhilaration that comes with performing before an audience. In this chapter, we provide tips on how to do this: finding jam sessions, forming a band, getting paid gigs, playing through a microphone, putting on a good show, and observing "playing etiquette."

Jamming

There are two ways to get out and play with, and in front of, others. The first is the neighborhood (often called "porch") jam and the second is the club jam. While they're quite different, both types of jamming help you learn how to play with other musicians and give you practice playing in front of an audience. They're also fun.

The porch jam usually is a collection of neighbors who've played some form of music in their life. They usually aren't professional musicians, and they generally don't play in any organized setting, but they're often quite extraordinarily talented. How do you find a porch jam? Check your neighborhood newsletter and the bulletin boards at local stores.

Porch jams generally are devoid of ego problems, and all levels of musicians are welcome, regardless of talent or skill level, as long as they play by the rules. The rules are relatively simple. The group sits in a circle and takes turns choosing and starting songs. People generally choose well-known songs that everyone

Blues Clues

Ask around to find porch jams; word of mouth is the most common mode of advertising these events. Try driving around your neighborhood with your windows rolled down, and listen for music (porch jams often are conducted outside). As a last resort, why not start one up yourself?

def•i•ni•tion

Stepping on vocals or solos is one of the greatest faux pas a harpist can commit. When someone's singing or another instrumentalist is playing a solo, you need to back off and play rhythm, or, in some cases, a subdued countermelody. Wait for your turn to solo; then show your stuff.

can pick up quickly. The "starter" plays the melody the first time around while others play backup. Then the melody gets passed around the circle for anyone who cares to give it a try. Only one musician at a time plays the melody; the others play rhythm or other backup. Usually, one or more of the musicians will take a crack at singing the words to a song. Pretty simple. All you have to do is play your best, and make sure you don't hog the melody or play too loudly when it's someone else's turn to take the melody.

Club jams are a little more structured and a little more pressure-filled. They're also more valuable in terms of developing a performance technique and getting used to playing before an audience. Club jams generally are held on slow nights at clubs or bars that cater to a particular kind of music (blues is a favorite). The idea is to increase the club's business that night by getting a band to host a jam session; that draws in a large number of musicians who'll spend money while they're waiting for their turn to play. You sign up, sit down, wait until your turn, and then play your songs (you usually get three). You'll be given a chance in each of the songs to do a solo passage. On a slow night, you might get up more than once, but don't count on it. The best thing to do is arrive early so you can be near the top of the list, play your songs, and network; however, be careful how much you drink. You'll usually get only 15 minutes on stage, but it can be a very valuable 15 minutes. The networking can be even more valuable, because that's how you might find future band members. The host band won't always be as encouraging or helpful as your porch-jam mates (particularly if you play the harp better than their harpist). You'll get booted off the stage faster than you can imagine if you *step on* the lead singer's vocals. It'll help to read the section in this chapter on playing well with others ("A Little Harp Can Go a Long Way") before you attend a club jam.

You can find club jams listed or advertised in the music section of your local newspaper (particularly one of those "alternative" newspapers that cater to people such as musicians, artists, environmentalists, and other liberals). They're also posted at music stores. The club will try to make the local musical community aware of its jams, as that's the only way it can make any money from them. Try checking out www.nationalbluespages.com, which makes an effort to list on a regional basis as many blues jams as possible. Also, local music societies often sponsor monthly or weekly jam sessions for their members. They're very similar to club jams, with the main advantage being that they usually aren't held in a smoky club or bar where you're expected to spend money.

A Little Harp Can Go a Long Way

As you get out and start playing with other musicians, you want to be welcome to go back and play with them again, so it's important that you know the specific "etiquette" your fellow musicians will expect you to observe. Here are some tips on how to play well with others:

- Remember that you're not the whole show. The idea is to be part of creating a "total sound," not just *your* sound. You have a role to play in the group, and you need to understand what that role is. It will probably be different for different songs. On some of them, you'll play exclusively backup; you'll lead with solos on others, and you'll play some songs where you do both. Get them clear in your head.

◆ As a general rule, you want to play a backup rhythm (usually at the low end of your harmonica) when someone is singing or another instrumentalist is playing a solo. The vocal line is the centerpiece of the song; it's how the story is told. An instrumental solo is an ornament. It gives the song flavor and energy, and gives the instrumentalist a chance to shine. Don't ruin solos by playing loudly over them and stepping on them.

◆ As you get familiar with a song, it might be good to add a subtle counter-melody under a vocal line or during someone else's solo. But play it softly so that it's a complementary background sound.

◆ Another good (and acceptable) technique is to play a call-and-response to the vocal or solo line. They're described in Chapter 15. Just make sure you don't start your "response" too early or let it drag into the next "call." And don't try to fit too many notes into your response; its pattern should track the pattern of the call.

◆ Do *not* try to overwhelm the other musicians or the audience with technique. It's great if you can play a lot of fast notes accurately and you have some skill in the complex techniques taught in this book. Sometimes, though, you need to play sweet, simple, and subtle. This seems to be a constant challenge for some harpists.

◆ Don't feel that you need to fill every space with notes, or that you need to be playing in every section. It really is okay to just stand there and do nothing if that's what sounds the best.

◆ Listen to what's going on around you. Maintain eye contact with the other musicians. Feel the music. Go for that *total sound*.

Have all these tips in mind when you're playing with a group, and chances are you'll get invited back.

> **Don't Harp On It**
>
> Please make sure you're playing a harp in the correct key for the song. Get it sorted out in advance. You can't stand up there after the song starts, "testing" different harps to figure out which one is in the right key. Also, be alert to key changes in a song that mean you either have to switch harps, change positions on your harp, or simply quit playing until the key changes back.

Forming a Band and Getting Gigs

If you really enjoy your jam sessions, perhaps music truly is in your blood. You might think about putting together or joining a band and actually getting paid to do something you're quite willing to do for free. Do *not* do this because you want, or need, to make a lot of money. Playing local gigs doesn't pay well, and you'll probably end up spending more money on equipment, CDs, websites, and other odds and ends than you'll ever make with your band. You should start a band only because you love your music and are willing to spend an inordinate amount of time and money to share it with the world.

Finding Musicians

Where do you find band members? The usual places. Place an ad in an alternative newspaper or post a message at a local music store. Network at jams and music performances. Check to see if there's a website that caters to the local

> **Blues Clues**
>
> You'll be much more valuable to a band if you can do something in addition to playing the harmonica. Most bands don't view the harmonica as a mainstream instrument that needs to be played on every song, so you'll do better if you can play an additional instrument or sing.

music or entertainment scene; you can probably post an ad and find musicians' postings on the site, and it may have a chatroom.

As you start to put your group together, make sure you're a good fit both musically and personally, and that you all have the same expectations and goals regarding commitment, music styles, money matters, and so on. You might also try to find some band members who already have equipment as well as experience playing in bands.

Getting Organized

When you have your group together and organized, you'll need to practice and work up several *sets*. We really mean this. You have to practice as a group or you probably won't get gigs, and you certainly won't get repeat gigs. Club owners are not going to pay you to make it up as you go along.

Now is the time when it is easy to go crazy buying equipment. You may need all or some of the following: a PA system, a mixer, speakers, microphones, monitors, cords, lights, and on and on. Spend wisely and slowly. Check out used equipment (did we mention that most bands break up and end up selling their like-new equipment for much less than they paid for it?). Get some advice from someone you trust (and who isn't trying to sell you his or her equipment). And definitely don't "under-power" yourself. A sound system that blows out the windows at the music store or in your living room may be barely audible in a club with several hundred noisy patrons.

Playing Amplified

If you're playing with drums and electric instruments, you'll probably need amplification, not only so people can hear you but also so you can hear yourself. There are two ways that amplification enhances your harp sound: it makes it louder, and it can alter the timbre of the instrument. To what degree your amplification system changes the acoustic tone of the instrument depends on three basic factors: your microphone, your amplifier and, last but not least, your monitor.

The microphone is where your amplification circuit starts. Basically, it converts sound fed into it into electrical signals, which are then routed to an amplifier that converts the electric signals back into sound again. When choosing a microphone, decide whether you want the microphone to alter the actual tone of the instrument.

If you want to maintain your acoustic sound (also known as a "clean" sound), you'll probably want to use a microphone favored by vocalists, such as a Shure SM-58. These are commonly known as "vocal mics." If you want a distorted or "dirty" sound (and most rock and blues-harp players do), there are several microphones designed for that purpose. Among the most popular are the Shure Green Bullet and the Astatic JT-30. Distortion is commonly considered a bad thing, but not when it comes to harmonica. For us, distortion has great musical benefits: it can make the harp sound darker, punchier, fuller, and give each note more *sustain*, which makes melodic lines sound fluid.

def•i•ni•tion

A **set** is a portion of a gig. A gig often runs for three to four hours, during which you'll play three or four sets. A set is typically 50 to 60 minutes long with a short break between each one.

def•i•ni•tion

Sustain is the characteristic timbre and volume of sounds produced by a particular instrument following its initial activation of the note.

In addition to the microphone itself, the way you hold it has a big effect on the signal it receives. Cup the microphone firmly in both hands so that you form an airtight seal around its face. Cupping tightly projects all the sound produced by your harmonica into the microphone. A loose grip allows sound to disperse outside the pickup area of the microphone, resulting in a less intense input signal. If you're going for a clean sound, this may be just what you want. You may even want to put the microphone on a stand and play standing near it.

When the electrical signal from the microphone gets sent to the amplifier, two things can happen: it can either cleanly be converted back to sound, or it can overload or "overdrive" the amplifier, causing it to distort, which can add warmth, depth, and fluidity to your harp sound. Whereas any amp can be overloaded, not all amps will distort your sound in the same way. Most harmonica players prefer an amp that uses vacuum tubes to amplify incoming electrical signals rather than solid-state transistors. These two types of amps are commonly referred to as "tube amps" and "transistor amps." Tube amps tend to produce a softer, rounder distortion when overdriven, while transistor amps generally have an edgier, harder distortion.

Other important factors to consider when choosing an amplifier are its power or wattage, the size of the speakers, and the number of speakers. There are three power ranges: small (5 to 35 watts), medium (35 to 50 watts), and large (50 watts or more). Wattage determines volume limits and distortion characteristics. Lower wattage means less input signal is required to get distortion. This can be good if you want a dirty sound at a low volume. You can't get distortion out of a high-wattage amp without cranking it up to "11." This is acceptable for a large room or concert hall, but doing so in a small room will make peoples' eardrums bleed!

Speaker sizes can also be categorized as small (8-inch), medium (10-inch), and large (12- to 15-inch). Large speakers put a lot of bass frequency in your sound but are harder to overdrive. Smaller speakers offer more overdrive but have less bass frequency, which may make your sound slightly tinny. Most harp players prefer 10-inch speakers, which offer a good compromise between the two extremes. Higher-wattage amps frequently have more than one speaker. The Fender Bassman, a very popular harmonica amp, has four 10-inch speakers.

If you want a clean sound through an amplifier, you will probably want to choose one with medium to high wattage and larger speakers. An even better way to get a clean sound is to play through the venue's amplification or PA system using a vocal microphone.

Whether playing through your own amplification system or the "house PA," you've got to be able to hear yourself and the other people you're playing with. If you can't hear yourself, you'll likely tense up and play too hard. PA systems typically have monitors, which are speakers positioned onstage facing the band. Their function is to enable the band to hear itself. If you're playing harp through a PA, make sure you can hear yourself in the monitors, but be willing to negotiate the harmonica monitor level you want with the other players: they very likely don't need to hear you as much as you want to hear you! If you're playing through an amp, you'll typically be using the amp as both your amplifier and your monitor, and you need to consider where to position it. Bad positioning will make it difficult for you to hear yourself. It's best to place the amp to either the right or left of you and at least a couple of feet away. If using a small low-powered amp, put it on a crate so that the sound coming out of it is closer to your ears. And above all else, sound test your positioning before your gig to make sure you (and the audience) don't suffer from that most dreaded of all microphone faux pas: ear-splitting feedback.

Harp players tend to devote a lot time to acquiring and tweaking their amplification systems. The right amplification system can do wonders for your sound, but nothing will help your sound more than developing an acoustic tone you like.

Getting the Word Out: Marketing

Just as important as practicing and getting the right equipment is marketing your new band. You'll need a sheet or packet describing your band and the members' backgrounds and talents. Include a picture that's both interesting and makes you all look as good as possible. You also must include a demo CD or tape of three or four of your best songs. You simply are not going to get gigs without one. These demos are a lot simpler and less expensive to produce than they used to be. You can rent the equipment and produce one at home yourself, or a lot of studios will do special "cheap and easy" demo CDs. You won't get any mixing or editing, but if you have your songs down and ready to play right the first time, you'll get a good enough demo CD to use for getting gigs.

In addition to the packet and demo CD, you might think about creating an inexpensive website and posting your band details on bulletin boards at music stores. And don't pass up any early opportunities to play for people, even if they aren't exactly who you had in mind. It's an additional way to market your band. Aunt Edna's summer barbecue might seem like a bad gig, but you need the practice and someone might be there who'll hire you for a *real* gig.

You then have to get the packet, picture, and demo CD into the hands of someone who's in a position to hire your band. You may want to try getting it to some music agents, but they're not likely to be interested until you have a reputation, a fan following, and a track record of successful gigs. (In other words, you probably won't get an agent interested in you until you don't need one.) In the early stages, you're going to have to get gigs the old-fashioned way: networking and visiting all the venues where you'd like to play to introduce yourself and drop off your materials. This can take time and also can be a very humbling experience. The same people you're trying to reach get approached by bands every day. They're not likely to give you much time, so make your point, leave your materials, and try to get a commitment from the person in charge to follow up on a specific day. Always be very polite and businesslike (remember, you want to look like you've done this before).

When you get that first precious gig, do everything you can to make it a success. Practice. Tell all your friends. Post notices telling people where and when you're playing. Get the venue to do a mailing or e-mail blast and put it on their website. Call that local alternative newspaper and radio station and get them to include it in their weekly schedule of music events. You want a crowd there and you want them to stay. The truth is that the owner *kind of* wants you to play good music, but he or she *really* wants you to bring in people who'll stay and spend a lot of money. Don't fail to do everything you can to make that wish come true. The owner may well have a tin ear but knows exactly how much food and drink must be sold to justify the expense of a band. A great performance will not get you a repeat gig if the place is empty.

Taking Care of Business

Unfortunately, you'll soon discover that being successful with your music turns it into a business. And *business* is exactly what you were trying to get away from. But if you're spending and making money, you're engaged in a business.

When booking your first gig, don't let your ego run ahead of your talent. Remember: *bulls make money, bears make money, but pigs get gored.* Be prepared to do that first gig as a "loss-leader." If it goes well, you'll get more money the next time. The amount of money you'll make is extremely variable and depends on the length of your performance, the night you're playing on, the size of the venue, and other factors that the owner probably will keep secret from you. Band fees often are paid as a mixture of a fixed fee and some agreed-on percentage of the cover charge or night's revenues. As (and if) you develop a reputation, a fan following, and steady bookings, you'll be able to command higher fees.

You'll also need to deal with issues of music ownership (copyrights), protecting your band name (trademarks), various music organizations such as the American Society of Composers, Authors, and Publishers (ASCAP) and Broadcast Music, Inc. (BMI), insurance, tax IDs, tracking income and expenses, musicians' unions, contracts, and much more. These topics are beyond the scope of this book, but there are numerous good books available that will help you understand and deal with them. Several are listed in Appendix B.

Leave 'em Screaming for More

When you've secured your first gig, you want to make sure there's a second one. The following tips will make your performance a memorable one:

- **Practice.** Have we mentioned this before? Establish the order of your music beforehand. Know how you'll play each song.
- **Test everything.** Set up all your equipment beforehand at home. Make sure it works and that you know what all the little lights and switches do.
- **Arrive early.** Leave yourself time to get everything set up and to test the sound levels and deal with any feedback or other problems.
- **Set up the stage.** Make sure that all the musicians have eye contact. There's a lot of nonverbal communication going on while you play.
- **Start on time.** Don't shortchange your audience and the owner.
- **Play 50- to 60-minute sets.** Don't break for too long between sets. You don't want to lose your audience.

Blues Clues

Be responsive to the other musicians and to the audience. For example, the lead guitarist may want to change the tempo or extend a passage that the audience is responding to. Watch for visual signals.

♦ **Start and end each set with some of your best songs.** The first song gets the audience's attention and the last one keeps them there for the next set.

♦ **Choreograph the flow.** Pace your music and energy to maximum audience effect. Give the audience peaks and valleys. Build to a high energy level and then back off a little. Mix your songs with the goal of achieving variety in your presentation.

♦ **Keep in constant eye contact with the other band members.** Music performances always involve a lot of spontaneity.

♦ **Don't be stiff.** Be alive. Show the audience that you love your music and you're having fun.

♦ **Be interested in the audience and show them your appreciation.** Introduce yourself during breaks and thank them for coming.

♦ **Try to respond to special requests.** If a song is requested that you don't know, you might offer to learn it for the next performance if they'll come back to hear it.

♦ **Save a good song for an encore.** Pray that you get a chance to play it.

It may sound a bit difficult to pull off all these performance tips right now, but you'll find that after you play a couple of gigs it'll all become second nature. That's when you'll know that you've gone beyond just playing an instrument and become a real musician. You'll be having so much fun it won't even occur to you to be nervous.

The Least You Need to Know

♦ Jams are an invaluable first step to getting out and playing in the music world.

♦ Learn and practice the etiquette of playing music with others.

♦ Starting a band and getting gigs is hard, slow work. Don't get discouraged or give up too quickly.

♦ There's no better feeling in the world than lighting up an audience with your music.

Music Break Number 2

In This Chapter

- ◆ Apply the techniques learned since Music Break Number 1
- ◆ Use the position chart to play in all 12 keys
- ◆ Build your skills by playing several blues études
- ◆ Play some more Appalachian fiddle tunes

The more advanced tunes in this chapter enable you to apply the techniques you've learned since Music Break Number 1 (Chapters 10-16). Consider them as a means to refining various technical skills and as launching pads for your own creative expression, building into Chapter 19.

Putting It All Together

All the tunes in this chapter are written for a C harp, but of course can be played in any key you like using the harp tablature we provide. The following chart summarizes the implied key of each of the seven positions for all 12 keys.

Key	1st	2nd	3rd	4th	5th	6th	12th
C	C	G	D	A	E	B	F
Db	Db	Ab	Eb	Bb	F	C	Gb
D	D	A	E	B	F#	C#	G
Eb	Eb	Bb	F	C	G	D	Ab
F	F	C	G	D	A	E	Bb
Gb	Gb	Db	Ab	Eb	Bb	F	Cb
G	G	D	A	E	B	F#	C
Ab	Ab	Eb	Bb	F	C	G	Db
A	A	E	B	F#	C#	G#	D
Bb	Bb	F	C	G	D	A	Eb
B	B	F#	C#	G#	D#	A#	E

The first three tunes present yet another dimension of blues harp. They are three boogie-woogie choruses in the three harp positions most frequently used by blues players—second, third, and first. They can be played in either "shuffle" or "straight-eight" feel (described in Chapter 14). Also note that each boogie actually takes you through all three principal blues-harp positions to better fit the standard 12-bar blues chord progression.

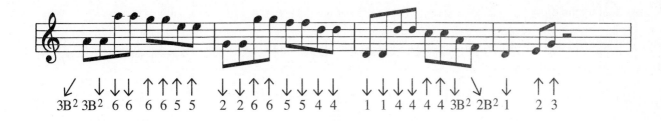

🎵 First Position Boogie

The next three tunes are vehicles for refining your bending technique in all three blues-harp positions. The squiggly lines indicate a slur between two notes. In each case, gradually raise the bent pitch to the target pitch within the indicated time interval. This stuff looks simple on paper but is a major technical challenge. Don't expect to perfect it right away!

Bent by the Blues

Son of Bent by the Blues

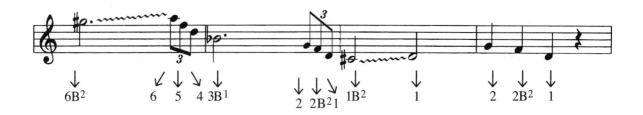

Bent Bluebird

The following tune, "Offbeat and Blue," should be played slowly. The rhythmic notation is approximate at best. The phrasing it alludes to is best represented by Little Walter's late-1950s work, such as "Quarter to Twelve," "My Babe," and "Key to the Highway," to name a few. The feel to go for is that of a trapeze artist who loses balance but regains it at the last second. Careful!

Offbeat and Blue

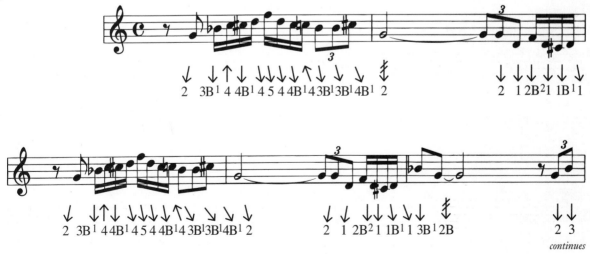

continues

continued

"Shakin' and Stirred" will help you work on your shake or warble technique.

🎵 **Shakin' and Stirred**

"Double Stop 'Til You Drop" requires you to use tongue-blocking to get most
of the double-stops. The rhythmic feel is a shuffle.

 **Double Stop 'Til You Drop**

"Red Haired Boy" is another Appalachian fiddle tune in Mixolydian mode, that is, second position.

Red Haired Boy

The 10 tunes in this chapter provide a variety of ways for you to consolidate the techniques you learned throughout the book in the musical styles most commonly played on the harp. Each one emphasizes a particular technique specific to the instrument or to a musical style. We think you'll have fun with them as is, and even more fun if you "complexify" or simplify them according to your own musical needs and tastes. Refine, reshape, and explore!

The Least You Need to Know

- Playing the tunes in this chapter will consolidate the techniques you've learned.
- You can learn to play in every key, using the position chart at the beginning of the chapter.
- Never hesitate to tailor the way you play a tune to your current level of technical proficiency.
- Always play at a comfortable tempo and make sure to keep it steady.
- When you play in a group, be aware of the musical conventions required, and always observe them.
- Learn to play the harmonica in a way that expresses your individual style.

Showtime! Finale: Putting It All Together

In This Chapter

- Mastering challenging new tunes
- Playing a variety of styles
- Demonstrating your newfound skills

Though commonly regarded as a limited instrument, diatonic harmonica is amazingly versatile. It works well with a wide range of musical styles both in spite of and because of its idiosyncrasies. Sometimes it works like a drum. At other times it sounds a lot like an accordion. And it can sing like a flute or growl like a saxophone muzzled with a trumpet mute. It's not uncommon for all these features to be combined in a single song. That's what happens in this chapter.

The Big Sendoff

Up to now, the music has been gauged to match your advancing skills on the instrument. This chapter follows suit but raises the ante a bit. We provide what may likely be challenging tunes in a variety of styles, keys, and harmonica tunings.

They were designed to be mastered phrase by phrase. Most phrases can be played in continuous loops. Doing so will build technical skills, physical stamina, rhythmic confidence, and refine breath control. Our advice is this:

- Bite off only as much as you can chew at a given time.
- Figure out how to simplify phrases that present overwhelming technical challenges and work on the problem areas in isolation.
- Make your phrase loops groove as much as possible.

Our support website, www.harpscomplete.com, provides a variety of approaches to this more advanced material so that you derive maximum enjoyment and skill building with minimum frustration. Getting there is at least half the fun, after all!

Each tune also provides indications for the key, recommended harmonica tuning (major, harmonic minor, natural minor, or Melody Maker), and the harmonica position found on the included CD. The conventional music notation is in the key of C for all tunes on the major diatonic. We did it this way to make it easier for you to follow the standard notation. The harmonica tab on the other hand indicates the correct hole and breath direction for each and every note. This way you will be able to easily play any of these songs in your preferred keys.

For example, our first tune is played on an A harmonica in second position but it's notated in the key of C. You can play the song on any major harmonica using the same harmonica tab, but to play along with our CD, you need to use an A harmonica.

Okay, onward!

Our first tune, "Train Time," focuses on chording and rhythmic skills. It imitates the chugging of a steam engine on an early twentieth-century locomotive. This song form was brought to a virtuosic level by many harp players throughout the rural American South. You can hear absolutely astonishing examples of this kind of playing on the CD *Harp Blowers (1925-1936)* from Document Records (see Appendix B). This version is played *in the key of E on an A-major harmonica in second position*. We recommend working on each of the lettered sections individually before putting them all together. Also, this is a very condensed version. Feel free to play each section as many times as you want. You'll also want to experiment with accelerating the tempo, but do it in a way that is musically convincing. Remember, you're imitating a train, not a train wreck!

 Train Time

"All Aboard" is another train piece but in *first position in the key of A on an A-major harmonica*. It's a good opportunity to practice playing octaves and blow bends in the upper register. Everything said about "Train Time" applies here as well.

All Aboard

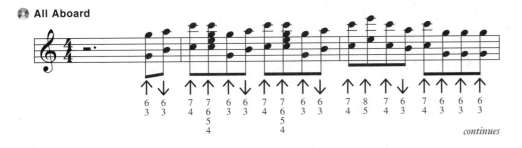

continues

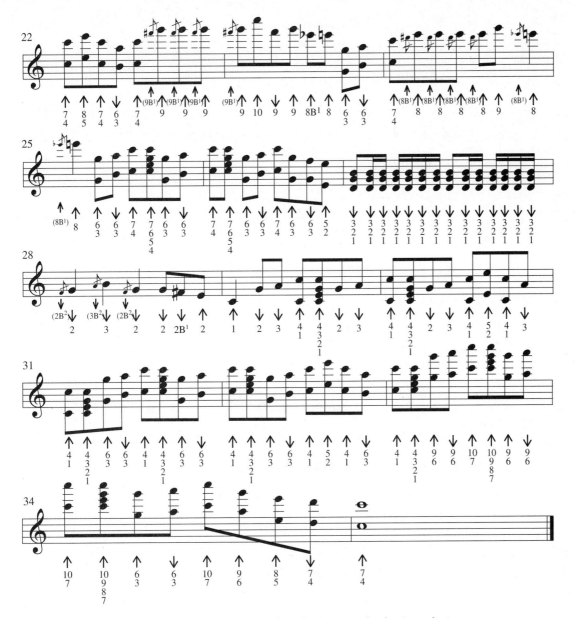

"Fox Chase" is another programmatic piece that focuses on rhythmic techniques. It is played in the *key of E on an A-major harmonica in second position.* Think bloodhounds and nervous foxes instead of locomotives when playing this one. DeFord Bailey, Wayne Rayney, Sonny Terry, and Lonnie Glosson have all recorded amazing versions of this song form. Make sure to include the indicated dog yelps!

Fox Chase

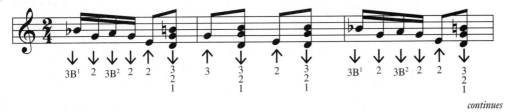

continues

continued

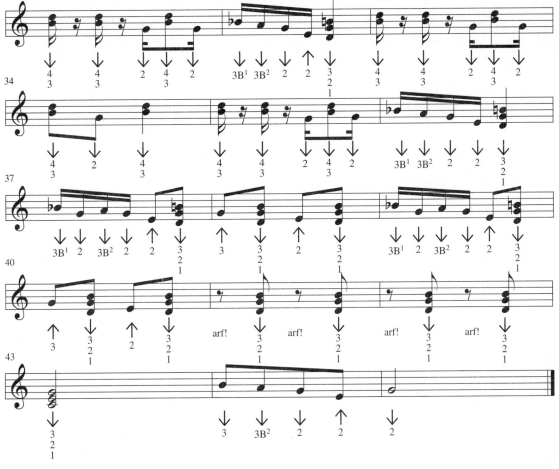

rrrrrrr (ing)

"Cluck Old Hen" is another harmonica rhythm piece that is also a standard Appalachian fiddle tune. This version draws from a great DeFord Bailey recording. You'll want to learn all the parts, but don't feel you have to play them in the indicated order with the indicated number of repetitions. It's played in the *key of A on an A-major harmonica in first position.*

Cluck Old Hen

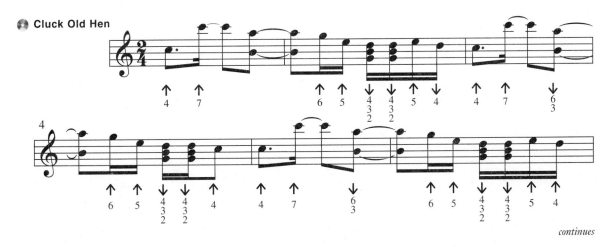

continues

continued

continues

continued

"Ducks on the Pond" is an Appalachian fiddle tune played in the *key of D minor on a C-major harmonica in Dorian mode, that is, third position.* Refer to the discussion of Appalachian fiddle tunes in Chapter 16 for pointers on rhythmic feel.

Ducks on the Pond

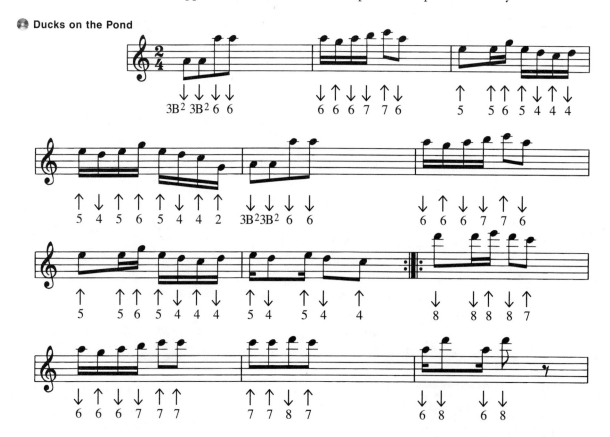

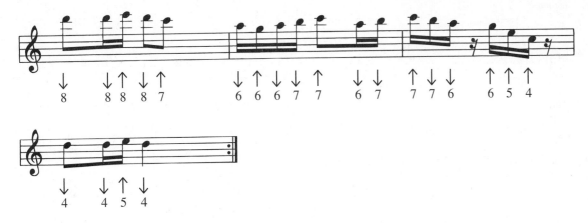

"Riverside Ramble" embellishes the folk tune "Down by the Riverside" with some pentatonic runs, octaves, and some chord figures thrown in for good measure. It is in the *key of G major on a C-major harmonica in second position.*

🎵 **Riverside Ramble**

continues

continued

"Harmonica Rag" is a ragtime piece referencing Chuck Darling's rendition included on the Yazoo anthology *Harmonica Blues* (see Appendix B). It is a good opportunity to refine your bending techniques (especially 3-hole draw bends). Play it on an *A-major harmonica in first position in the key of A major.*

Harmonica Rag

"Bayou Bounce" puts heavy emphasis on octaves. A key objective is to emulate the sound of a Cajun accordion. It is played in the *key of C major on a C-major harmonica in first position.*

Bayou Bounce

"New Orleans Thing," played in the *key of C major on a C-major harmonica in first position*, is similar in style and approach to "Bayou Bounce" but includes some syncopated rhythmic figures as well.

New Orleans Thing

continues

"Mokey Smokes" is a cakewalk with a turn-of-the-century (twentieth that is) Northern Brazilian flavor. It provides ample opportunity to work on extended melodic lines readily playable in *first position on a C-major harmonica in the key of C major.*

Mokey Smokes

continues

continued

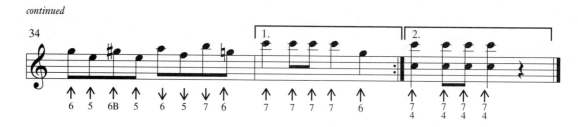

"HarmoniTropica" has a bossa nova feel. It, too, provides ample opportunity to work on melodic lines playable in first position. This is the first piece that follows a typical 32-bar AABA form and also has a couple of key modulations. Play it in the *key of B♭ major on a B♭-major harmonica in first position.*

 **HarmoniTropica**

"Verano Montuno" features an Afro-Latin feel. The chord changes are similar to those of the standard "Summertime." This tune really works your top-octave blow bends and explores some of the funkier options in fourth position. Play it on a *G-major harmonica in the key of E minor.*

Verano Montuno

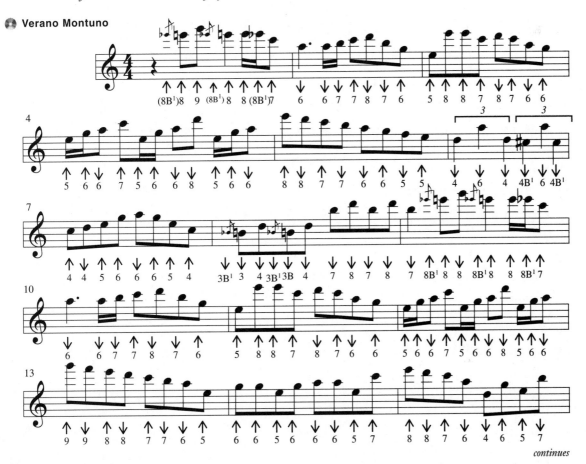

continues

continued

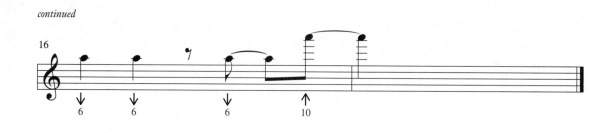

Don't Harp On It

Refer to Chapter 14 regarding discrepancies in manufacturers' key identification schemes for natural-minor harps before going out to buy one!

"Afro Reel" is an Afro-Cuban harmonica duet with an undulating "6/8" feel. The rhythm harmonica part is well suited to the layout of the natural minor harmonica and is played in the *key of G minor on a G-natural-minor harmonica in first position*. The biggest challenge in the lead part revolves around rhythmic placement. Striving to get both harmonica parts to seamlessly interlock is the most important objective of all. Pan your stereo balance controls to hear each part separately.

Afro Reel

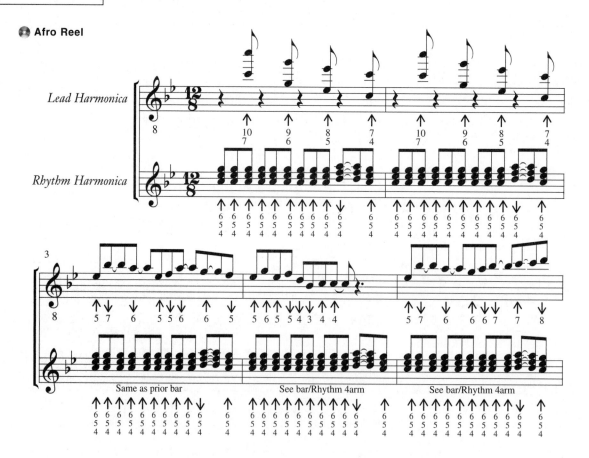

"Dorian Duet" is both our second duet and our second third position tune in this chapter. The big challenges here are getting the harmonica parts to seamlessly interlock, getting a good groove going with the rhythm part, and mastering the breath-control challenges posed by the last lead phrase. The piece is played in the *key of C minor on a B♭-major harmonica in third position.*

Dorian Duet

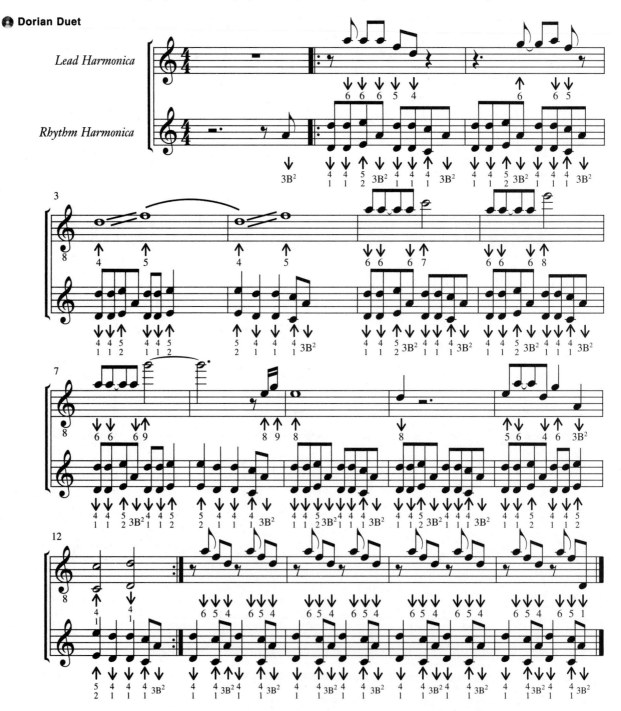

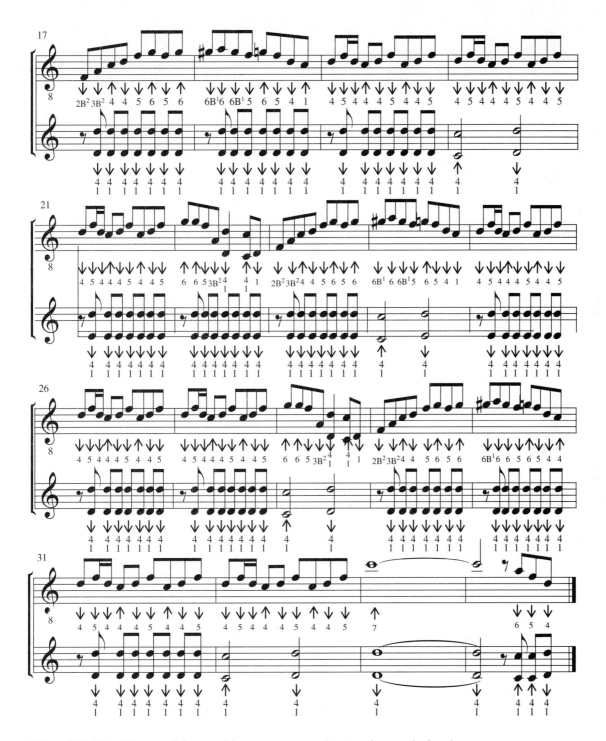

"Silver Wedding" is a well-known klezmer tune, and it is tailor-made for the harmonic minor tuning. The 3-hole draw bends can be a little tricky. It is played in the *key of G minor on a G harmonic-minor harmonica in first position.*

Silver Wedding

"The Swallow Tail Jig" is a popular Irish Jig in Dorian mode. The melodic ornaments that move from 5-6-5 draw and 6-7-6 draw and 5-6-5 blow look intimidating on the score but are actually fairly easy to play. Play "The Swallow Tail Jig" in the *key of E minor on a D-major harmonica in third position.*

The Swallow Tail Jig

"Gallagher's Frolic" is another Irish Jig in Dorian mode. As with "The Swallow Tail Jig," the ornaments play easier than they look. It is played on a *D-major harmonica in the key of E minor.*

Gallagher's Frolic

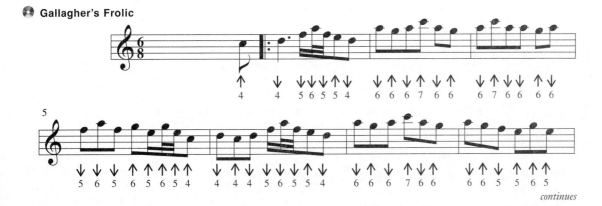

continues

continued

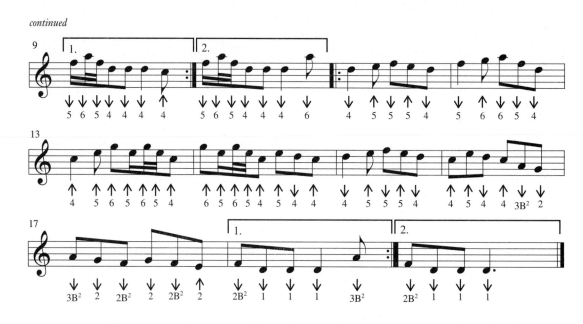

"Porgianna" demonstrates how Melody Maker tuning can both sing and wail on a soulful, harmonically complex ballad. Play it in the *key of C major on a C Melody Maker harmonica in second position*.

Porgianna

"Fifth-Position Moan" demonstrates how nice minor pentatonic melodies can sound when played in fifth position on the major diatonic. This melody also works in second position. But here we present it with a minor-key accompaniment, D minor to be exact. Play the piece on a *B♭-major diatonic harmonica in fifth position.*

Fifth-Position Moan

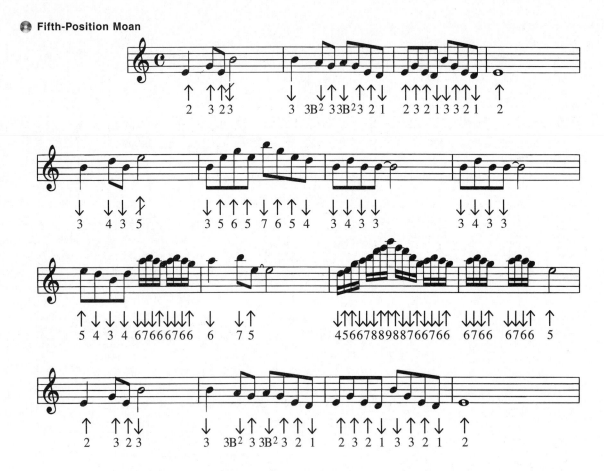

"Glory in the Rockhouse" mangles the Appalachian fiddle tune "Glory in the Meeting House" into a rocked-out harmonica anthem in second position. Now is your opportunity to hear how you sound with full band accompaniment. It is played here on an *A-major diatonic harmonica in the key of E major.*

Glory in the Rockhouse

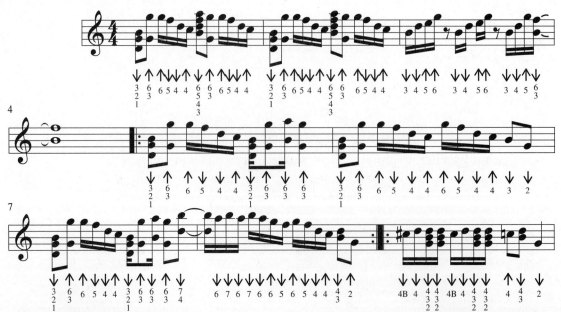

As we've emphasized throughout the book, the diatonic harmonica is a very personal instrument: the individualistic, the idiosyncratic, and the downright weird are welcome members of the harmonica community. On the other hand, conformity is not necessarily a bad thing if you want to be more than a solo act. As we've discussed, playing with others is a cooperative effort; musical cooperation frequently requires you to follow musical conventions so that you don't step on your fellow musicians' toes. We hope we've gotten that message across, too. You're not just a harp player: you're a musician! Whatever your aspirations, we wish you well and thank you for allowing us to introduce you to the most fun you can fit in your shirt pocket. Blow (and draw) on!

The Least You Need to Know

◆ These tunes are meant to be challenging.

◆ They were designed to be mastered phrase by phrase. Most phrases can be played in continuous loops. Doing so will build technical skills, physical stamina, and rhythmic confidence, plus it will also refine breath control.

◆ The website www.harpscomplete.com provides guidance on how to break the tunes down and practice as prescribed above.

◆ These tunes are also meant to be fun. Enjoy!

Complete Glossary of Harp Terms

12-bar blues A pattern of chords repeated over 12 measures that is the basis for most blues music.

accidental A sharp, flat, or natural that is not in the key signature.

Aeolian The Aeolian mode corresponds to the fourth position on a harmonica. The sixth note of the scale to which the harmonica is tuned becomes the root note. The Aeolian mode is popular in Celtic music. See Chapters 13 and 15 for a full discussion.

arpeggio A chord in which the notes are played one after the other instead of simultaneously, usually starting with the lowest note. It is also called a broken chord.

aura The name for Christian Buschman's musical box, patented in 1822, which generally is considered to be the first harmonica.

backup Playing an accompaniment, usually rhythm, chords, or harmony, to an instrumental or vocal solo.

bar line A vertical line that divides measures on a staff.

bass harmonica A harmonica (usually two harmonicas hinged together), which is designed to play in the low range of the musical scale. Bass harmonicas contain a full chromatic range of notes.

bending A technique used to alter the actual pitch of a note. See Chapter 12 for a full discussion.

call-and-response A musical technique involving a solo passage or riff (call) played or sung by a vocalist or instrumentalist, followed by a complementary (answering) passage or riff by another musician. Also called call-and-answer.

chamber The open area of a harmonica's comb into which the player breathes. The reeds vibrate into the chamber, producing a tone.

chord A group of three or more notes played at the same time, we hope, producing a harmonious sound together.

chord harmonica A harmonica on which notes are clustered together in chords to enable the player to more easily play chord accompaniment. Chord harmonicas are not intended for playing single notes or solos.

chord progression A series of chords in a repeating pattern, often in 8-bar, 12-bar, or 16-bar groupings. These patterns repeat themselves throughout a song.

chromatic harmonica A harmonica on which the entire 12-note chromatic scale can be played without bending notes. Chromatic harmonicas have a button on the side, which, when pushed, produces a half-step rise in pitch on each hole, thus providing the ability to play sharps and flats.

chromatic scale A scale that includes all the 12 different notes found in Western music. Each note is a half-step raised in pitch from the preceding note.

circle of fifths A term used to describe the interval movements based on a perfect fifth that determine the positions on a harmonica. Each position on a harmonica has a root note that is a perfect fifth higher than the root note of the preceding position. See Chapter 13 for a full discussion.

clef A sign at the beginning of each staff that identifies the note names for each line and space on the staff. The treble clef is the one most commonly found in music written for harmonica.

comb The plastic, wooden, or metal part that is sandwiched between the reed plates and cover plates on a harmonica, and into which the harpist breathes.

country scale A major pentatonic scale, consisting of the first, second, third, fifth, and seventh notes of a major scale. This scale is commonly used in country music.

Country-tuned diatonic A harmonica by Hohner that is tuned the same as the traditional major diatonic, except that the 5-draw note is raised a half step. As the name implies, this is a good harp for playing country music.

cover plates The two metal plates that constitute the outside covering of a harmonica.

cross harp A style of playing the harmonica in which it is played in a key five notes higher than the key it is tuned to. For example, a song in the key of G would be played on a C-tuned harmonica. This style of playing consists primarily of drawing notes, as opposed to blowing, and is characterized by pulling the tone of the notes downward to create a bending effect. This position is also known as the second, or blues-harp, position.

diatonic harmonica A harmonica that contains only the seven diatonic notes of the key to which the harmonica is tuned.

diatonic scale A scale that contains only seven notes. The most common diatonic scales are the major scale and the minor (natural and harmonic) scale.

Dorian The Dorian mode corresponds to the third position on a harmonica. The second note of the scale to which the harmonica is tuned becomes the root note. The Dorian mode is popular in Celtic music. See Chapters 13 and 16 for a full discussion.

double stop The playing of two notes simultaneously with equal strength.

dropoff   A glissando, moving either right or left, without a definite ending note. Dropoffs usually involve moving your harmonica quickly to the right in a descending direction. Thus, you "drop off" a definite starting note in a descending direction, but have no definite ending note. You generally continue to drop off until you run out of notes at the low end.

flat   A sign that lowers a note a half step.

free-reed instrument   An instrument that uses free-standing reeds to create different tones. The reed is a strip of leather or metal that is attached at one end and free to vibrate at the other. The flow of air makes the free end vibrate. The length of the strip determines the tone: a longer reed produces a lower tone, and conversely, a shorter reed produces a higher tone.

gap   The open space between the reed and the reed plate. Gapping involves adjusting this space to the correct distance. Generally, the size of the gap should be equal to the thickness of the reed.

gig   A booking or paid engagement for a musician, usually for a single performance.

glissando   A sliding of the harmonica either right or left with the effect of rapidly sliding through notes while still blowing or drawing. It includes both slides and dropoffs.

half-step   The smallest interval between any two notes in Western music. It is the distance between every note on a piano keyboard and the closest white or black key. Also called a semi-tone.

harmonic minor-tuned diatonic   A diatonic harmonica tuned to play the notes of a harmonic minor scale. For example, on a C-minor diatonic harmonica, all Es are lowered to E flats, and all As are lowered to A flats. This is a great harp for playing Eastern European, "gypsy," Greek, and other ethnic music that requires the classic minor tuning. This harp is designed for playing in straight-harp position and is labeled in its straight-harp key.

improvisation   Creating music spontaneously without any predetermined arrangement.

interval   The distance between two notes. The interval between every note on a piano keyboard is a half step.

Ionian   The Ionian mode corresponds to the first position on a harmonica. When playing in the Ionian mode or first position, you're playing in the same key as the one to which the harmonica is tuned. See Chapter 13 for a full discussion.

jam   A gathering of musicians and vocalists who play many different songs spontaneously. Usually, the participants take turns selecting the songs and will rotate playing the lead melodies. Some jam sessions encourage improvisations over songs or even free-form improvisation.

key   The key indicates the root note of the scale on which a song is based and the sharps and flats that are included in that scale.

key signature   A sign at the beginning of a song or section that indicates which key the music is written in.

ledger lines   Short lines used to indicate notes above or below a staff.

Locrian   The Locrian mode corresponds to the sixth position on a harmonica. The seventh note of the scale to which the harmonica is tuned becomes the root note. See Chapter 13 for a full discussion.

Lydian   The Lydian mode corresponds to the twelfth position on a harmonica. The fourth note of the scale to which the harmonica is tuned becomes the root note. See Chapter 13 for a full discussion.

major-tuned diatonic   The traditional tuning for a diatonic harmonica, based on Josef Richter's original tuning from the 1820s. It is clearly the most commonly played tuning for a harmonica and is used for blues, rock, country, bluegrass, folk, and just about every other style of music.

measure   A unit that is used to separate notes into rhythm patterns and a uniform number of beats. There typically will be three or four beats per measure, though there can be more or less. The measures establish a rhythm and accent pattern for the music. A measure is also referred to as a bar.

Melody Maker–tuned diatonic   A variation of the traditional major diatonic tuning by Lee Oskar specifically designed for playing single-note melodies. Three notes are altered from the standard major-tuned diatonic harmonica. It's designed for playing in the cross-harp position, so it's labeled with its cross-harp key rather than the straight-harp key.

metronome   A clock-like device that can be set to tick at various beats per minute, thus providing the precise speed of a song and a reliable reference point for the chosen tempo while playing. More important, it assists a musician in maintaining a steady tempo without rushing or dragging.

Mixolydian   The Mixolydian mode corresponds to the second position on a harmonica. The fifth note of the scale to which the harmonica is tuned becomes the root note. When played in cross harp at the low end of the harmonica, this mode corresponds to the classic blues-harp position. The Mixolydian mode also is used to play Celtic music at the higher end in straight harp (starting at the 6-hole). See Chapters 13 and 16 for a full discussion.

natural   A sign that cancels a sharp or flat.

natural minor-tuned diatonic   Five notes are flattened from the traditional major diatonic tuning for this harp, with the result that both blow and draw chords are minor. This harmonica is used for minor blues, rock, and reggae music. The natural minor diatonic is designed for playing in cross harp and thus is labeled in its cross-harp key.

octave harmonica   A diatonic harmonica with a double set of reeds, with the upper and lower reeds being tuned to notes which are exactly an octave apart.

ornament   A note or technique that is used to embellish a melody line. It's also sometimes referred to as a decoration. An ornament will create an effect or special sound. Methods of ornamentation differ greatly between musical styles and contribute greatly to their respective identities. Grace notes, trills, slides, dropoffs, tongue blocking, and bends are techniques that can be used as ornaments.

overbending   A technique for raising the pitch of a note on a diatonic harmonica, to enable the player to hit the remaining chromatic notes that cannot ordinarily be played on a diatonic harmonica. See Chapter 12 for a full discussion.

Paddy Richter–tuned diatonic   A specially-tuned diatonic harmonica, developed by Brendan Power, which raises the pitch of the 3-hole blow note one full step. This tuning is ideal for playing Celtic music.

pentatonic scale   A five-note scale. The two most common pentatonic scales are the major pentatonic (the first, second, third, fifth, and seventh notes of a major scale) and the minor pentatonic (the first, third, fourth, fifth, and seventh notes of a natural minor scale).

Phrygian   The Phrygian mode corresponds to the fifth position on a harmonica. The third note of the scale to which the harmonica is tuned becomes the root note. See Chapter 13 for a full discussion.

pitch   The sound of a note that identifies it as a specific note. The pitch of a note is determined by the speed of the vibrations that are creating the note. For example, the pitch of a note on a harmonica is determined by the speed of the cyclic sound-wave patterns produced by the reed vibrations. Pitch is expressed as "vibrations or cycles per second," such as A = 440 Hz. Hz stands for Hertz, and Hertz is shorthand for cycles per second.

positions   Playing a harmonica in different "positions" enables the harpist to play it in different keys than the key it is tuned to. It involves using a different root note for each position. The first (straight-harp) and second (cross-harp) positions are the most common. See Chapter 13 for a full discussion.

puckering   A technique for playing single notes that involves shaping the lips and blowing and drawing air in the same style as when whistling or blowing air through a straw. Also called the whistle or lip-blocking technique. See Chapter 6 for a full discussion.

reed   The thin piece of metal connected to the reed plate over the slot that vibrates to create a tone.

reed plate   The metal plate with slots to which the reeds are attached.

relative minor or major   Any major and minor keys that have the same key signature are relative to each other.

resolution   A place in a song where the music returns to the root note of the key in which the song is written. This usually happens at the end of a verse or chorus and almost always at the end of the song.

rest   Sign that indicates a period during which the musician is silent.

rhythm   The beat of the music. Also used to refer to a style of back-up accompaniment in which the musician plays notes or chords that correspond to the beat of the music.

Richter-tuned diatonic   The most common tuning for a diatonic harmonica, as developed by Josef Richter in the 1820s.

riff   A short solo or interlude in which an instrumentalist plays the melody line or other improvised lead. Riffs often are played between, and complementary to, vocal lines or as transitions between verses. Riffs also are sometimes called licks (or motifs, by classical musicians).

sharp   A sign that raises the pitch of a note a half step.

slide   A glissando, moving either right or left, with a definite ending note. A slide may or may not start with a definite note, but it always ends with one.

slot   The openings on a reed plate over which the reeds are positioned.

slur   The playing of two notes simultaneously where one of the notes is a primary note and the other is a softer, secondary note.

solo-tuned diatonic   A diatonic harmonica in which all the blow and draw notes are positioned as an ascending diatonic scale (like a chromatic harmonica without the slide button).

staff   The five lines and four spaces on which Western music is written.

Steve Baker Special–tuned diatonic   This version of the Hohner Marine Band model, developed by Steve Baker, is an extension of the standard major diatonic tuning. Three holes added at the low end provide an additional octave for playing low bend notes.

straight harp   A style of playing the harmonica, also called the first position, in which the harmonica is played in the same musical key as it is tuned to. This style of playing consists primarily of blowing notes, as opposed to drawing, and is the dominant style of play for folk, bluegrass, and Celtic music.

sustain   The characteristic timbre and volume of sounds that an instrument produces after the note is first played.

tablature   Any notation system that does not use standard music notation to designate the notes and rhythms to be played. Harmonicas, guitars, and drums all have tablature systems that are used as an alternative to standard music notation. There are several different styles of harmonica tablature.

time signature   The sign at the beginning of a song or a section of a song that indicates the number of beats, and the length of each beat, in a measure.

tongue blocking   A technique for playing single notes that involves using the tongue to block the flow of air to all holes except one. Tongue blocking also is used to create different sounds, such as tongue-block slaps, lifts, octaves, and tremolos. See Chapters 7 and 11 for a full discussion.

tremolo harmonica   A diatonic harmonica with a double set of reeds, with the upper and lower reeds tuned to slightly different pitches of the same note, thus producing a tremolo or wavering sound when played together.

trill   The alternation of two adjacent notes on the harmonica caused by either moving the harmonica quickly sidewise with the hand or shaking the head quickly from side to side, depending on which technique is preferred. The notes will blend together and sound almost like a single note. Also called a shake, or warble.

triplet   A group of three notes to be played within the same time ordinarily used to play two notes of the same type.

tritone   A musical interval that spans three whole tones.

U-blocking   A technique for playing single notes that involves curling the tongue into a "U" shape. Also called the tube-tongue method.

valved diatonic   On a traditional diatonic harmonica, it's possible to produce draw bends on holes 1 through 6 and blow bends on holes 7 through 10 to play notes that are not available with the harmonica's standard tuning. With a valved diatonic, it's possible to produce blow bends on holes 1 through 6 and draw bends on holes 7 through 10 to achieve a chromatic capability through bending. Suzuki manufactures a valved diatonic called the ProMaster.

vibrato   A slight tremulous or oscillating effect characterized by rapid variations in pitch or volume. On a harmonica, it can be created using the hand, tongue, throat, or diaphragm.

whole step   An interval between two notes that is equal to two half steps.

Resources

Harmonica Websites

www.angelfire.com/tx/myquill

Very good diatonic harmonica reference, instruction, and information site by Mike Will.

www.bassharp.com/bh_itin.htm

The Harper's International Gig List, a listing of gigs by harmonica players and harmonica events.

www.bluesharp.ca

Informative blues harmonica site.

www.bluesharp.org

Instruction, news, links, listings of harp teachers, and more.

www.coast2coastmusic.com

Covers a broad range of harmonica topics and instruction.

www.gindick.com

Jon Gindick's Harmonica Central website with instruction, Q&A, events, information, and so forth. One of the best and most complete around.

www.harp-l.com

Website for Harp-L, a mailing list and discussion group for harpists.

www.harmonicalessons.com

Very good instructional site, with a lot of harmonica information from beginner to advanced levels; offers links and an online store.

www.harmonicalinks.com

One of the most comprehensive harmonica sites, with many links to other sites.

www.harmony-central.com/Bands

Very good information on forming bands, getting gigs, performance tips, and the music business in general.

www.harpinon.com

Another good site with links, instruction, CDs, information, news, and reviews.

www.spah.org

The official site of the Society for the Preservation and Advancement of the Harmonica, with an abundance of harmonica information and links to other sites.

www.planetharmonica.com

Online magazine (available in English and French) with news, reviews, links, and a wealth of other harp information.

www.hunterharp.com

Richard Hunter's website, loaded with harmonica information, links, reviews, news about players, and so on.

www.stevebaker.de

Steve Baker's international website, with your choice of German or English language. Listings of his gigs, a discography, news of all kinds, and lots of worldwide links.

Harmonica Organizations

The Society for the Preservation and Advancement of the Harmonica (SPAH)

P.O. Box 865
Troy, MI 48099-0865
www.spah.org

The first national harmonica organization. SPAH holds an annual convention and publishes a quarterly newsletter. Its website is one of the best sources for harmonica information, resources, and links.

There are hundreds of local harmonica clubs throughout the United States and other countries. The SPAH website has a listing and contact information for most of them.

Harmonica Instruction Books, Videos, and CDs

There are many very good instruction books for learning to play the harmonica. The following all focus on a particular style of playing or provide instruction on topics or techniques that are supplementary to those covered in this book. They can easily be found and purchased at one or more of the harmonica and paraphernalia distributors listed later in this appendix.

General Instruction and Series

Barrett, David. *Harmonica Masterclass* (multi-book and video series covering beginner to advanced levels). Mel Bay Publications (www.melbay.com).

Buffalo, Norton. *Harmonica Power: Norton Buffalo's Bag of Tricks* (video). Homespun Video.

Duncan, Phil. *Harmonica Chord Chart*. Mel Bay Publications.

—. *Mel Bay's Complete Harmonica Book*. Mel Bay Publications.

Gindick, Jon. *The Natural Blues and Country Western Harmonica Series*. Cross Harp Press.

Levy, Howard. *New Directions for Harmonica—Expanding Your Technique* (advanced video). Homespun Video.

Martin, Richard. *The Harmonica Educator Series* (wide range of instruction books covering many topics). Available through The Harmonica Educator, P.O. Box 340, North Hampton, OH 45349-0340; 937-964-1115; email: Ri58066217@aol.com.

Amplified Playing

Hagerty, Kevin. *Amplified Harmonica Playing Made Possible*. Potential Publications.

Sheridan, Pete. *The Quest for Tone in Amplified Blues Harp*. Available through Kevin's Harps.

Blues

Baker, Steve. *Interactive Blues Harp Workshop*. Mel Bay Publications (www. melbay.com).

Ball, Tom. *Sonny Terry Licks*. Centerstream Publishing.

—. *Sourcebook of Little Walter/Big Walter Licks*. Hal Leonard Publishing.

Barrett, David. *Complete Classic Chicago Blues Harp*. Mel Bay Publications.

—. *Masters of the Chicago Blues Harp*. Mel Bay Publications.

Bell, Carey, and Barrett, David. *Carey Bell: Deep Down*. Mel Bay Publications.

Buffalo, Norton. *Harmonica Power: Norton Buffalo's Blues Techniques* (video). Homespun Video.

Duncan, Phil. *Blues Harp for Diatonic and Chromatic Harmonica*. Mel Bay Publications.

—. *You Can Teach Yourself Blues Harp*. Mel Bay Publications.

Gindick, Jon. *Rock and Blues Harmonica*. Cross Harp Press.

Glover, Tony. *Blues Harp*. Oak Publications.

Howell, Lonnie Joe. *Sixty Hot Licks for Harmonica*. Mel Bay Publications.

Huang, Cham-Ber. *Blues and All That Jazz*. CBH Harmonica Research Labs (Insignia International).

Michelsen, David. *Blues Harmonica Classics*. Mel Bay Publications.

Musselwhite, Charlie. *Charlie Musselwhite: Power Blues Harp*. Mel Bay Publications.

Celtic

Conway, Pat. *Irish Songs for Harmonica*. Music Sales Corporation.

—. *Scottish Songs for Harmonica*. Music Sales Corporation.

Duncan, Phil. *Irish Melodies for Harmonica*. Mel Bay Publications.

Power, Brendan. *Play Irish Music on the Blues Harp* and *Play Irish Music on the Chromatic Harmonica*. Available at the Brendan Power website, www. brendanpower.com.

Christmas

Duncan, Phil. *Christmas Songs for Harmonica*. Mel Bay Publications.

Holman, Bobby Joe. *Christmas Carols and Hymns for Harmonica*. Hal Leonard Publishing.

Country

Harp, David. *How to Play Country & Western Harmonica*. Musical I. Press.

Howell, Lonnie Joe. *Texas Harmonica Styles*. Mel Bay Publications.

McCoy, Charlie. *Beginning Country Harp*. Wise Publications.

—. *Learn to Play All-American Harp*. Music Sales Corporation.

Fiddle Tunes

Weiser, Glenn. *Irish and American Fiddle Tunes for Harmonica*. Centerstream Publishing.

Folk, Bluegrass, and Gospel

Duncan, Phil. *Bluegrass and Country Music for Harmonica*. Mel Bay Publications.

—. *Gospel Harp*. Mel Bay Publications.

—. *Hymns for Harmonica*. Mel Bay Publications.

Gindick, Jon. *Harmonica Americana*. Cross Harp Press.

—. *Gospel Plow*. Cross Harp Press.

Sterling, Clarence. *Bluegrass Harmonica*. Creative Concepts Publishing.

Stevens, Mike. *Bluegrass Harmonica*. Centerstream Publishing.

Play-Along CDs

Agresta, Ralph. *Harmonica Jam Trax*. Amsco Music.

Baker, Steve. *Blues Harmonica Playalongs*. Mel Bay Publications (www.melbay.com).

Gindick, Jon. *The Jam Lessons*. Cross Harp Press.

Reading Music and Music Theory

Cooper, Helen. *Basic Guide to How to Read Music*. Perigee.

Evans, Roger. *How to Read Music*. Three Rivers Press.

Harp, David. *Harmonica Positions*. Musical I. Press.

—. *Music Theory Made Easy*. Musical I. Press.

Scott, Andrew. *Progressive Music Theory Grade One and Grade Two*. Koala Publications.

Shanet, Howard. *Learn to Read Music*. Simon & Schuster.

Stewart, Dave. *The Musician's Guide to Reading and Writing Music*. Backbeat Books.

Two free websites:

◆ *Gary Ewer's Easy Music Theory*, www.musictheory.halifax.ns.ca.

◆ Introduction to Reading Music, www.datadragon.com/education/reading.

Other Harmonica and General Interest Books

Baker, Steve. *The Harp Handbook*. Wise Publications.

Field, Kim. *Harmonicas, Harps, and Heavy Breathers*. Cooper Square Press.

Krampert, Peter. *The Encyclopedia of the Harmonica*. Tatanka Publishing.

McPherson, Brian. *Get It in Writing: The Musician's Guide to Music Business*. Hal Leonard Publishing.

Mitchell, Billy. *The Gigging Musician: How to Get, Play, and Keep the Gig*. Backbeat Books.

Tate, Douglas, *Make Your Harmonica Work Better*. Centerstream Publishing.

Weissman, Dick. *Making a Living in Your Local Music Market*. Hal Leonard Publishing.

Wilson, Lee. *Making It in the Music Business: The Business and Legal Guide for Songwriters and Performers*. Allworth Press.

Harmonica Magazines

American Harmonica Newsmagazine. Al Eichler, Editor, and Phil Lloyd, Contributing Editor. 104 Highland Ave., Battle Creek, MI 49015-3272; (269-962-2989; e-mail: philharpn@aol.com.) A very good monthly publication that has been in existence for 14 years. Focused on all aspects and styles of harmonica playing, with reviews, interviews, and other information.

Easy Reeding (Hohner). Hohner, Inc., P.O. Box 15035, Richmond, VA 23227-0435; www.hohnerusa.com (click on "Harmonicas", and then "Easy Reeding").

The Harmonica Educator. Richard Martin, P.O. Box 340, North Hampton, OH 45349-0340 (937-964-1115; email: Ri58066217@aol.com). A well-rounded quarterly that covers a diverse range of harmonica topics.

Harmonica Happenings. P.O. Box 865, Troy, MI 48099-9965. SPAH's quarterly newsletter.

Harmonica Information Press. 203 14th Ave., San Francisco, CA 94118-1007 (415-751-0212; www.angelfire.com/music2/harmonicainfo).

Distributors of Harmonicas and Related Paraphernalia (Online and Catalogue)

All the following offer good prices and fast delivery for harmonicas and related paraphernalia:

Best Li'l Harp House

210 Farnsworth Ave
Bordentown, NJ 08505
1-877-274-2776; www.harphouse.com

Coast2Coast Music

P.O. Box 1857
Ellicott City, MD 21041-1857
410-750-3570
www.coast2coastmusic.com

Elderly Instruments

1100 N. Washington
Lansing, MI 48906
517-372-7890
www.elderly.com

Harley's Harps (specializing in unique, unusual, and rare harps)

741 Cedar Field Ct.
Chesterfield, MO 63017
312-434-8875
www.harleysharps.com

Harmonicaspot-Encore Music Co.

P.O. Box 191
22133 Main Street
Woodburn, IN 46797
1-888-554-5581
www.harmonicaspot.com

Harp Depot

P.O. Box 567
New Palestine, IN 46163
317-861-9484
www.harpdepot.com

Hering Harmonicas USA

25 SE 2nd Ave., Suite 435
Miami, FL 33131
305-358-0004
www.heringharp.com

Huang Harmonicas

Cham-Ber Huang
257 Benson Ave.
Elmont, NY 11033
e-mail: haungharps@yahoo.com

Lee Oskar Harmonicas

P.O. Box 50225
Duvall, WA 98019
425-844-9889
www.leeoskar.com

M. Hohner, Inc.

P.O. Box 15035
Richmond, VA 23227
804-515-1900
www.hohnerusa.com

Suzuki Corporation

P.O. Box 261030
San Diego, CA 92126-9877
619-566-9710
www.suzukimusic.com/harmonicas

Custom Harmonicas and Repair

Joe Filisko

1313 Colorado Ave.
Joliet, IL 60435-3704
815-725-9095;
www.customharmonicas.com

Dick Gardner

7024 Jocelyn Ave. S.
Cottage Grove, MN 55016
612-458-1193
harmonicats@juno.com

James Gordon

P.O. Box 461
Bellows Fall, VT 05101
802-463-3737
joegordon@customharmonicas.com

John Infande

8506 E-SW 93rd St.
Ocala, FL 34481
352-873-0303
infande@hotmail.com
www.infandecustomharmonicas.com

Vern Morgus

P.O. Box 899
Shelton, WA 98584
306-426-6877

Steve Pruitt

P.O. Box 280
Topeka, IN 46571-0280
219-593-3777
steve@srp-harmonicas.com

Bill Romel

Custom Craft Harmonicas, Ltd.
8524 Summer Vista Ave.
Las Vegas, Nevada 89128
702-256-7470
romel@earthlink.net

Richard Sleigh

R.R. 1, Box 345
Philipsburg, PA 16866
814-342-9722
rsleigh@customharmonicas.com

Harmonica Workshops, Camps, and Events

A more comprehensive and up-to-date listing with links can be found at the
SPAH website: www.spah.org.

Bean Blossom Blues Festival
Bean Blossom, Indiana
www.beanblossomblues.com

Buckeye Harmonica Festival
Columbus, Ohio
www.buckeyeharmonica.org

**David Barrett's Harmonica Master-
class Workshops**
(multi-site intense three-day workshops
for intermediate to advanced harpists)
P.O. Box 1723
Morgan Hill, CA 95038
1-877-427-7252
www.harmonicamasterclass.com

Jon Gindick Harmonica Jam Camp
1-800-646-9245
jon@gindick.com
www.harmonicajamcamp.com

SPAH Annual Convention
(information available at SPAH website: www.spah.org)

**Yellow Pine Annual Harmonica
Festival and Competition**
P.O. Box 32
Yellow Pine, ID 83677
208-633-3300
www.harmonicacontest.com

Blues jams around the country are
listed at www.nationalbluespages.com.

Harmonica CDs

There are hundreds of harmonica CDs available. The Coast2Coast Music
Harmonica CD Page (www.coast2coastmusic.com) lists over 650 of them for
you to choose from. Following are some of our all-time favorite harp CDs:

George Harmonica Smith. *Blowing the Blues*. El Segundo: ESR98001.

Sheng Organ for the Mouth. Melisma Music: MELI 3048-2.

Paul De Lay. *Paulzilla*. Criminal Records: CR33-15.

Little Walter. *The Essential Little Walter*. Chess: CHD2-9312.

Blues Masters Volume 4: Harmonica Classics. Rhino: R2 71124.

Harmonica Blues. Yazoo: 1053.

Harmonica Masters. Yazoo: 2019.

Harp Blowers (1925–1936). Document Records DOCD-5164.

Mark Graham. *Southern Old-Time Harmonica*. Graham: CD80001.

Junior Wells. *Hoodoo Man Blues*. Delmark: CD612.

Black White and Hillbilly Music (Early Harmonica Recordings from the 1920's and 1930's). Trikon: US-0226.

Wayne Rayney. *That Real Hot Boogie Boy: The King Anthology*. Ace: CDCHD 857.

About the CD and Website

Most tracks on the CD feature both harmonica and instrumental accompaniment. If you want to hear either the accompaniment or the harmonica in isolation, you can pan your stereo's balance control hard left or hard right.

We couldn't include everything we'd like on the CD so please check out www.harpscomplete.com for additional musical examples from the book and other useful study tools. Among these are downloadable, extended versions of all the accompaniment tracks with count-off bars at the beginning to help you get in the groove.

Track #	Track Title	Songs Included	Page #
1	Some Familiar Tunes	Twinkle Twinkle Mary Had a Little Lamb When The Saints Go Marching In	45
2	Playing High Notes	Red River Valley	65
3	Trilling Tunes	She'll Be Coming Around the Mountain Oh, Susanna My Old Kentucky Home	67
4	Moon Dance		70
5	For He's a Jolly Good Fellow		71
6	Hannon for Harp	Hannon Harp 1 Hannon Harp 2	72
7	Down in the Valley		76
8	Swannee River		76
9	Shenandoah		76
10	Yellow Rose of Texas		77
11	Aura Lee		77
12	Spancil Hill		78
13	Silent Night		78
14	William Tell Overture		79
15	Red River Valley		79

continues

continued

Index

tablature system, 43
    bending, 44
tongue blocking, 55-58
tongue-blocking, 109
    octaves, 109-111
Nyu-kwa, empress of China, 11

O-P

octaves, 22
    tongue-blocking, 109-111
ornaments
    blues, 158-159
    grace notes, 69
    rolls, 167
Oskar, Lee, 17
overbending notes, 126-127

Paddy Richter–tuned diatonic harmonica, 167
"Peg O' My Heart", 15
Perkins, Carl, 154
phrases, mastering, 193-194
phrasings (rhythmic), 158
Phrygian mode (fifth position), 136
Piazza, Rod, 17
pitch, 88
pitch pipes, 107
placement (rhythmic), 158
Pope Pius XI, 7
Popper, John, 17
"Porgianna", 218
positions
    Aeolian mode (fourth position), 135
    circle of fifths, 129-131
    Dorian mode (third position), 134
    Ionian mode (first position), 131
    Locrian mode (sixth position), 137
    Lydian mode (twelfth position), 137-139
    Mixolydian mode (second position), 132-133
    Phrygian mode (fifth position), 136
posture, importance of, 48
Power, Brendan, 167
practice
    importance of, 6
    strategies, 7-10

pranayama, 50
prices, harmonicas, 22
ProMaster harmonica, 127
puckering, 55-57
Pythagoras, 130

Q-R

quills, 14

Rayney, Wayne, 197
reading music notation, 107-108
    beats, 96-100
    chords, 94-96
    keys, 103-107
    lines and dots, 92-93
    naturals, 89-90
    notes, 88-91
    reasons for, 87-88
    rests, 91-92
    signs, 100-102
Reagan, Ronald, 5
recording yourself, 9
"Red Haired Boy", 190
reed plates, replacing, 36
Reed, Jimmy, 158
reed-plate replacement kits, 21-22
reeds, replacing, 35-36
reels (Celtic), 166
repairing harmonicas, 33-36
rests, music notation, 91-92
rhythmic placement and phrasing, 158
Ricci, Jason, 17
Richter, Josef, 12
riffs, 31
    blues, 148-150
    call-and-response, 150-155
"Riverside Ramble", 203
rock music, playing, 165
rolls, 167
routines (practice), developing, 8
Ruth, Peter "Madcat", 17

S

saxophones, 12
Schirra, Wally, 16
Sebastion, John, 16
second position (Mixolydian mode), 132-133

sets, gigs, 178
shakes, 52, 65-67, 159
shapes, music notation, 89-91
sharps, music notation, 89-90
shengs, 11-12
shuffle rhythm, 149
signatures (keys), 104-105
signs, music notation, 100-102
"Silver Wedding", 215
Single-Note Exercise Number 1, 57
Single-Note Exercise Number 2, 58
Single-Note Exercise Number 3, 58
sixth position (Locrian mode), 137
slide buttons, chromatic harmonicas, 44-45
slides, 70-71, 159
Smith, George "Harmonica", 158
Society for the Preservation and Advancement of the Harmonica (SPAH), founding of, 17
"Son of Bent by the Blues", 158
songs
    "Afro Reel", 212
    "Bayou Bounce", 206
    "Boatmen", 172
    "Cluck Old Hen", 199
    "Dance of the Naked Druid Maidens", 167
    "Dorian Duet", 214
    "Ducks on the Pond", 202
    "Fifth-Position Moan", 219
    "Fox Chase", 197
    "Gallagher's Frolic", 217
    "Glory in the Rockhouse", 220
    "Harmonica Rag", 204
    "HarmoniTropica", 210
    "Irish Washerwoman, The", 114
    "Mokey Smokes", 208
    "New Orleans Thing", 207
    "Porgianna", 218
    "Red Haired Boy", 190
    "Riverside Ramble", 203
    selection of, 6
    "Silver Wedding", 215
    "Spancil Hill", 78
    "Swallow Tail Jig, The", 217
    "Swanee River", 76
    "Train Time", 194
    "Verano Montuno", 211
    "Yellow Rose of Texas, The", 77
sound quality (harmonicas), 21